STAR WARS®

L E G A C Y

LEGACY

(Forty years after the Battle of Yavin and beyond)

As this era began, Luke Skywalker had unified the Jedi Order into a cohesive group of powerful Jedi Knights. It was a time of relative peace, yet darkness approached on the horizon. Now, Skywalker's descendants face new and resurgent threats to the galaxy, and to the balance of the Force.

The events in this story begin approximately 137 years after the Battle of Yavin.

STAR WARS®
LEGACY

VOLUME SEVEN
STORMS

STORY
**John Ostrander and
Jan Duursema**

SCRIPT
John Ostrander

PENCILS
**Jan Duursema and
Omar Francia**

INKS
**Dan Parsons and
Omar Francia**

COLORS
Brad Anderson

LETTERS
Michael Heisler

COVER ART
Omar Francia

BACK COVER ART
**Jan Duursema and
Brad Anderson**

DARK HORSE BOOKS

PUBLISHER
Mike Richardson

EDITOR
Randy Stradley

COLLECTION DESIGNER
Scott Cook

ASSISTANT EDITOR
Freddye Lins

Special thanks to Elaine Mederer, Jann Moorhead, David Anderman, Leland Chee, Sue Rostoni, and Carol Roeder at Lucas Licensing.

STAR WARS: LEGACY VOLUME SEVEN—STORMS

This volume collects issues #32, #33, #36, #34, and #35 of the Dark Horse comic-book series *Star Wars: Legacy*.

Published by
Dark Horse Books
A division of Dark Horse Comics, Inc.
10956 SE Main Street
Milwaukie, OR 97222

darkhorse.com
starwars.com

To find a comics shop in your area, call the Comic Shop Locator Service toll-free at 1-888-266-4226

First edition: December 2009
ISBN 978-1-59582-350-2

1 3 5 7 9 10 8 6 4 2
Printed in China

In revenge for their aiding the remnant fleet of the Galactic Alliance in destroying the Empire's shipyards and stealing its greatest battle cruiser, Sith Emperor Darth Krayt ordered the extermination of the population of the planet Dac. But in exposing the Empire's black heart, Krayt has frightened some systems into joining his enemies.

Emboldened by this, and by reports of Krayt's death—following a battle with Imperial Knights, Jedi, and the notorious Cade Skywalker—Admiral Gar Stazi of the Galactic Alliance and Emperor-in-Exile Roan Fel plot to join forces and strike at their common foe.

Though victorious in their fight with Darth Krayt and his Sith, Skywalker and his allies did not all survive unscathed. He and his crew, along with Jedi Shado Vao, make for the planet Kiffex, where they hope a wounded friend may be saved from grave injuries . . .

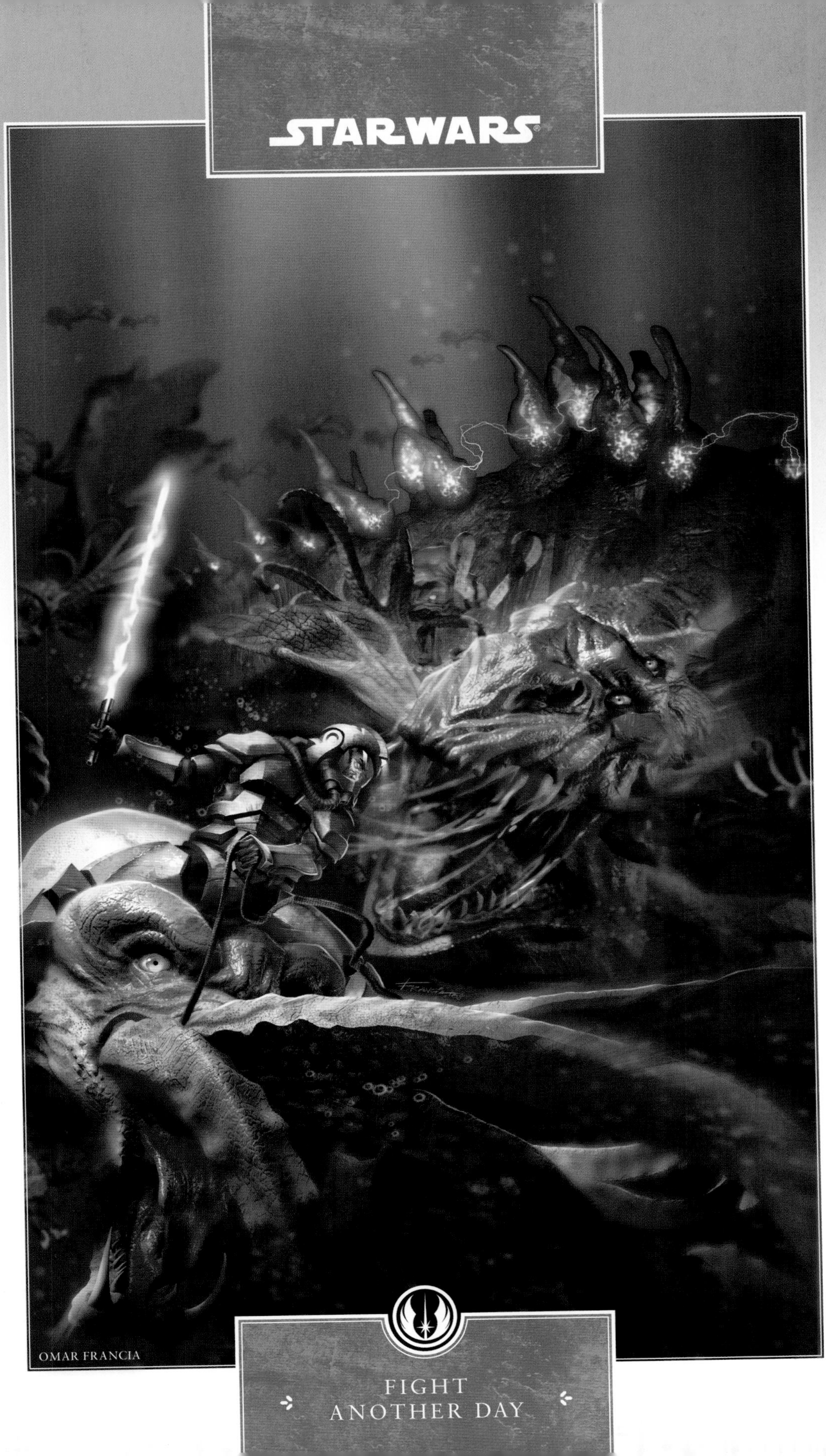
STAR WARS
OMAR FRANCIA
FIGHT
ANOTHER DAY

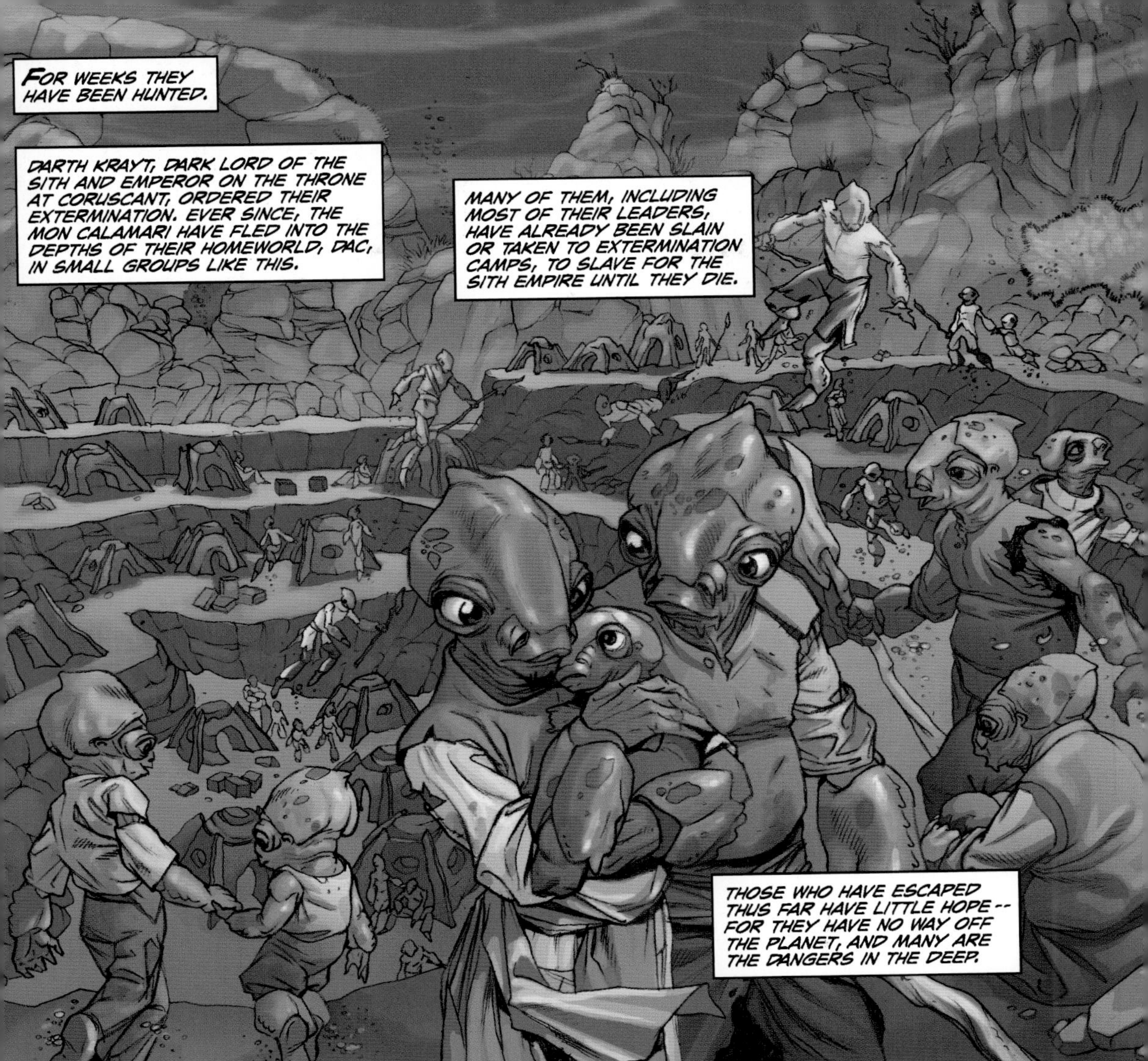
FOR WEEKS THEY HAVE BEEN HUNTED.
DARTH KRAYT, DARK LORD OF THE SITH AND EMPEROR ON THE THRONE AT CORUSCANT, ORDERED THEIR EXTERMINATION. EVER SINCE, THE MON CALAMARI HAVE FLED INTO THE DEPTHS OF THEIR HOMEWORLD, DAC, IN SMALL GROUPS LIKE THIS.
MANY OF THEM, INCLUDING MOST OF THEIR LEADERS, HAVE ALREADY BEEN SLAIN OR TAKEN TO EXTERMINATION CAMPS, TO SLAVE FOR THE SITH EMPIRE UNTIL THEY DIE.
THOSE WHO HAVE ESCAPED THUS FAR HAVE LITTLE HOPE -- FOR THEY HAVE NO WAY OFF THE PLANET, AND MANY ARE THE DANGERS IN THE DEEP.
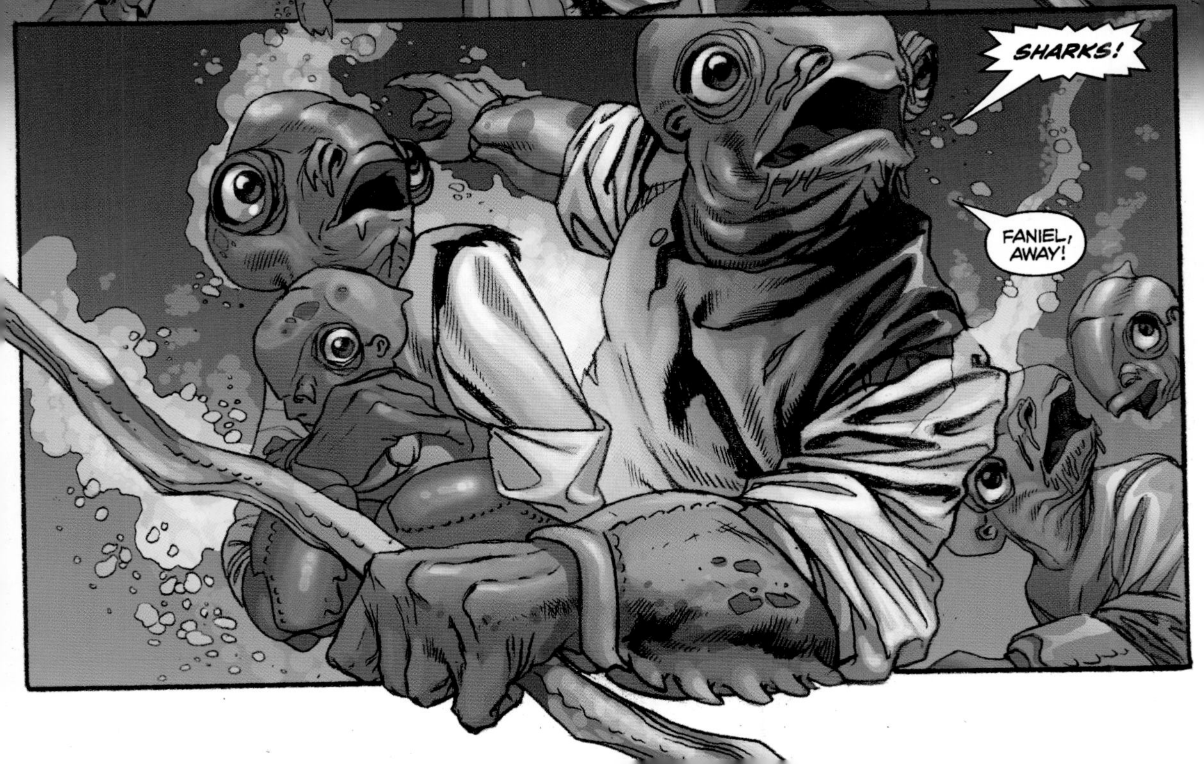
SHARKS!
FANIEL, AWAY!

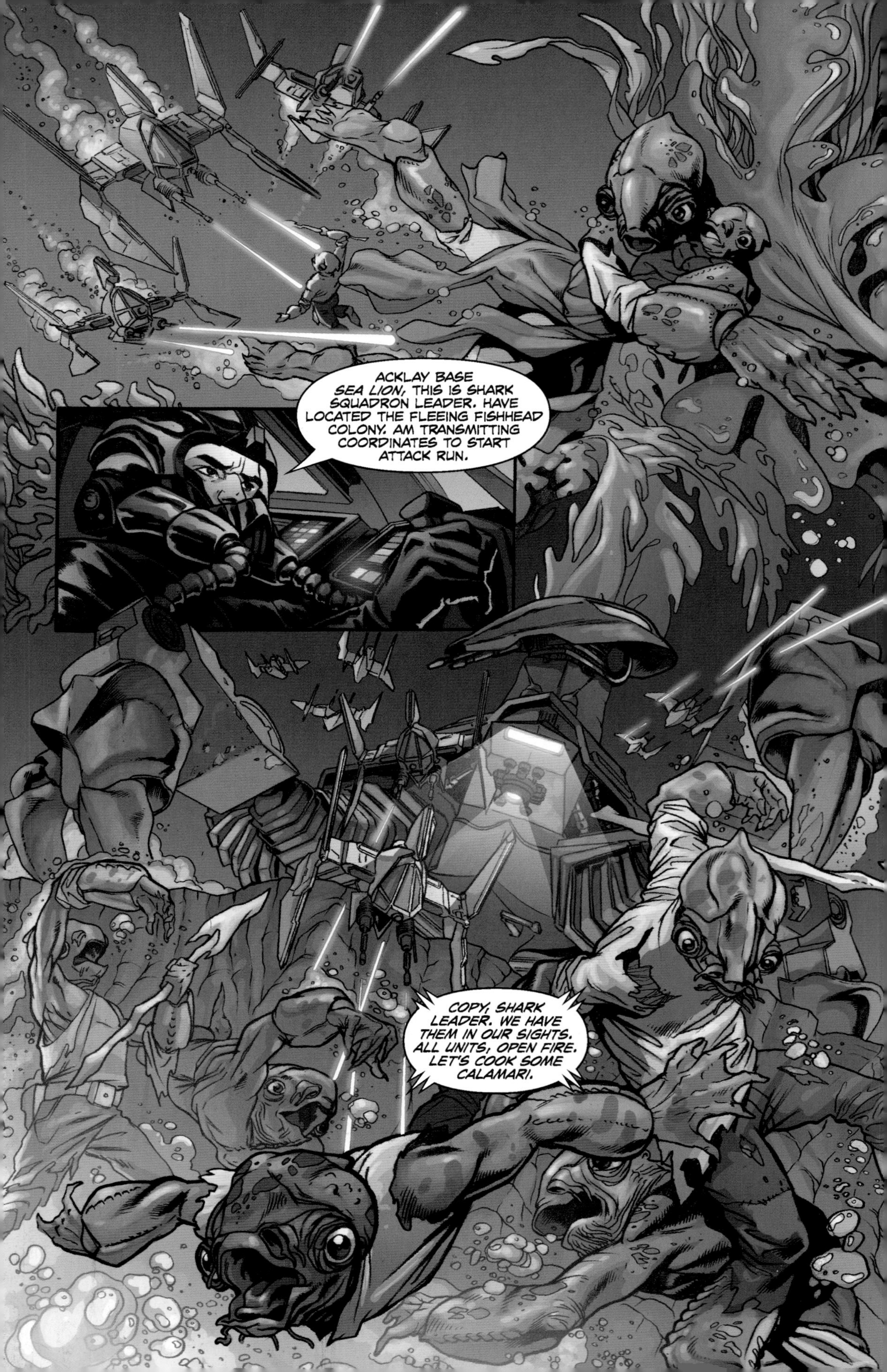
ACKLAY BASE *SEA LION*, THIS IS SHARK SQUADRON LEADER. HAVE LOCATED THE FLEEING FISHHEAD COLONY. AM TRANSMITTING COORDINATES TO START ATTACK RUN.
COPY, SHARK LEADER. WE HAVE THEM IN OUR SIGHTS. ALL UNITS, OPEN FIRE. LET'S COOK SOME CALAMARI.

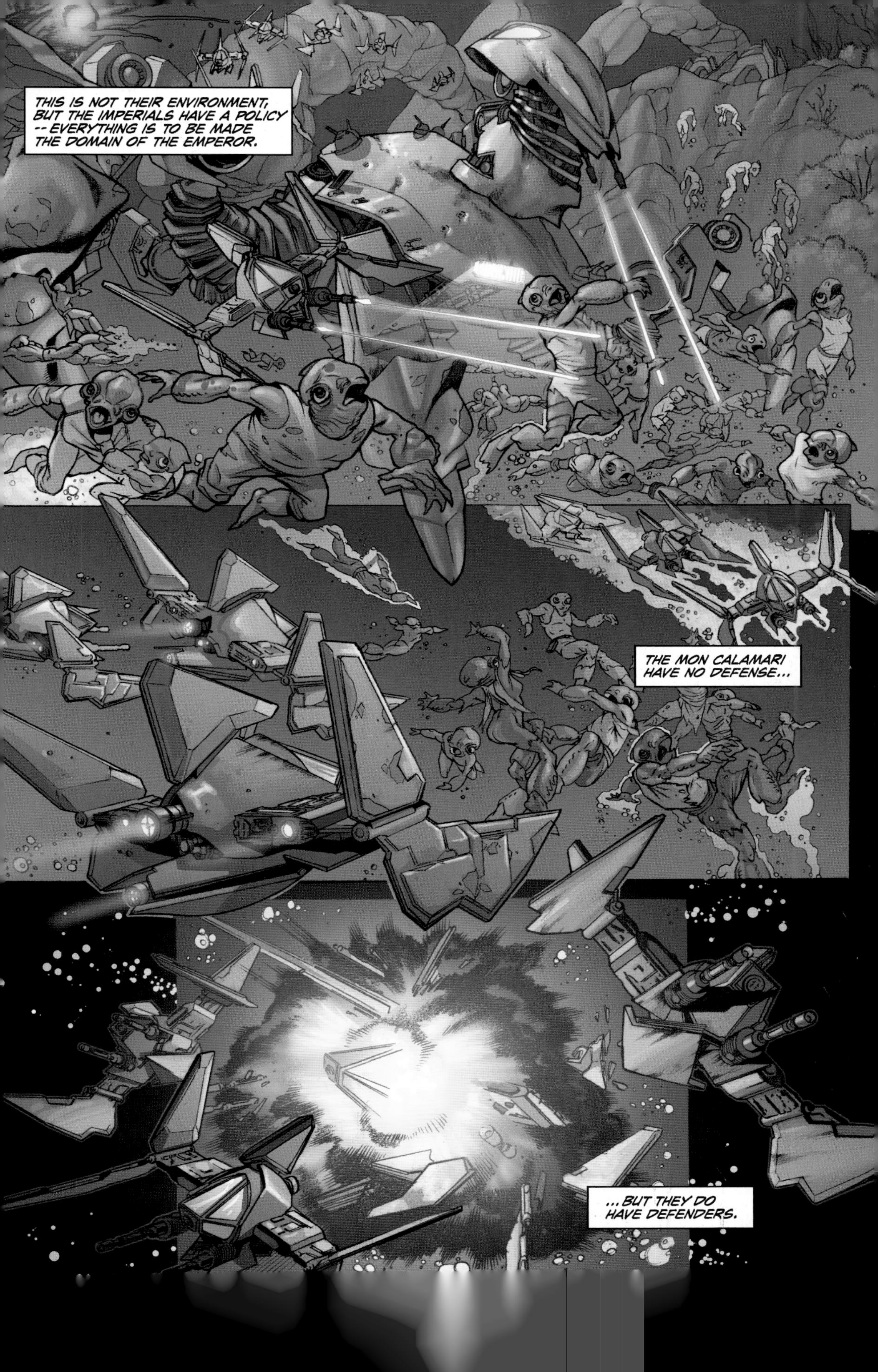
THIS IS NOT THEIR ENVIRONMENT, BUT THE IMPERIALS HAVE A POLICY -- EVERYTHING IS TO BE MADE THE DOMAIN OF THE EMPEROR.
THE MON CALAMARI HAVE NO DEFENSE...
...BUT THEY DO HAVE DEFENDERS.

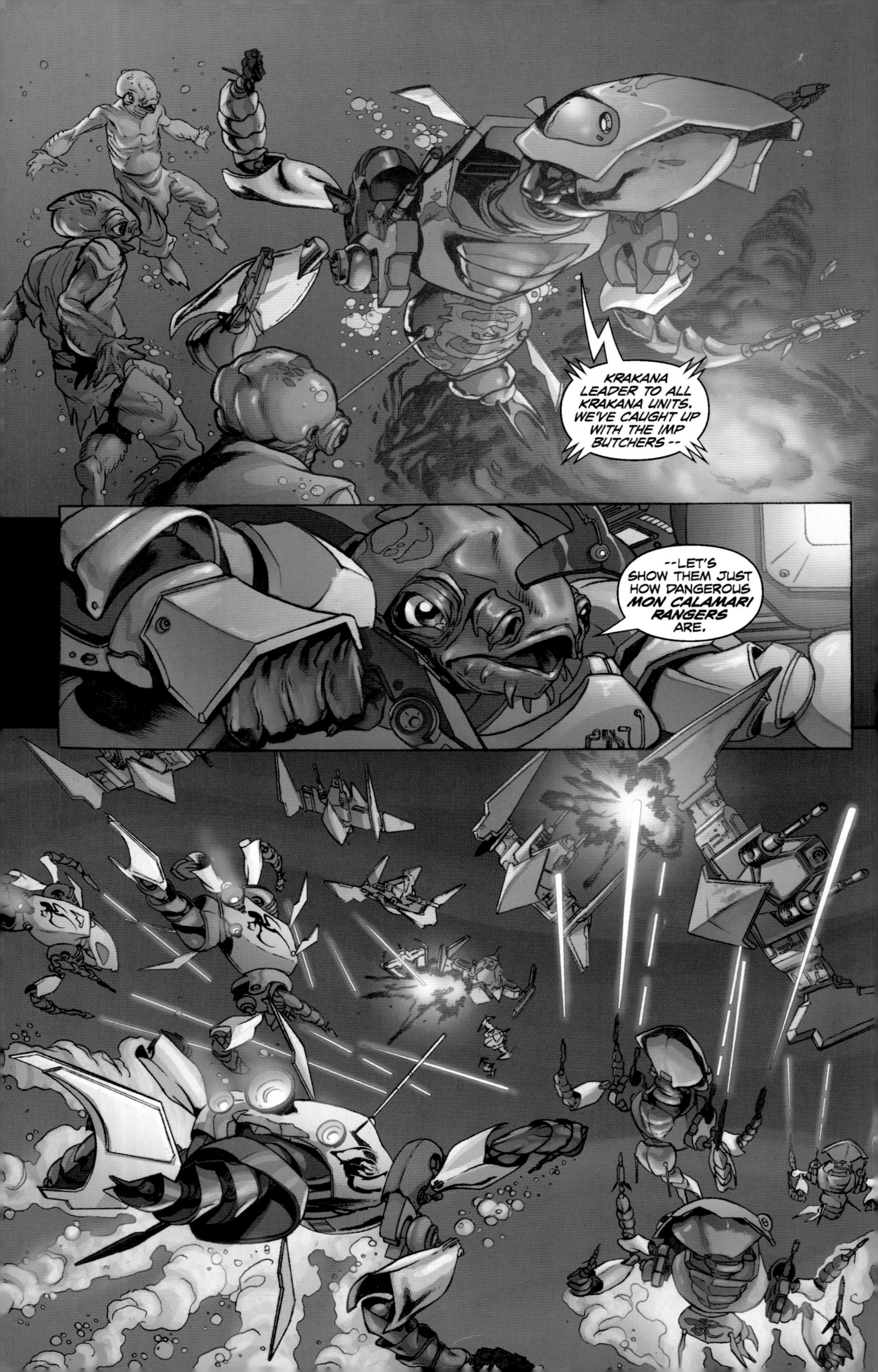
KRAKANA LEADER TO ALL KRAKANA UNITS. WE'VE CAUGHT UP WITH THE IMP BUTCHERS --
--LET'S SHOW THEM JUST HOW DANGEROUS ***MON CALAMARI RANGERS*** ARE.

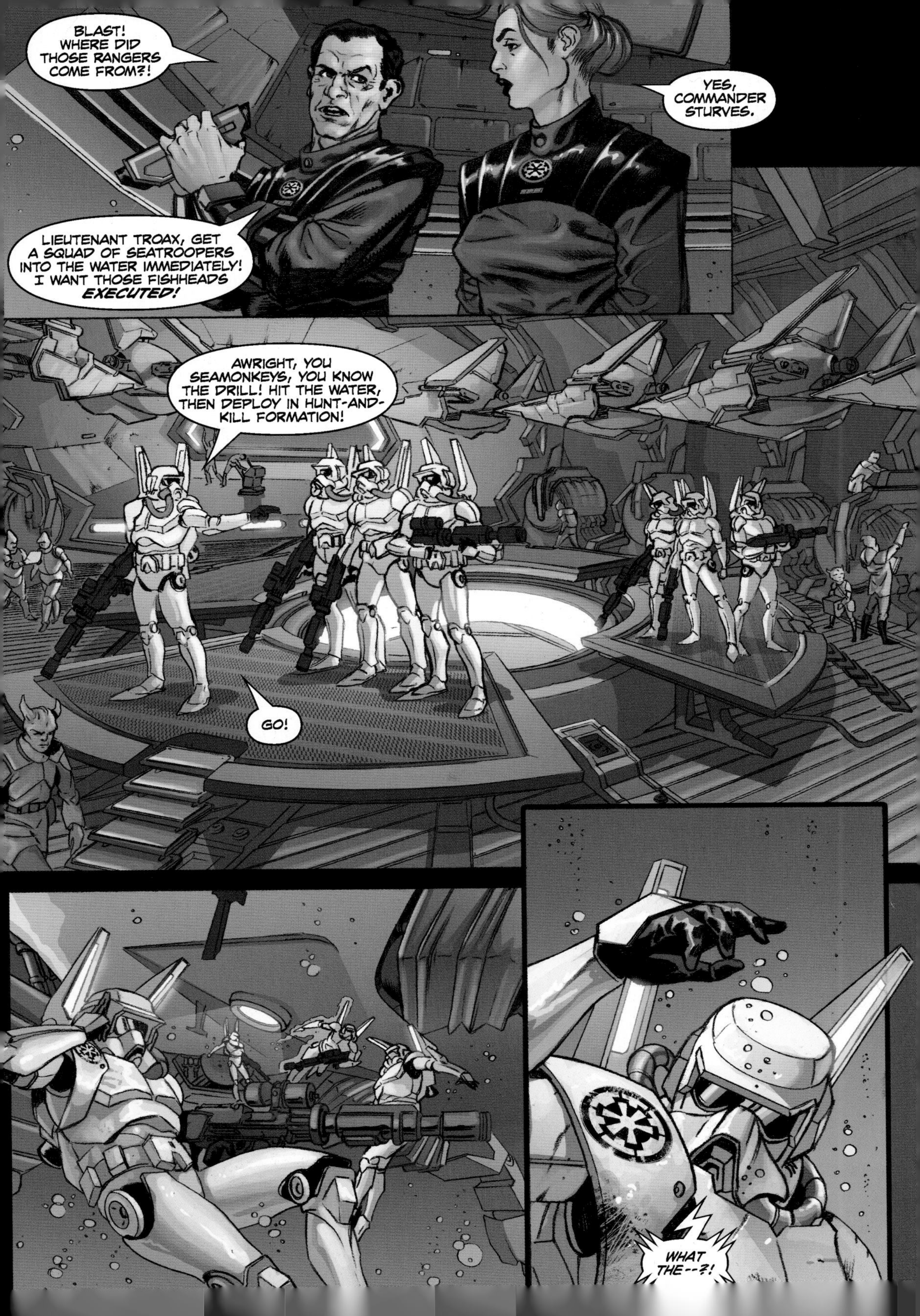
BLAST! WHERE DID THOSE RANGERS COME FROM?!
YES, COMMANDER STURVES.
LIEUTENANT TROAX, GET A SQUAD OF SEATROOPERS INTO THE WATER IMMEDIATELY! I WANT THOSE FISHHEADS EXECUTED!
AWRIGHT, YOU SEAMONKEYS, YOU KNOW THE DRILL! HIT THE WATER, THEN DEPLOY IN HUNT-AND-KILL FORMATION!
GO!
WHAT THE--?!

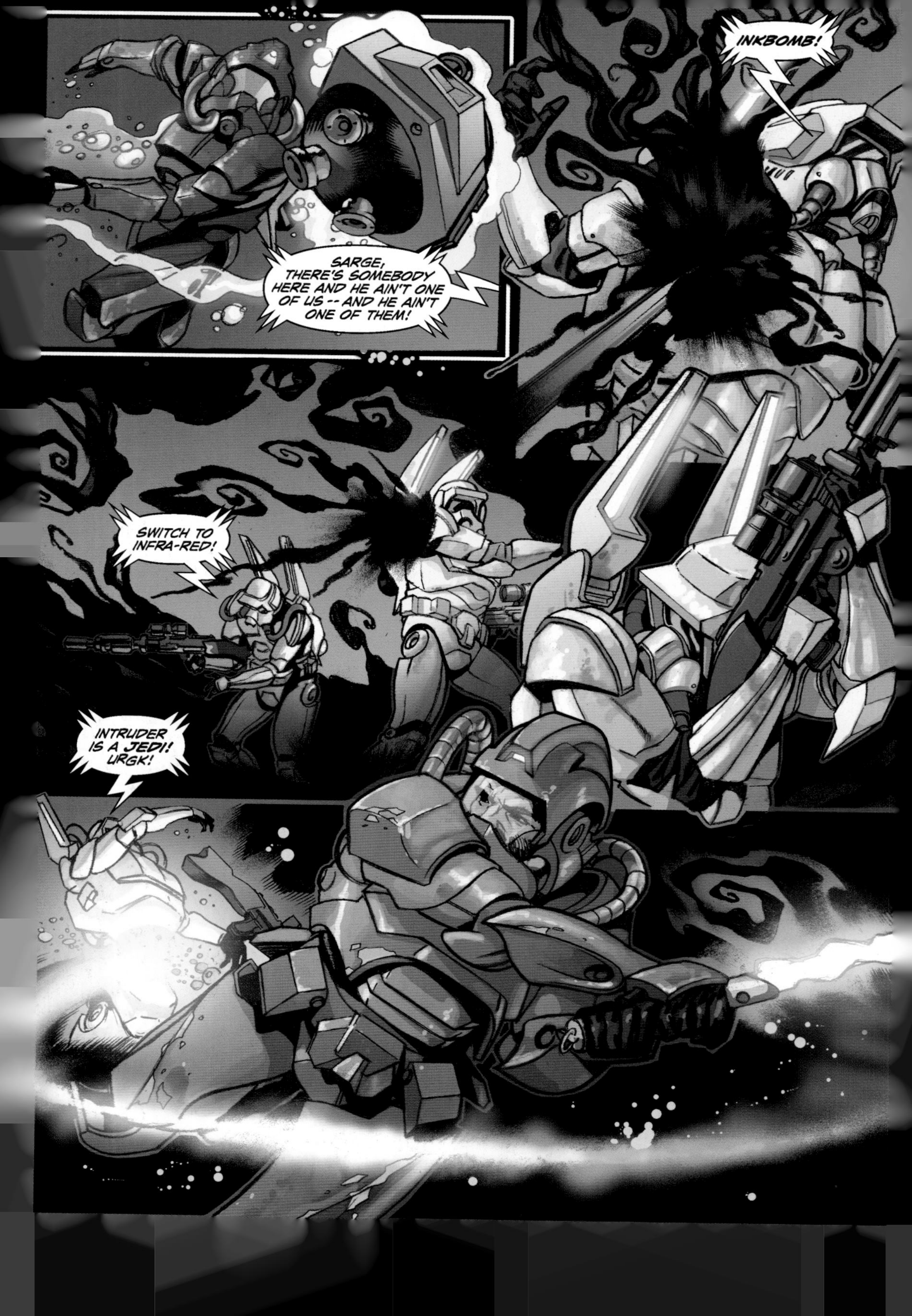
SARGE, THERE'S SOMEBODY HERE AND HE AIN'T ONE OF US -- AND HE AIN'T ONE OF THEM!
INKBOMB!
SWITCH TO INFRA-RED!
INTRUDER IS A JEDI! URGK!

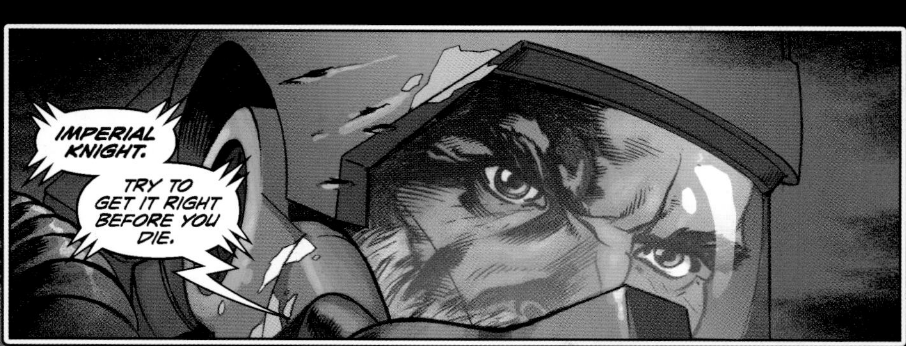
IMPERIAL KNIGHT.
TRY TO GET IT RIGHT BEFORE YOU DIE.

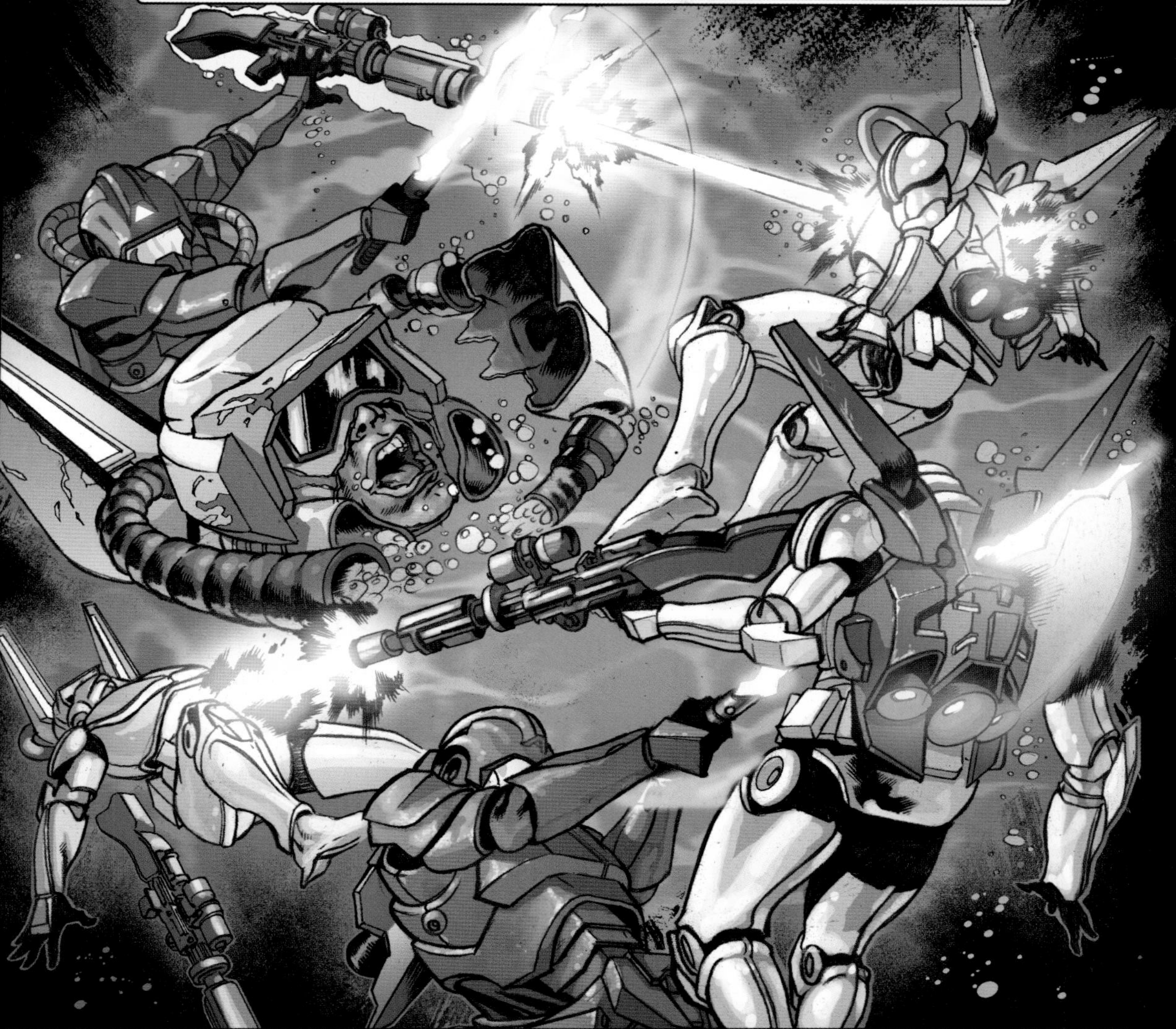

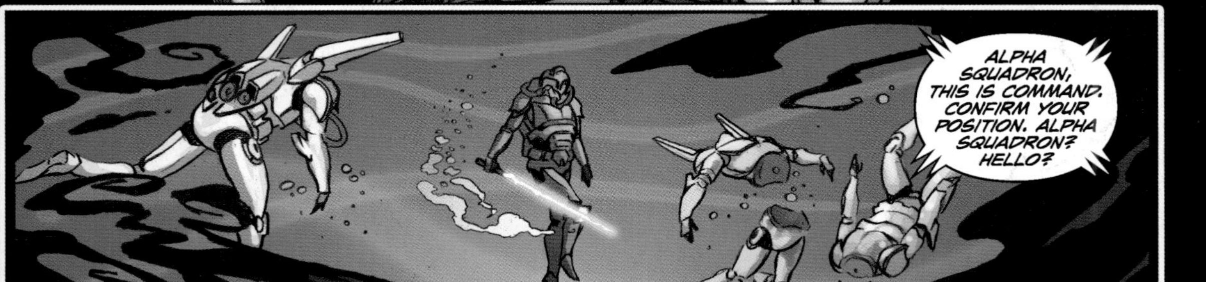
ALPHA SQUADRON, THIS IS COMMAND. CONFIRM YOUR POSITION. ALPHA SQUADRON? HELLO?

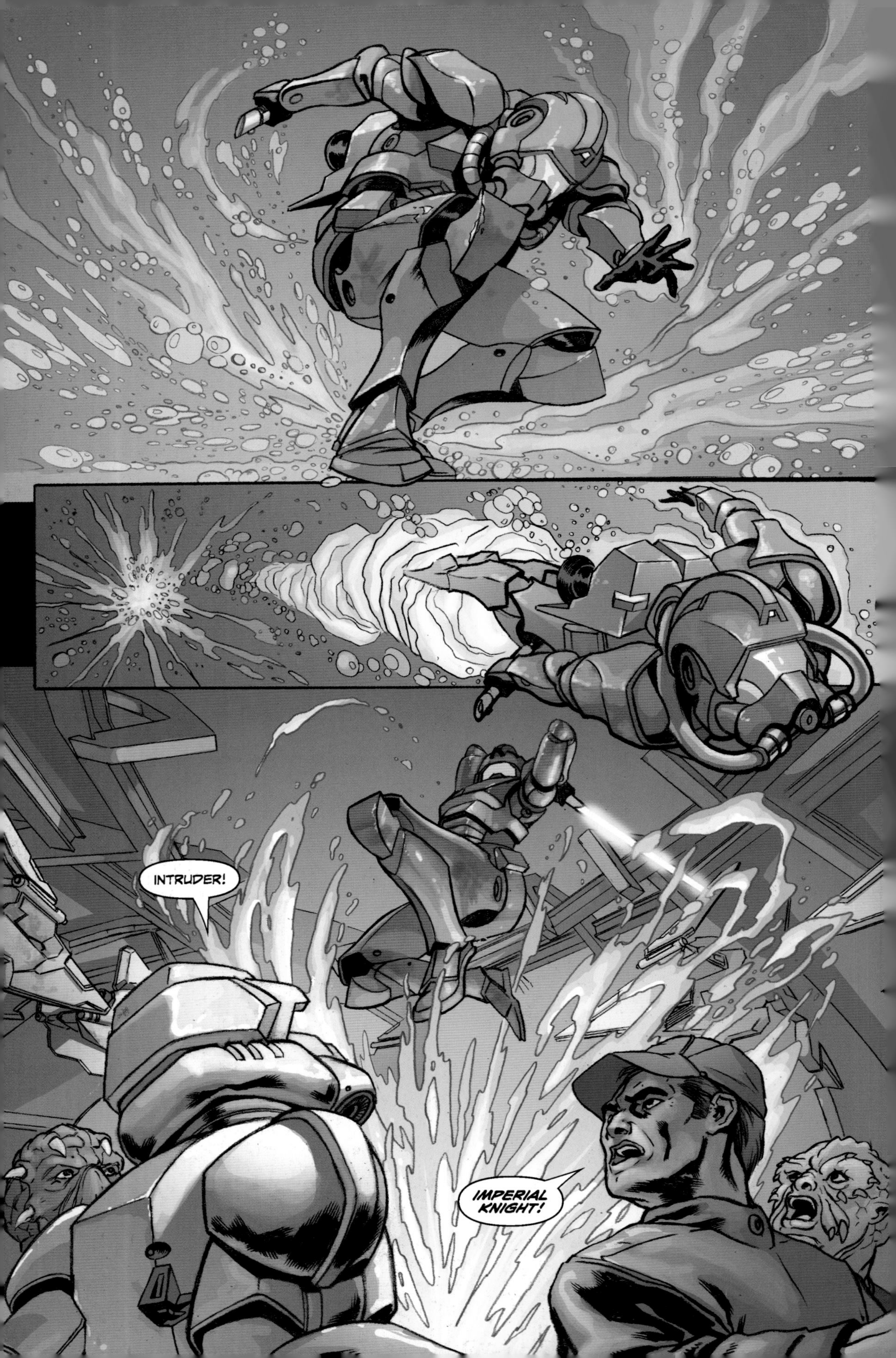
INTRUDER!
IMPERIAL KNIGHT!

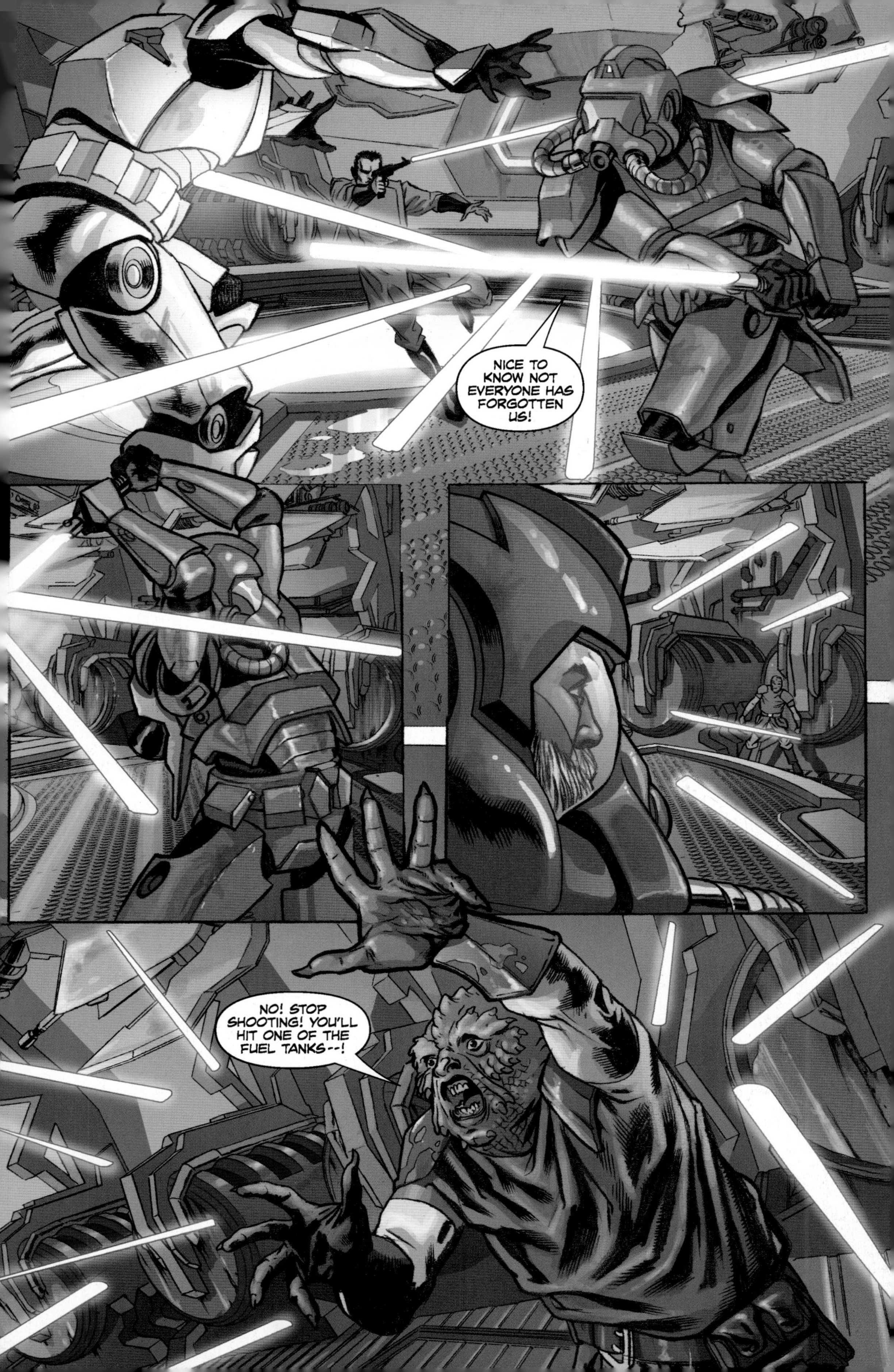
NICE TO KNOW NOT EVERYONE HAS FORGOTTEN US!
NO! STOP SHOOTING! YOU'LL HIT ONE OF THE FUEL TANKS--!

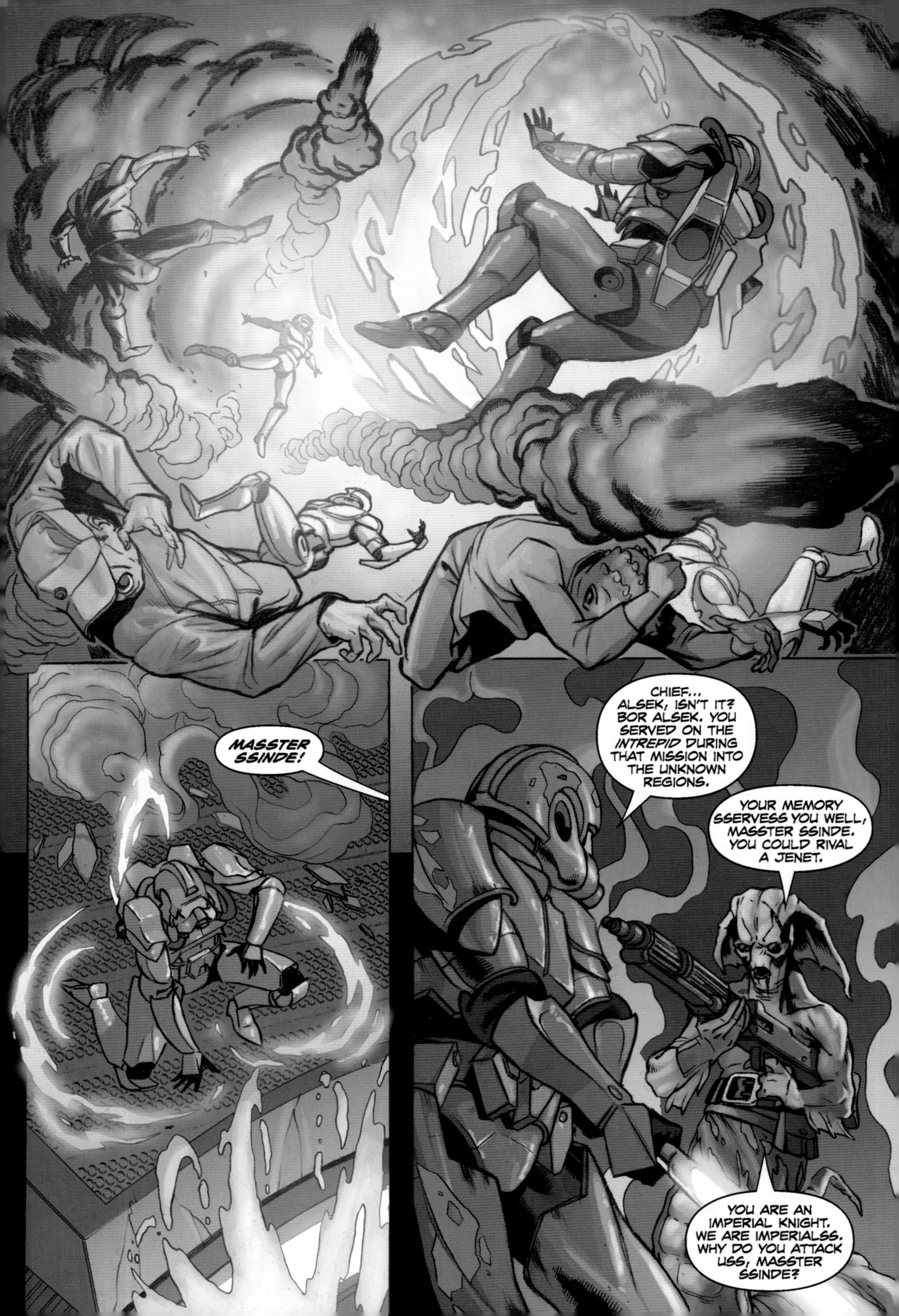
MASSTER SSINDE!
CHIEF... ALSEK, ISN'T IT? BOR ALSEK. YOU SERVED ON THE *INTREPID* DURING THAT MISSION INTO THE UNKNOWN REGIONS.
YOUR MEMORY SSERVESS YOU WELL, MASSTER SSINDE. YOU COULD RIVAL A JENET.
YOU ARE AN IMPERIAL KNIGHT. WE ARE IMPERIALSS. WHY DO YOU ATTACK USS, MASSTER SSINDE?

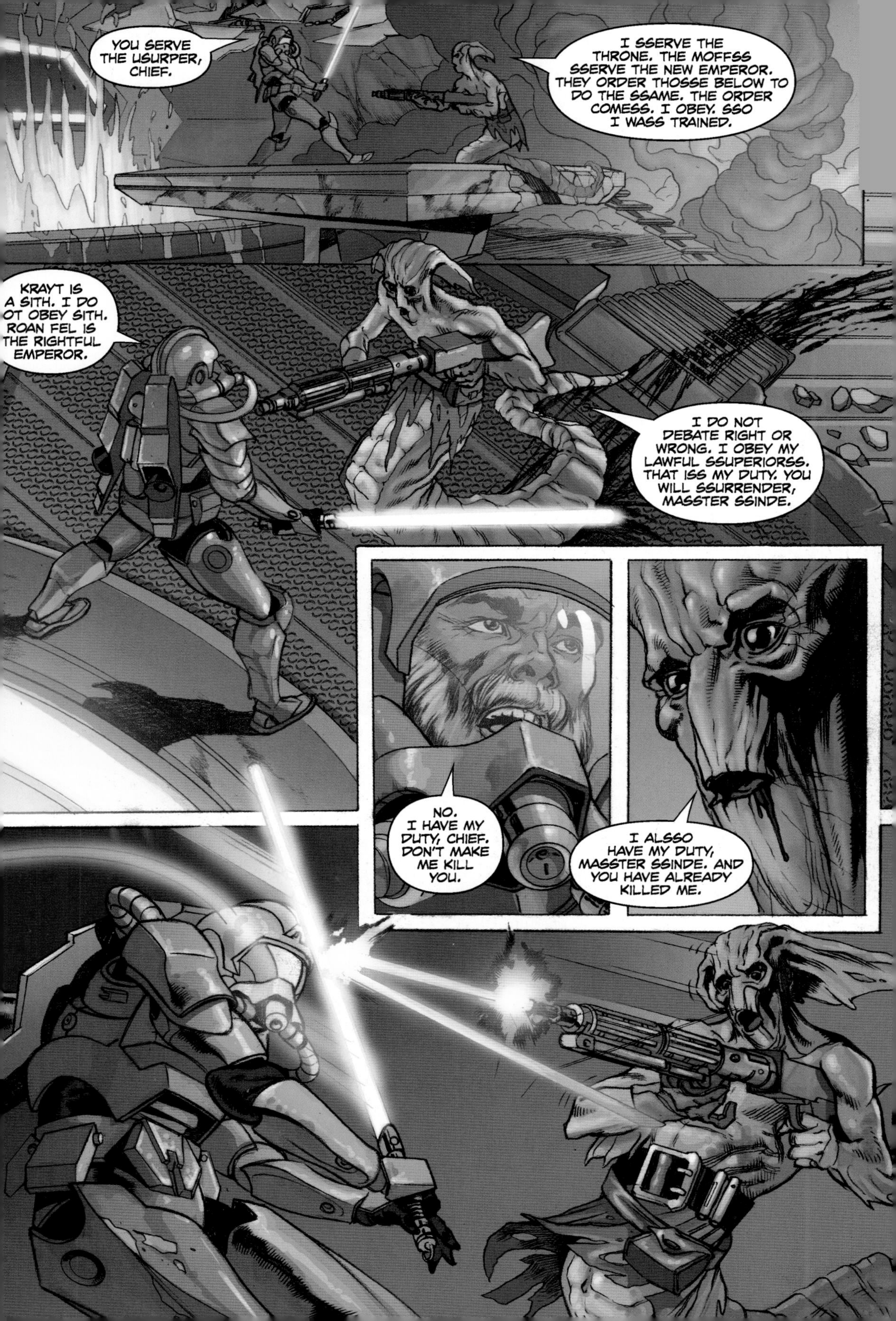
YOU SERVE THE USURPER, CHIEF.
I SSERVE THE THRONE. THE MOFFSS SSERVE THE NEW EMPEROR. THEY ORDER THOSSE BELOW TO DO THE SSAME. THE ORDER COMESS. I OBEY. SSO I WASS TRAINED.
KRAYT IS A SITH. I DO OT OBEY SITH. ROAN FEL IS THE RIGHTFUL EMPEROR.
I DO NOT DEBATE RIGHT OR WRONG. I OBEY MY LAWFUL SSUPERIORSS. THAT ISS MY DUTY. YOU WILL SSURRENDER, MASSTER SSINDE.
NO. I HAVE MY DUTY, CHIEF. DON'T MAKE ME KILL YOU.
I ALSSO HAVE MY DUTY, MASSTER SSINDE. AND YOU HAVE ALREADY KILLED ME.

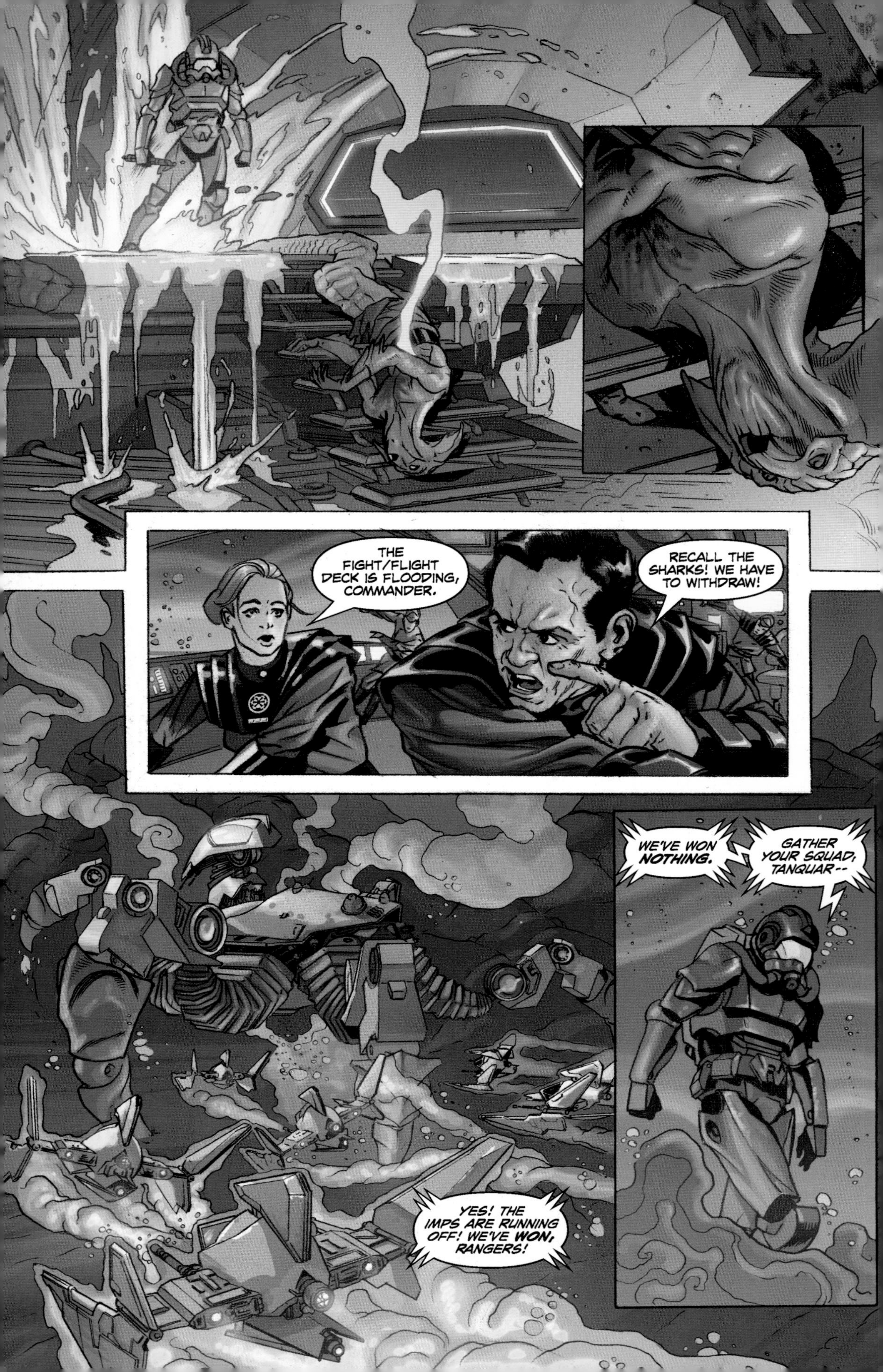
THE FIGHT/FLIGHT DECK IS FLOODING, COMMANDER.
RECALL THE SHARKS! WE HAVE TO WITHDRAW!
YES! THE IMPS ARE RUNNING OFF! WE'VE **WON**, RANGERS!
WE'VE WON **NOTHING**.
GATHER YOUR SQUAD, TANQUAR--

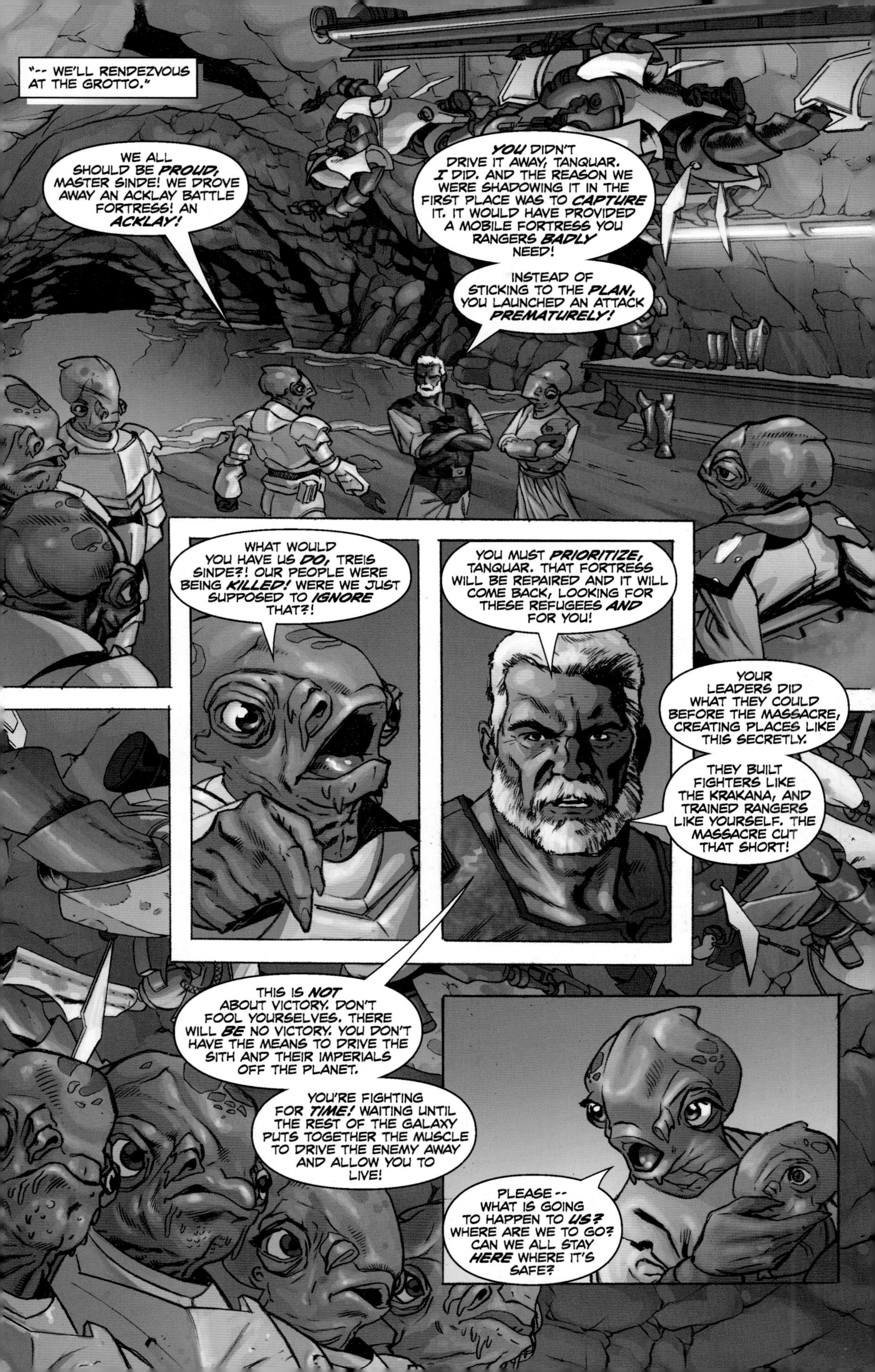
"-- WE'LL RENDEZVOUS AT THE GROTTO."
WE ALL SHOULD BE *PROUD,* MASTER SINDE! WE DROVE AWAY AN ACKLAY BATTLE FORTRESS! AN *ACKLAY!*
YOU DIDN'T DRIVE IT AWAY, TANQUAR. *I* DID. AND THE REASON WE WERE SHADOWING IT IN THE FIRST PLACE WAS TO *CAPTURE* IT. IT WOULD HAVE PROVIDED A MOBILE FORTRESS YOU RANGERS *BADLY* NEED!
INSTEAD OF STICKING TO THE *PLAN,* YOU LAUNCHED AN ATTACK *PREMATURELY!*
WHAT WOULD YOU HAVE US *DO,* TREIS SINDE?! OUR PEOPLE WERE BEING *KILLED!* WERE WE JUST SUPPOSED TO *IGNORE* THAT?!
YOU MUST *PRIORITIZE,* TANQUAR. THAT FORTRESS WILL BE REPAIRED AND IT WILL COME BACK, LOOKING FOR THESE REFUGEES *AND* FOR YOU!
YOUR LEADERS DID WHAT THEY COULD BEFORE THE MASSACRE, CREATING PLACES LIKE THIS SECRETLY.
THEY BUILT FIGHTERS LIKE THE KRAKANA, AND TRAINED RANGERS LIKE YOURSELF. THE MASSACRE CUT THAT SHORT!
THIS IS *NOT* ABOUT VICTORY. DON'T FOOL YOURSELVES. THERE WILL *BE* NO VICTORY. YOU DON'T HAVE THE MEANS TO DRIVE THE SITH AND THEIR IMPERIALS OFF THE PLANET.
YOU'RE FIGHTING FOR *TIME!* WAITING UNTIL THE REST OF THE GALAXY PUTS TOGETHER THE MUSCLE TO DRIVE THE ENEMY AWAY AND ALLOW YOU TO LIVE!
PLEASE -- WHAT IS GOING TO HAPPEN TO *US?* WHERE ARE WE TO GO? CAN WE ALL STAY *HERE* WHERE IT'S SAFE?

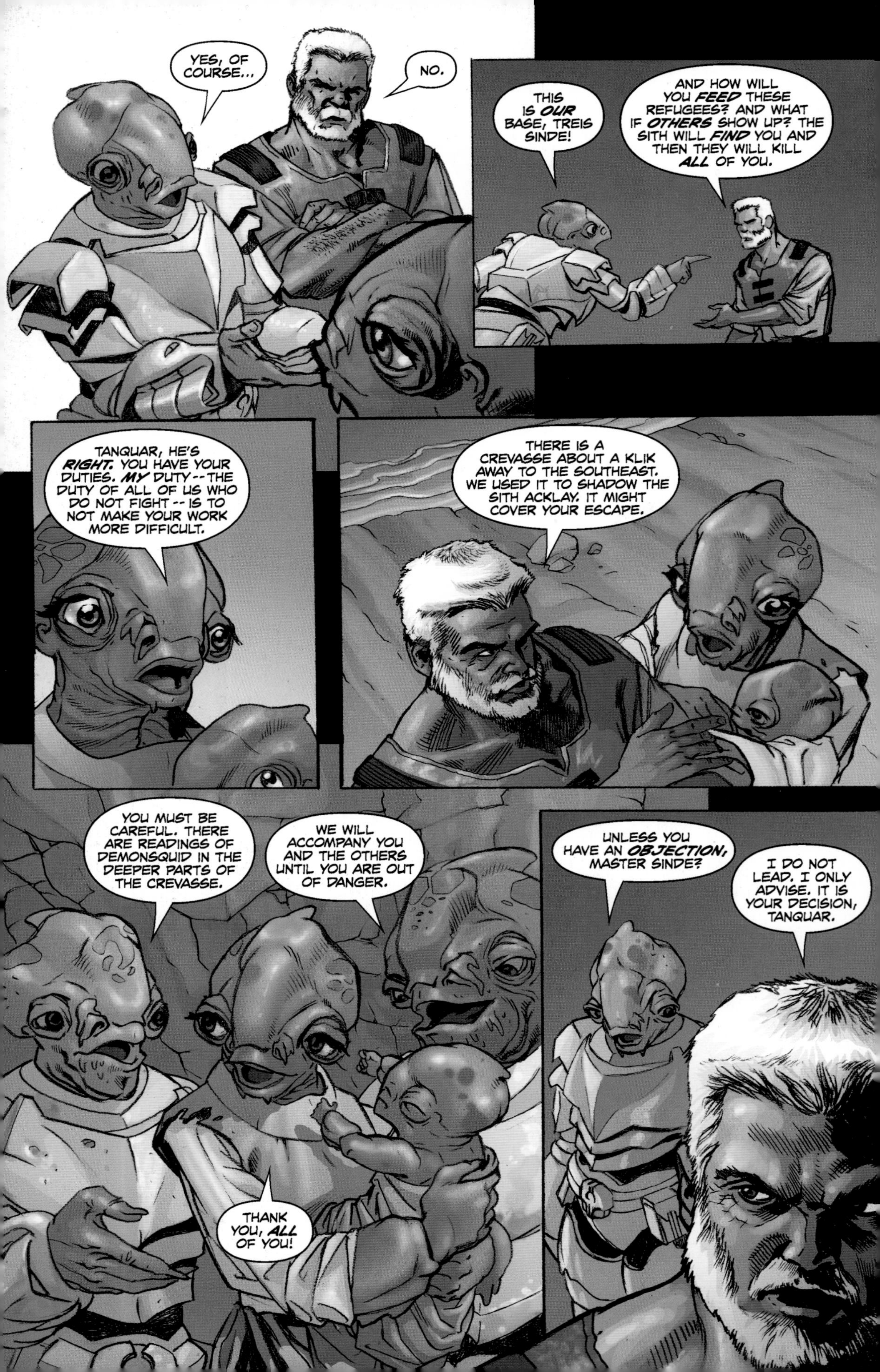
YES, OF COURSE...
NO.
THIS IS OUR BASE, TREIS SINDE!
AND HOW WILL YOU FEED THESE REFUGEES? AND WHAT IF OTHERS SHOW UP? THE SITH WILL FIND YOU AND THEN THEY WILL KILL ALL OF YOU.
TANQUAR, HE'S RIGHT. YOU HAVE YOUR DUTIES. MY DUTY -- THE DUTY OF ALL OF US WHO DO NOT FIGHT -- IS TO NOT MAKE YOUR WORK MORE DIFFICULT.
THERE IS A CREVASSE ABOUT A KLIK AWAY TO THE SOUTHEAST. WE USED IT TO SHADOW THE SITH ACKLAY. IT MIGHT COVER YOUR ESCAPE.
YOU MUST BE CAREFUL. THERE ARE READINGS OF DEMONSQUID IN THE DEEPER PARTS OF THE CREVASSE.
WE WILL ACCOMPANY YOU AND THE OTHERS UNTIL YOU ARE OUT OF DANGER.
THANK YOU, ALL OF YOU!
UNLESS YOU HAVE AN OBJECTION, MASTER SINDE?
I DO NOT LEAD. I ONLY ADVISE. IT IS YOUR DECISION, TANQUAR.

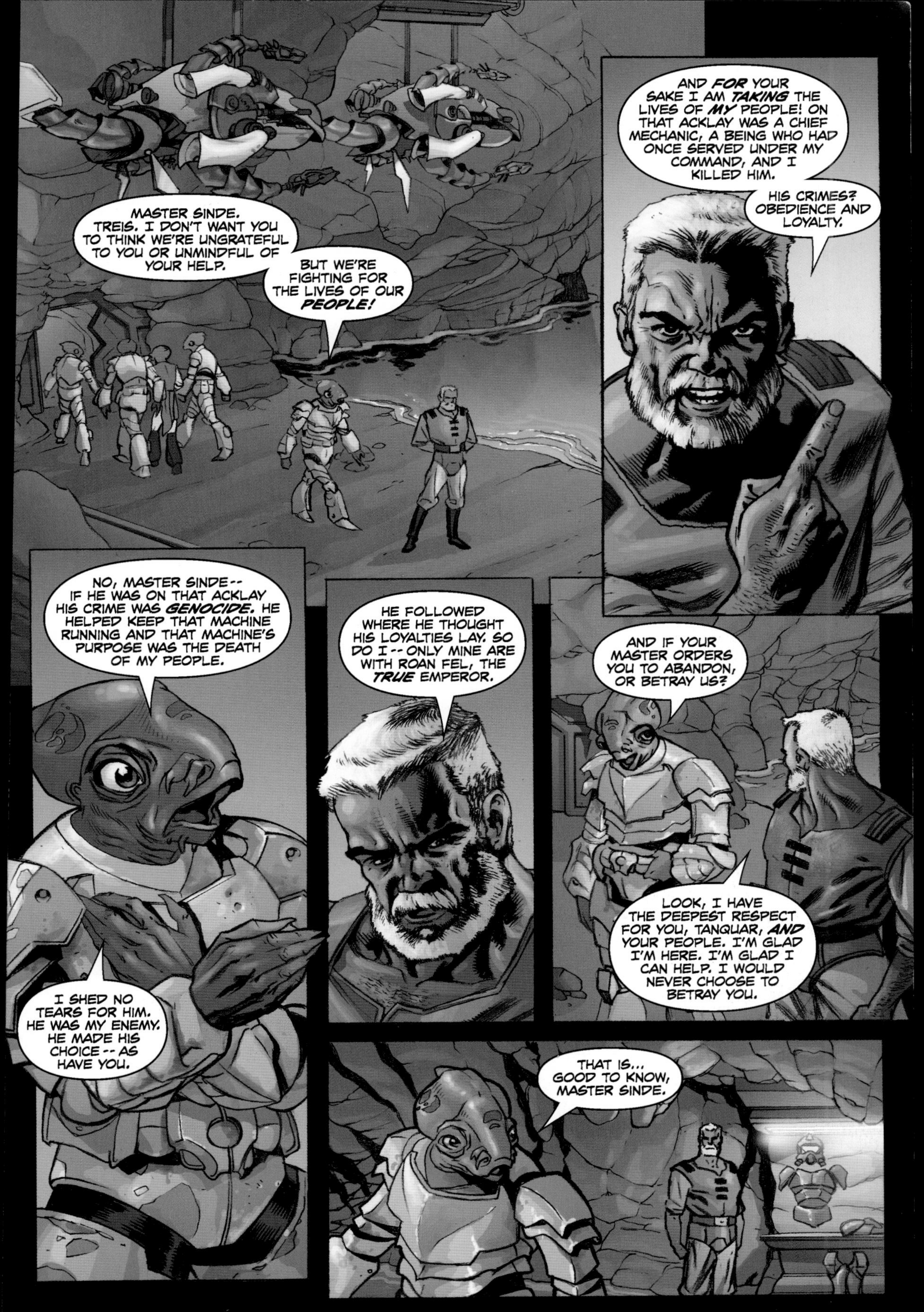
MASTER SINDE. TREIS. I DON'T WANT YOU TO THINK WE'RE UNGRATEFUL TO YOU OR UNMINDFUL OF YOUR HELP.
BUT WE'RE FIGHTING FOR THE LIVES OF OUR PEOPLE!
AND FOR YOUR SAKE I AM TAKING THE LIVES OF MY PEOPLE! ON THAT ACKLAY WAS A CHIEF MECHANIC, A BEING WHO HAD ONCE SERVED UNDER MY COMMAND, AND I KILLED HIM.
HIS CRIMES? OBEDIENCE AND LOYALTY.
NO, MASTER SINDE-- IF HE WAS ON THAT ACKLAY HIS CRIME WAS GENOCIDE. HE HELPED KEEP THAT MACHINE RUNNING AND THAT MACHINE'S PURPOSE WAS THE DEATH OF MY PEOPLE.
I SHED NO TEARS FOR HIM. HE WAS MY ENEMY. HE MADE HIS CHOICE--AS HAVE YOU.
HE FOLLOWED WHERE HE THOUGHT HIS LOYALTIES LAY. SO DO I--ONLY MINE ARE WITH ROAN FEL, THE TRUE EMPEROR.
AND IF YOUR MASTER ORDERS YOU TO ABANDON, OR BETRAY US?
LOOK, I HAVE THE DEEPEST RESPECT FOR YOU, TANQUAR, AND YOUR PEOPLE. I'M GLAD I'M HERE. I'M GLAD I CAN HELP. I WOULD NEVER CHOOSE TO BETRAY YOU.
THAT IS... GOOD TO KNOW, MASTER SINDE.

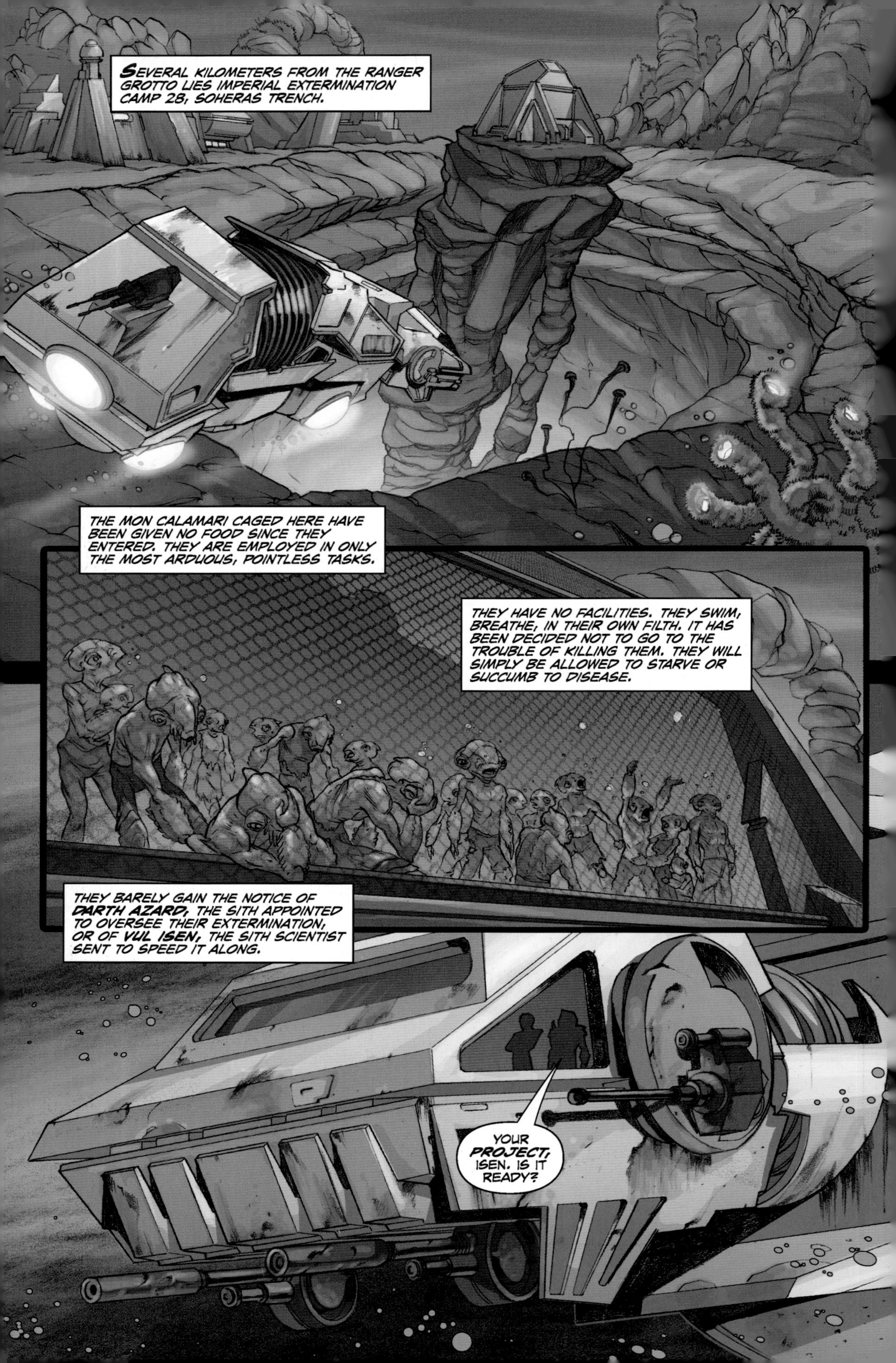
SEVERAL KILOMETERS FROM THE RANGER GROTTO LIES IMPERIAL EXTERMINATION CAMP 28, SOHERAS TRENCH.
THE MON CALAMARI CAGED HERE HAVE BEEN GIVEN NO FOOD SINCE THEY ENTERED. THEY ARE EMPLOYED IN ONLY THE MOST ARDUOUS, POINTLESS TASKS.
THEY HAVE NO FACILITIES. THEY SWIM, BREATHE, IN THEIR OWN FILTH. IT HAS BEEN DECIDED NOT TO GO TO THE TROUBLE OF KILLING THEM. THEY WILL SIMPLY BE ALLOWED TO STARVE OR SUCCUMB TO DISEASE.
THEY BARELY GAIN THE NOTICE OF DARTH AZARD, THE SITH APPOINTED TO OVERSEE THEIR EXTERMINATION, OR OF VUL ISEN, THE SITH SCIENTIST SENT TO SPEED IT ALONG.
YOUR PROJECT, ISEN. IS IT READY?

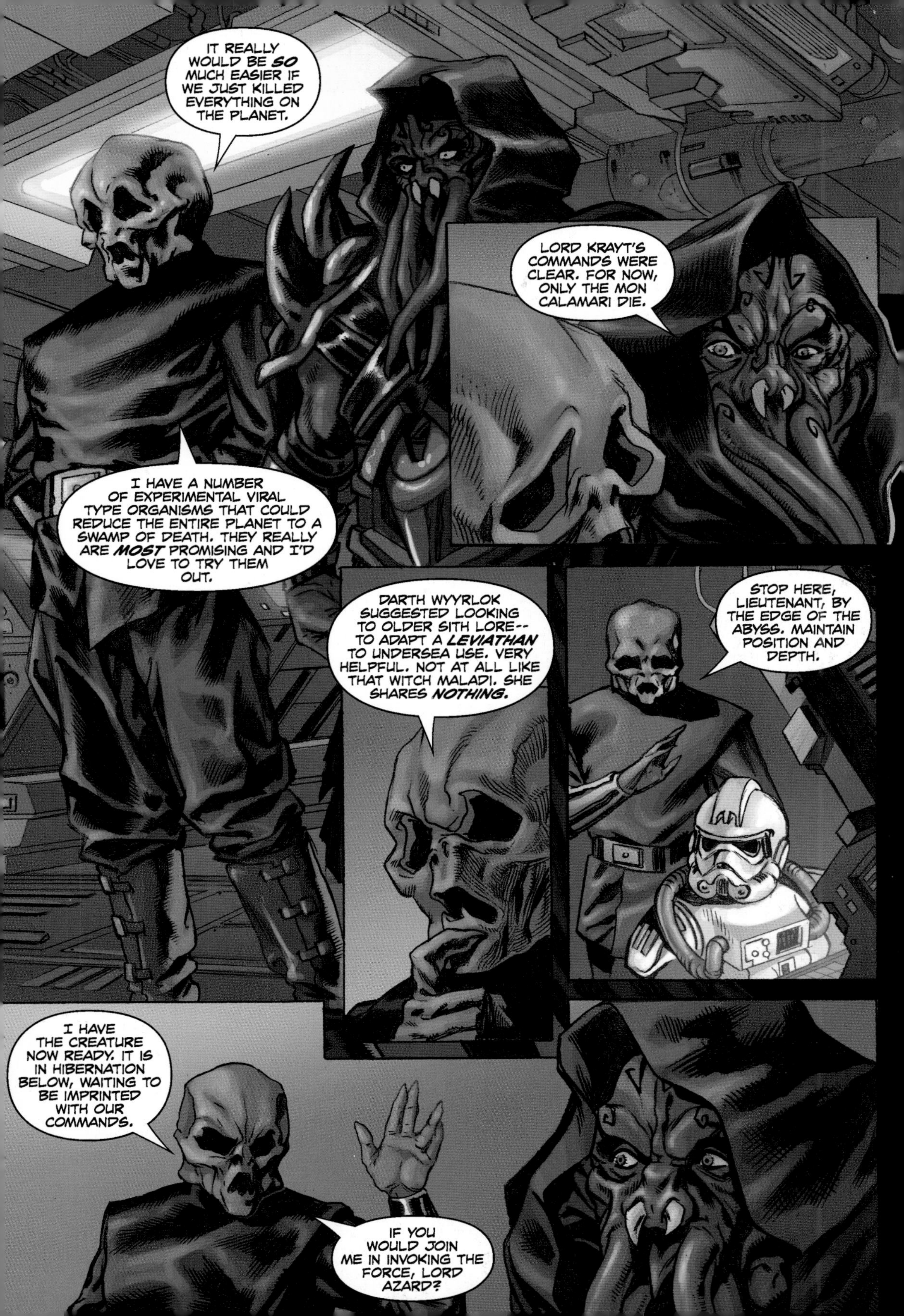
IT REALLY WOULD BE SO MUCH EASIER IF WE JUST KILLED EVERYTHING ON THE PLANET.
LORD KRAYT'S COMMANDS WERE CLEAR. FOR NOW, ONLY THE MON CALAMARI DIE.
I HAVE A NUMBER OF EXPERIMENTAL VIRAL TYPE ORGANISMS THAT COULD REDUCE THE ENTIRE PLANET TO A SWAMP OF DEATH. THEY REALLY ARE MOST PROMISING AND I'D LOVE TO TRY THEM OUT.
DARTH WYYRLOK SUGGESTED LOOKING TO OLDER SITH LORE-- TO ADAPT A LEVIATHAN TO UNDERSEA USE. VERY HELPFUL. NOT AT ALL LIKE THAT WITCH MALADI. SHE SHARES NOTHING.
STOP HERE, LIEUTENANT, BY THE EDGE OF THE ABYSS. MAINTAIN POSITION AND DEPTH.
I HAVE THE CREATURE NOW READY. IT IS IN HIBERNATION BELOW, WAITING TO BE IMPRINTED WITH OUR COMMANDS.
IF YOU WOULD JOIN ME IN INVOKING THE FORCE, LORD AZARD?

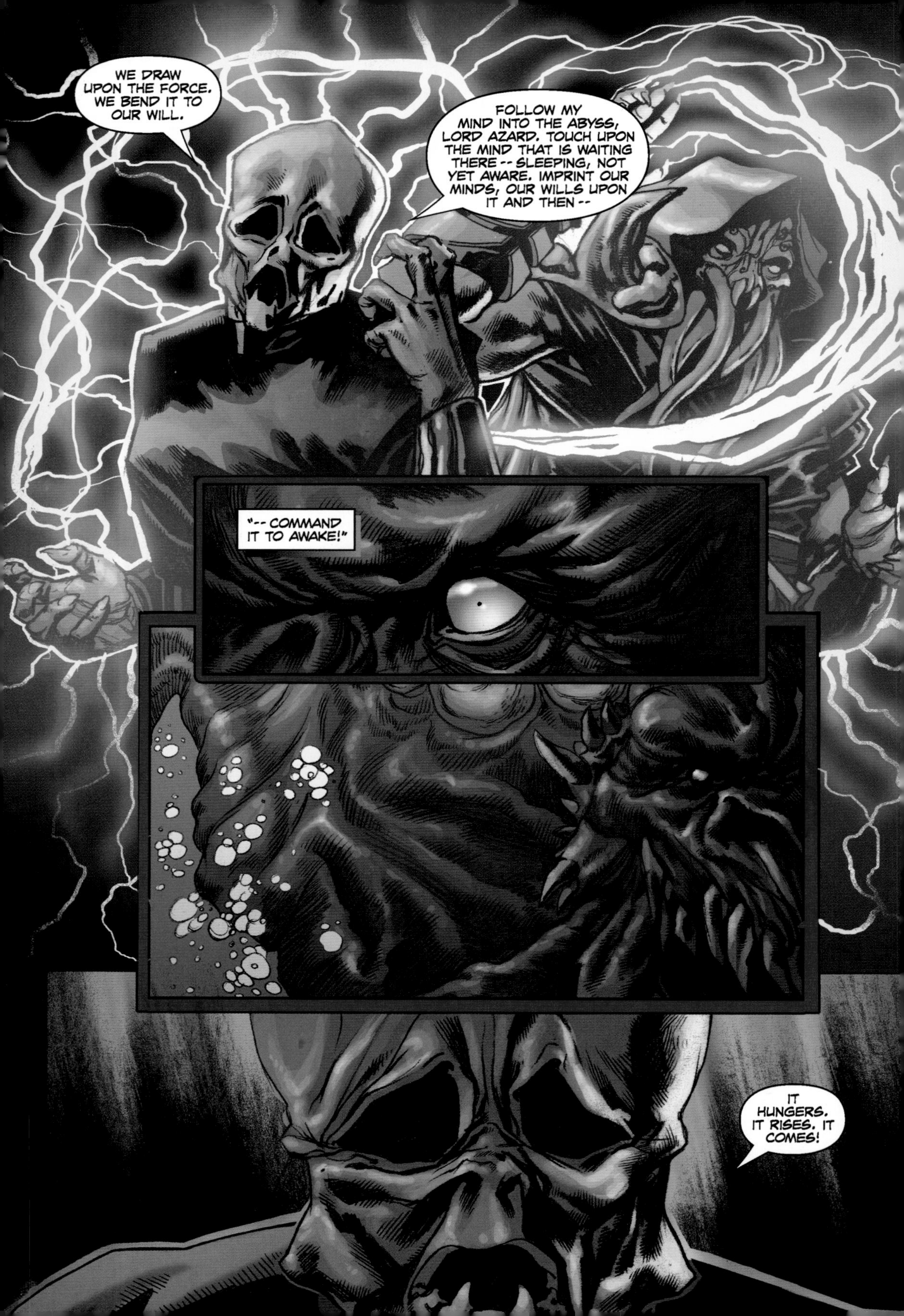
WE DRAW UPON THE FORCE. WE BEND IT TO OUR WILL.
FOLLOW MY MIND INTO THE ABYSS, LORD AZARD. TOUCH UPON THE MIND THAT IS WAITING THERE -- SLEEPING, NOT YET AWARE. IMPRINT OUR MINDS, OUR WILLS UPON IT AND THEN --
"-- COMMAND IT TO AWAKE!"
IT HUNGERS. IT RISES. IT COMES!

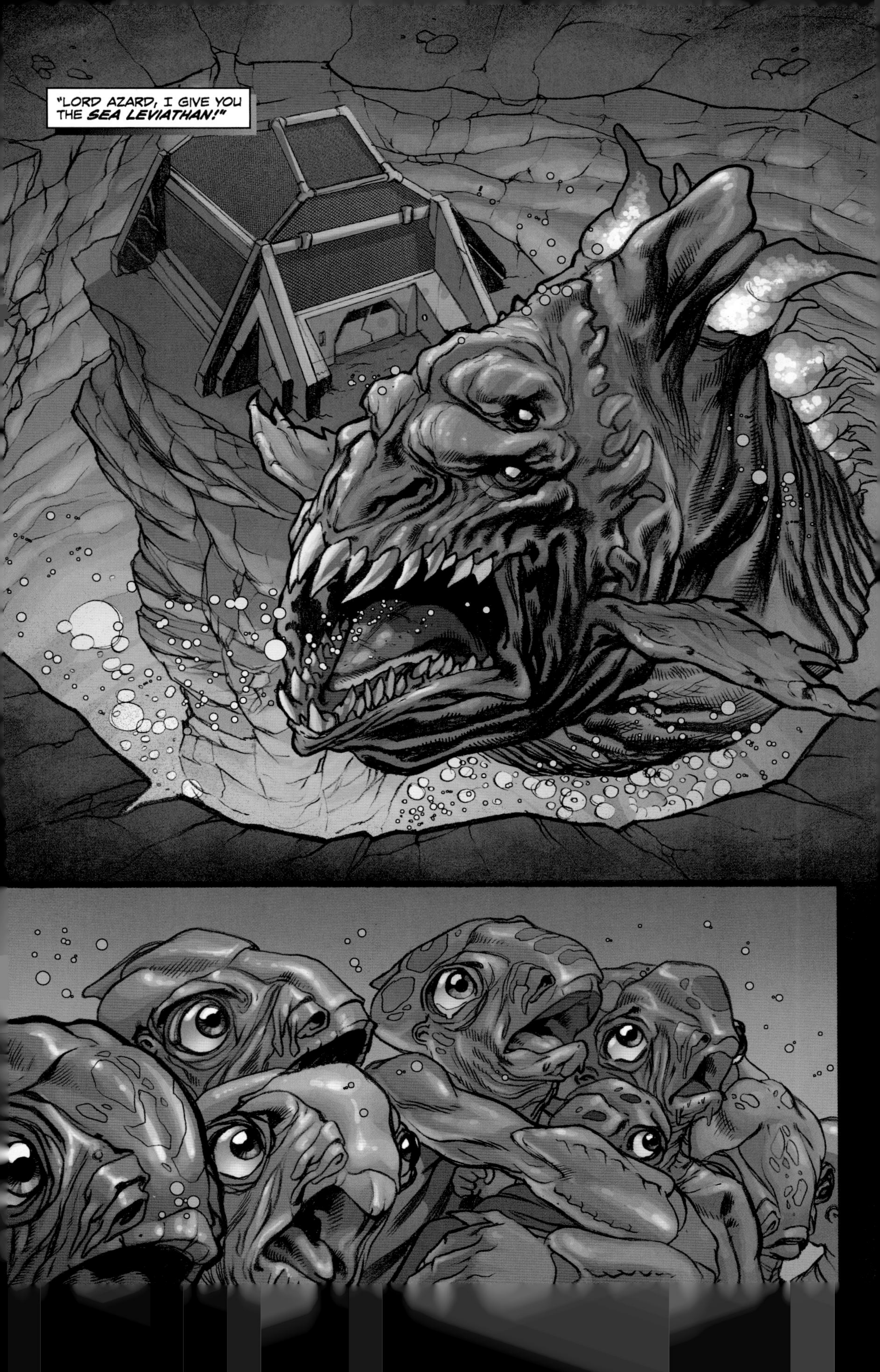
"LORD AZARD, I GIVE YOU THE SEA LEVIATHAN!"

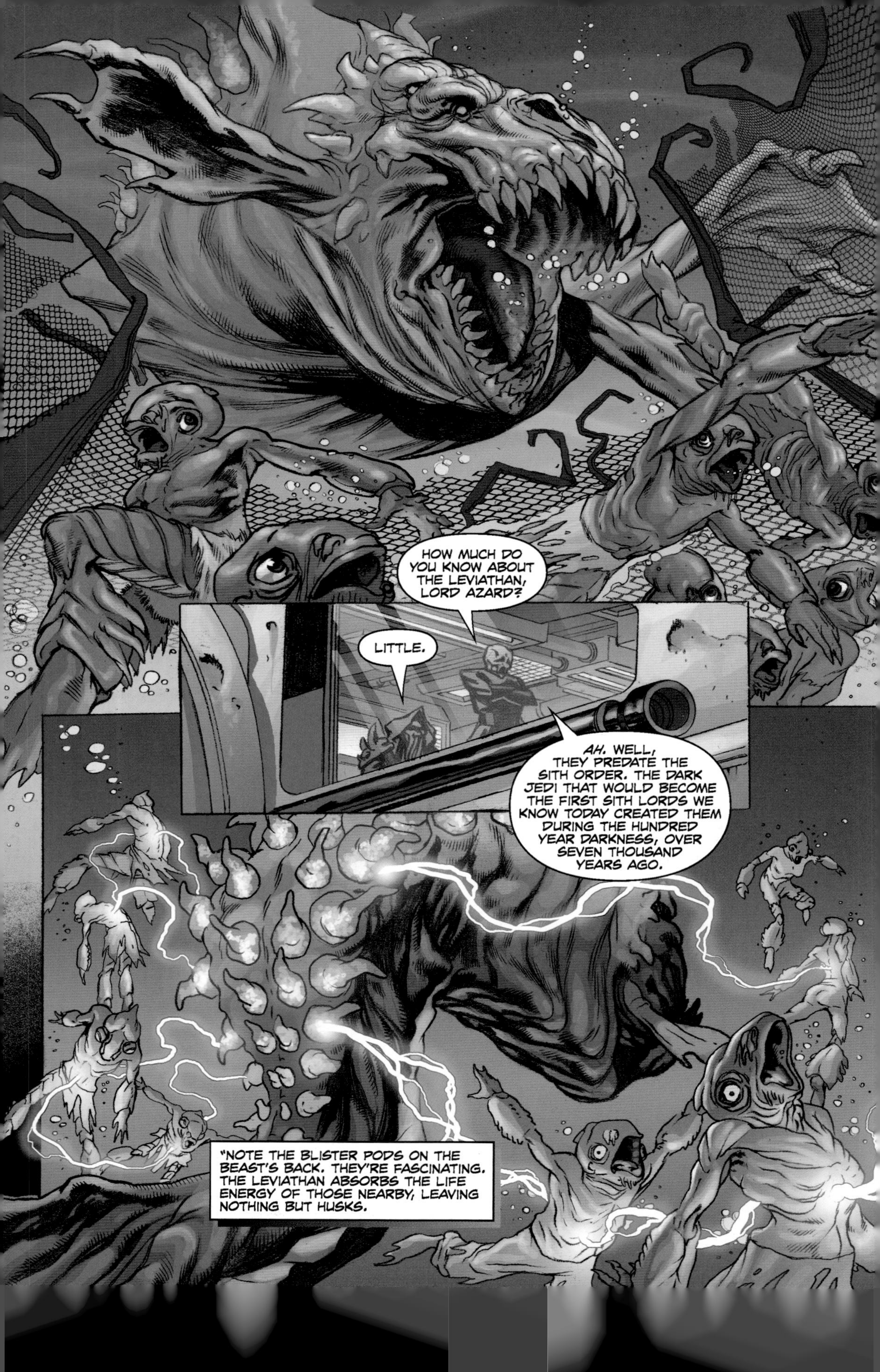
HOW MUCH DO YOU KNOW ABOUT THE LEVIATHAN, LORD AZARD?
LITTLE.
AH. WELL, THEY PREDATE THE SITH ORDER. THE DARK JEDI THAT WOULD BECOME THE FIRST SITH LORDS WE KNOW TODAY CREATED THEM DURING THE HUNDRED YEAR DARKNESS, OVER SEVEN THOUSAND YEARS AGO.
"NOTE THE BLISTER PODS ON THE BEAST'S BACK. THEY'RE FASCINATING. THE LEVIATHAN ABSORBS THE LIFE ENERGY OF THOSE NEARBY, LEAVING NOTHING BUT HUSKS.

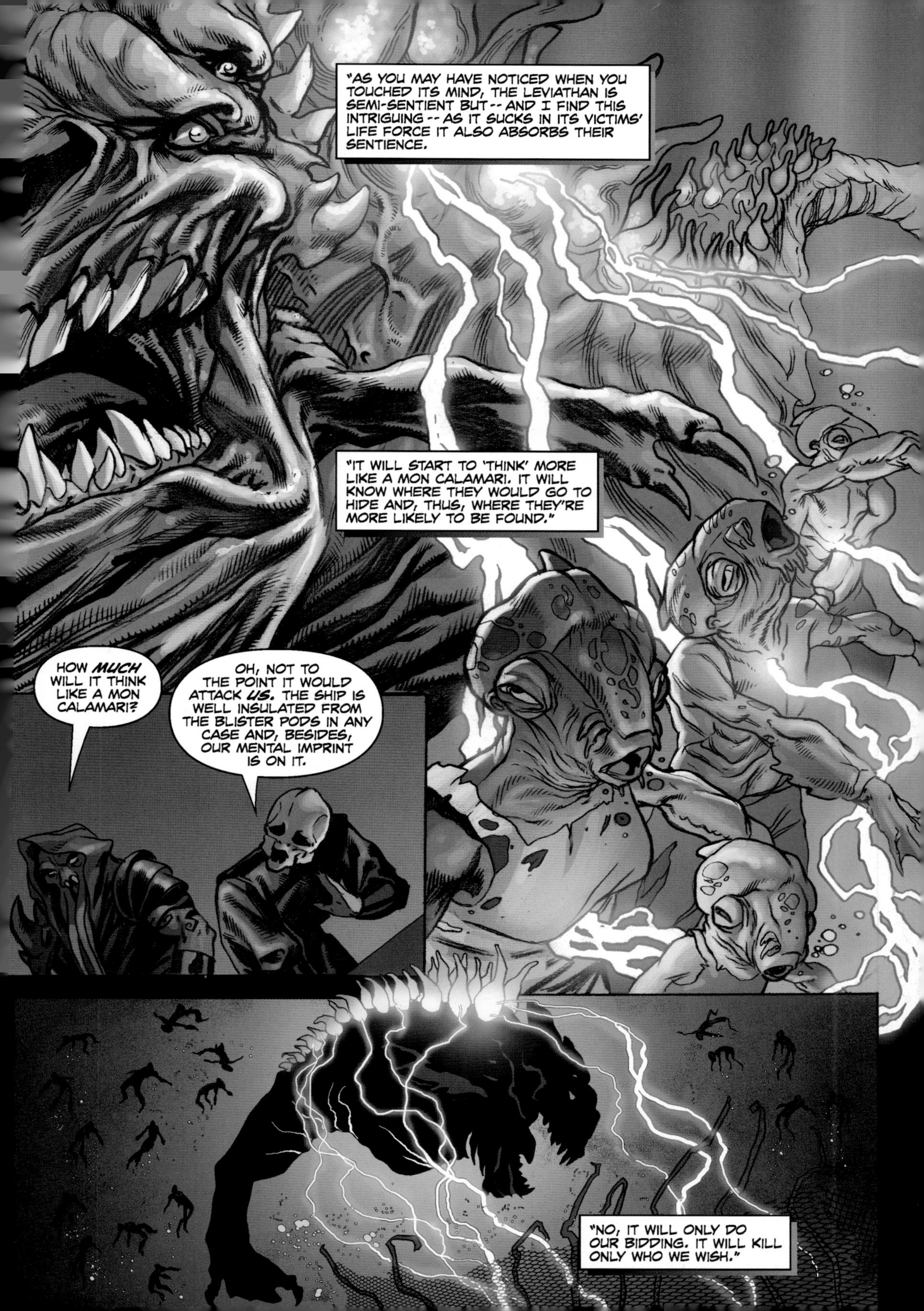
"AS YOU MAY HAVE NOTICED WHEN YOU TOUCHED ITS MIND, THE LEVIATHAN IS SEMI-SENTIENT BUT -- AND I FIND THIS INTRIGUING -- AS IT SUCKS IN ITS VICTIMS' LIFE FORCE IT ALSO ABSORBS THEIR SENTIENCE.
"IT WILL START TO 'THINK' MORE LIKE A MON CALAMARI. IT WILL KNOW WHERE THEY WOULD GO TO HIDE AND, THUS, WHERE THEY'RE MORE LIKELY TO BE FOUND."
HOW MUCH WILL IT THINK LIKE A MON CALAMARI?
OH, NOT TO THE POINT IT WOULD ATTACK US. THE SHIP IS WELL INSULATED FROM THE BLISTER PODS IN ANY CASE AND, BESIDES, OUR MENTAL IMPRINT IS ON IT.
"NO, IT WILL ONLY DO OUR BIDDING. IT WILL KILL ONLY WHO WE WISH."

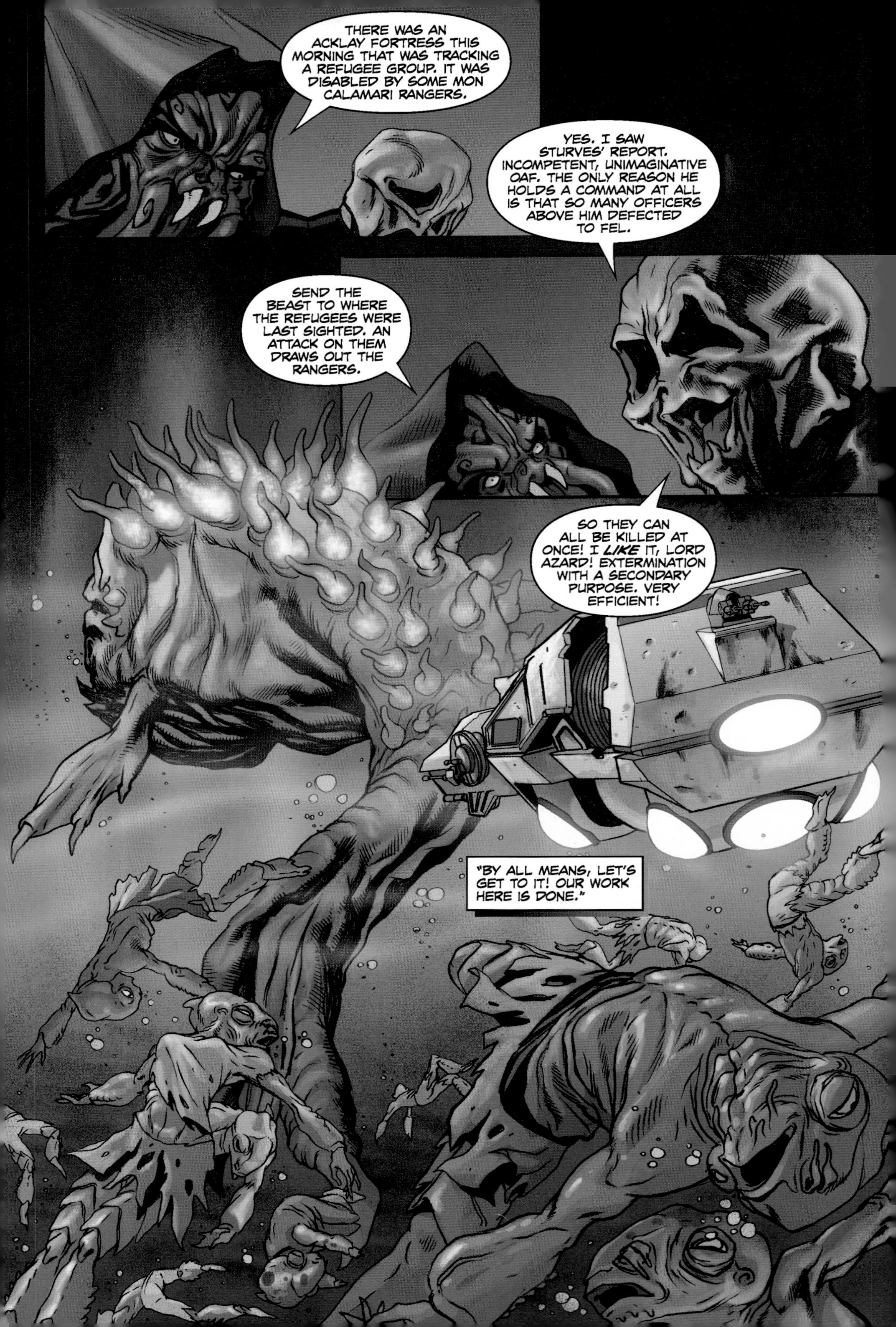
THERE WAS AN ACKLAY FORTRESS THIS MORNING THAT WAS TRACKING A REFUGEE GROUP. IT WAS DISABLED BY SOME MON CALAMARI RANGERS.
YES. I SAW STURVES' REPORT. INCOMPETENT, UNIMAGINATIVE OAF. THE ONLY REASON HE HOLDS A COMMAND AT ALL IS THAT SO MANY OFFICERS ABOVE HIM DEFECTED TO FEL.
SEND THE BEAST TO WHERE THE REFUGEES WERE LAST SIGHTED. AN ATTACK ON THEM DRAWS OUT THE RANGERS.
SO THEY CAN ALL BE KILLED AT ONCE! I *LIKE* IT, LORD AZARD! EXTERMINATION WITH A SECONDARY PURPOSE. VERY EFFICIENT!
"BY ALL MEANS, LET'S GET TO IT! OUR WORK HERE IS DONE."

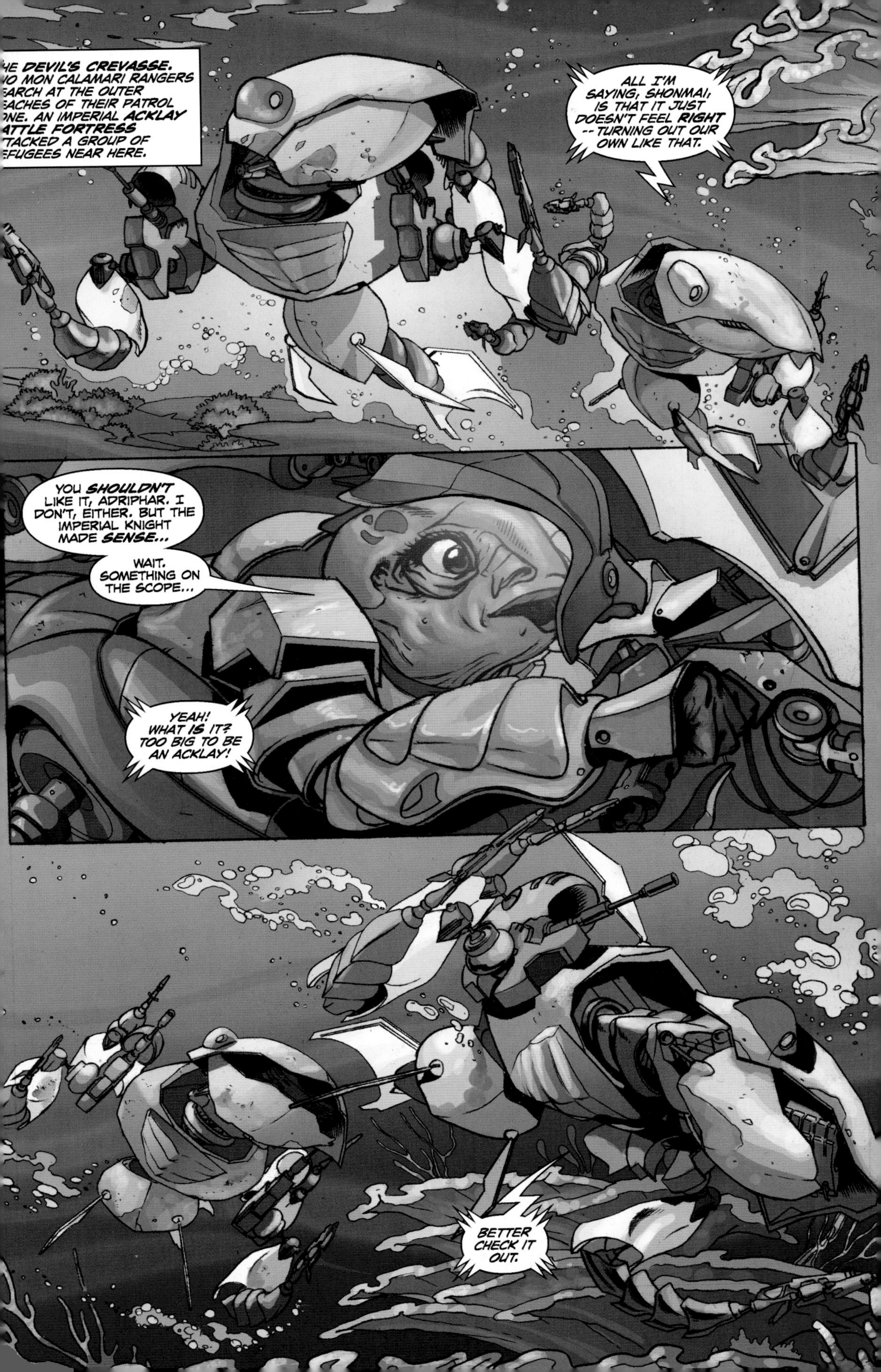
THE DEVIL'S CREVASSE. TWO MON CALAMARI RANGERS SEARCH AT THE OUTER REACHES OF THEIR PATROL ZONE. AN IMPERIAL ACKLAY BATTLE FORTRESS ATTACKED A GROUP OF REFUGEES NEAR HERE.
ALL I'M SAYING, SHONMAI, IS THAT IT JUST DOESN'T FEEL RIGHT -- TURNING OUT OUR OWN LIKE THAT.
YOU SHOULDN'T LIKE IT, ADRIPHAR. I DON'T, EITHER. BUT THE IMPERIAL KNIGHT MADE SENSE...
WAIT. SOMETHING ON THE SCOPE...
YEAH! WHAT IS IT? TOO BIG TO BE AN ACKLAY!
BETTER CHECK IT OUT.

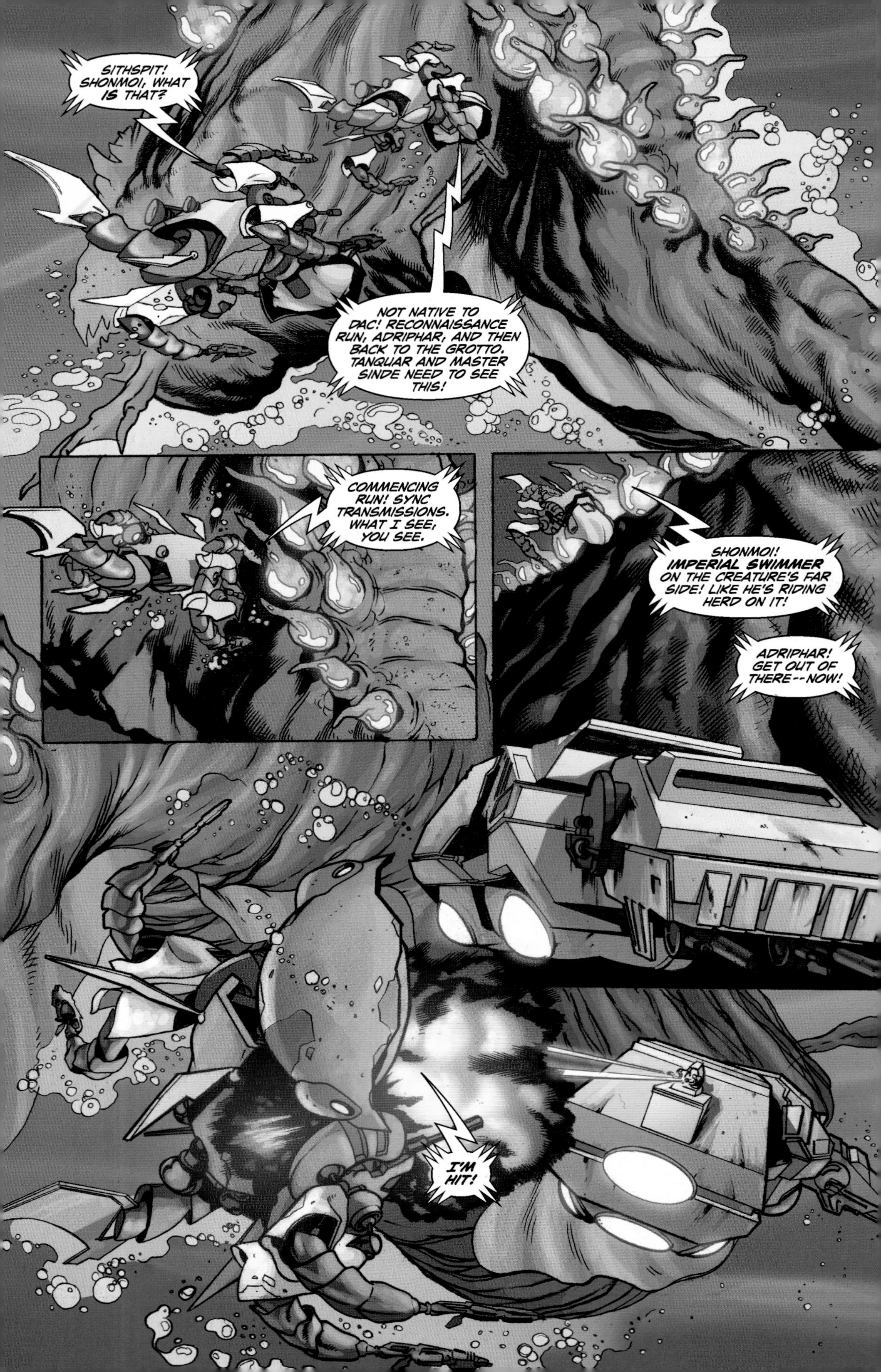
SITHSPIT! SHONMOI, WHAT IS THAT?
NOT NATIVE TO DAC! RECONNAISSANCE RUN, ADRIPHAR, AND THEN BACK TO THE GROTTO. TANQUAR AND MASTER SINDE NEED TO SEE THIS!
COMMENCING RUN! SYNC TRANSMISSIONS. WHAT I SEE, YOU SEE.
SHONMOI! IMPERIAL SWIMMER ON THE CREATURE'S FAR SIDE! LIKE HE'S RIDING HERD ON IT!
ADRIPHAR! GET OUT OF THERE--NOW!
I'M HIT!

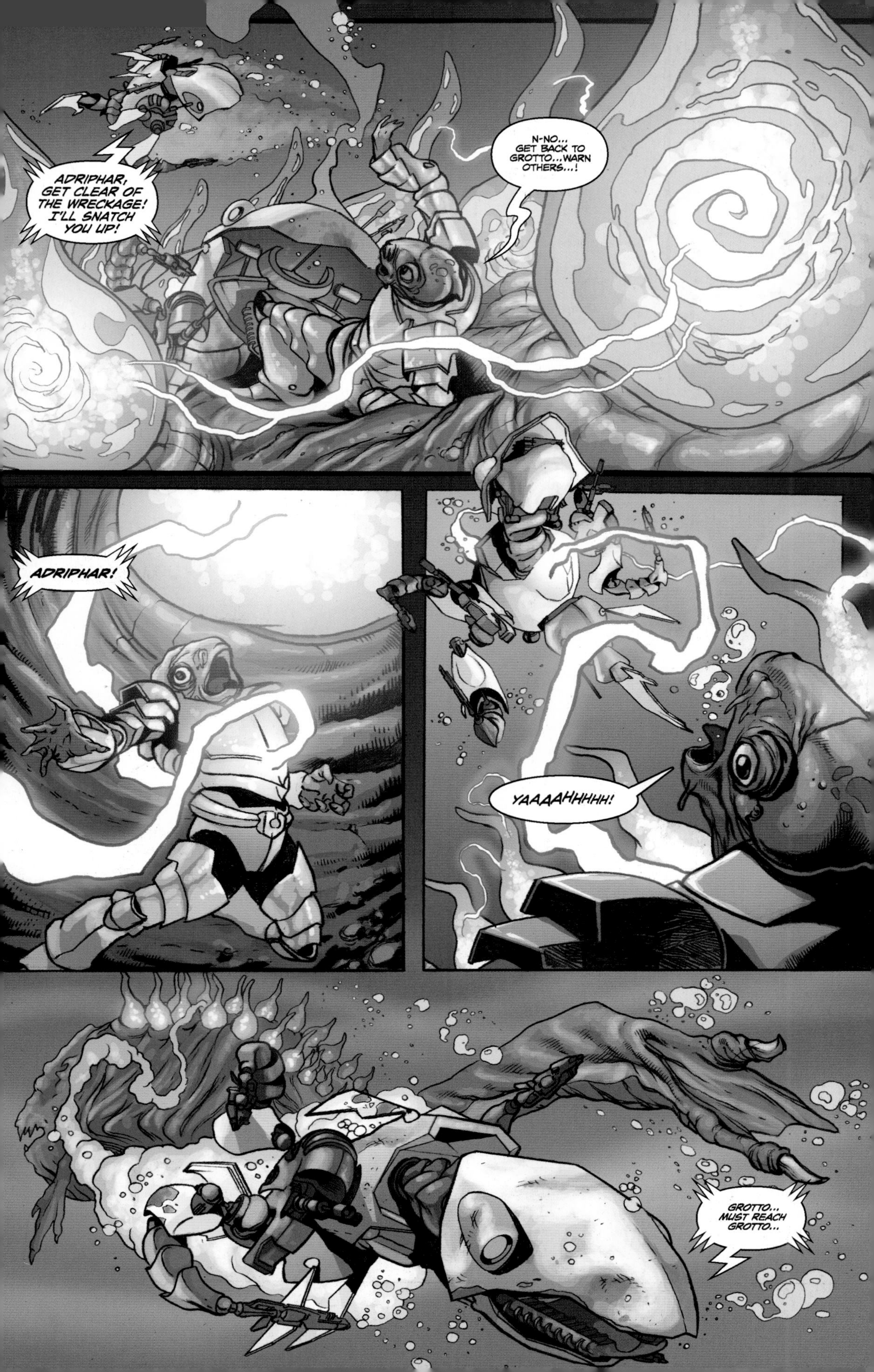
ADRIPHAR, GET CLEAR OF THE WRECKAGE! I'LL SNATCH YOU UP!
N-NO... GET BACK TO GROTTO...WARN OTHERS...!
ADRIPHAR!
YAAAAHHHHH!
GROTTO... MUST REACH GROTTO...

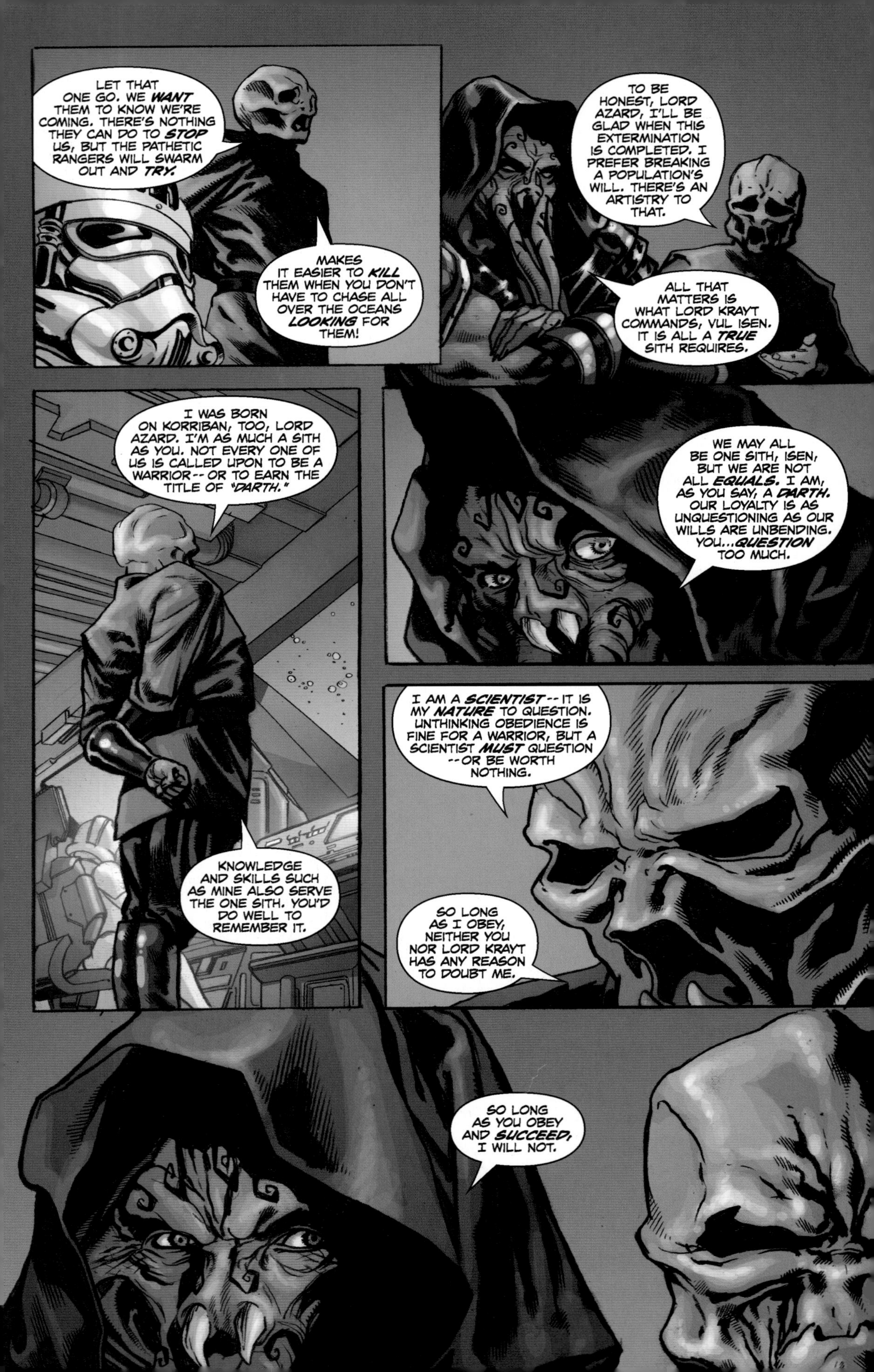
LET THAT ONE GO. WE WANT THEM TO KNOW WE'RE COMING. THERE'S NOTHING THEY CAN DO TO STOP US, BUT THE PATHETIC RANGERS WILL SWARM OUT AND TRY.
MAKES IT EASIER TO KILL THEM WHEN YOU DON'T HAVE TO CHASE ALL OVER THE OCEANS LOOKING FOR THEM!
TO BE HONEST, LORD AZARD, I'LL BE GLAD WHEN THIS EXTERMINATION IS COMPLETED. I PREFER BREAKING A POPULATION'S WILL. THERE'S AN ARTISTRY TO THAT.
ALL THAT MATTERS IS WHAT LORD KRAYT COMMANDS, VUL ISEN. IT IS ALL A TRUE SITH REQUIRES.
I WAS BORN ON KORRIBAN, TOO, LORD AZARD. I'M AS MUCH A SITH AS YOU. NOT EVERY ONE OF US IS CALLED UPON TO BE A WARRIOR--OR TO EARN THE TITLE OF "DARTH."
KNOWLEDGE AND SKILLS SUCH AS MINE ALSO SERVE THE ONE SITH. YOU'D DO WELL TO REMEMBER IT.
WE MAY ALL BE ONE SITH, ISEN, BUT WE ARE NOT ALL EQUALS. I AM, AS YOU SAY, A DARTH. OUR LOYALTY IS AS UNQUESTIONING AS OUR WILLS ARE UNBENDING. YOU...QUESTION TOO MUCH.
I AM A SCIENTIST--IT IS MY NATURE TO QUESTION. UNTHINKING OBEDIENCE IS FINE FOR A WARRIOR, BUT A SCIENTIST MUST QUESTION --OR BE WORTH NOTHING.
SO LONG AS I OBEY, NEITHER YOU NOR LORD KRAYT HAS ANY REASON TO DOUBT ME.
SO LONG AS YOU OBEY AND SUCCEED, I WILL NOT.

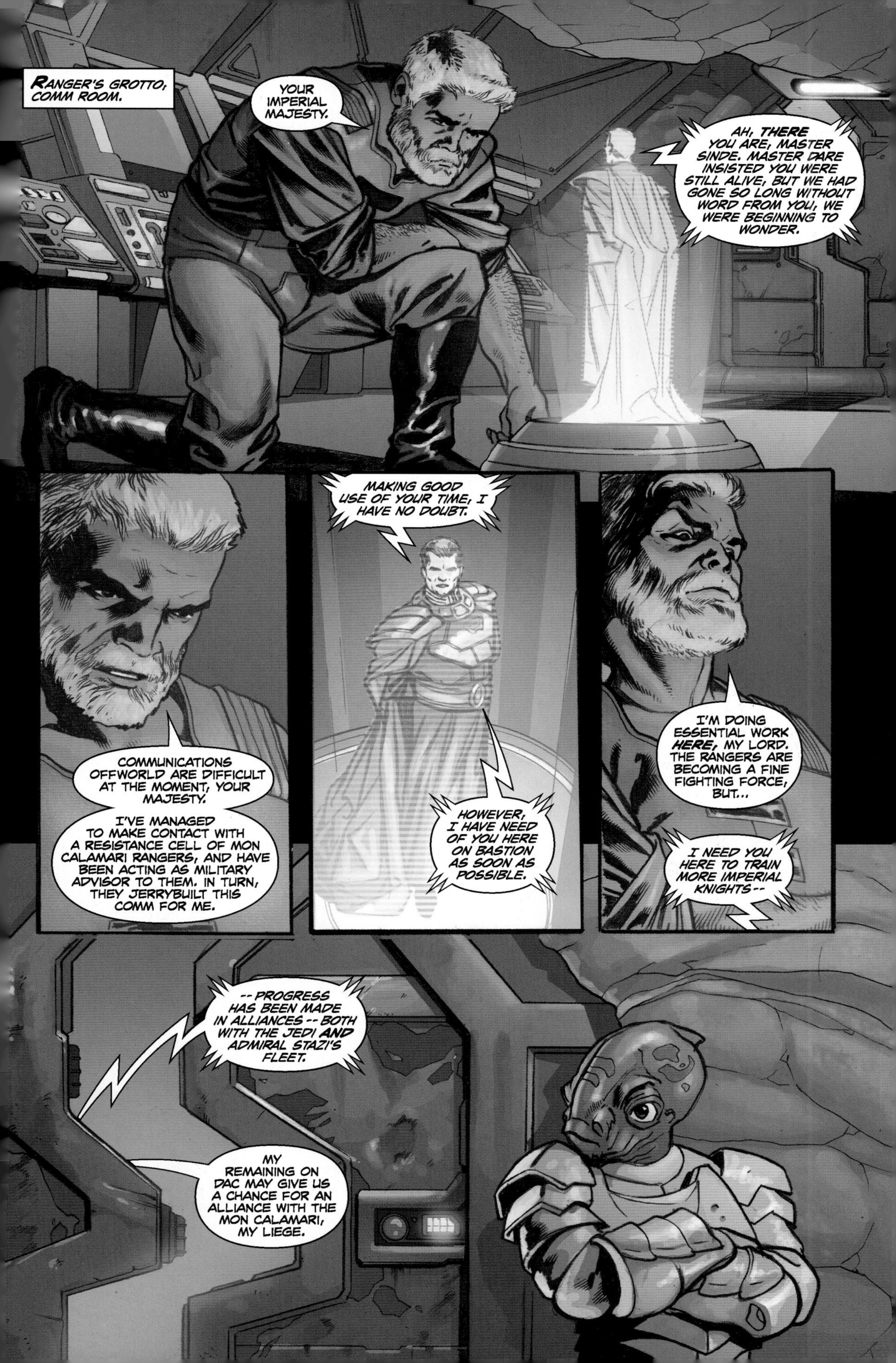
RANGER'S GROTTO, COMM ROOM.
YOUR IMPERIAL MAJESTY.
AH, THERE YOU ARE, MASTER SINDE. MASTER DARE INSISTED YOU WERE STILL ALIVE, BUT WE HAD GONE SO LONG WITHOUT WORD FROM YOU, WE WERE BEGINNING TO WONDER.
MAKING GOOD USE OF YOUR TIME, I HAVE NO DOUBT.
COMMUNICATIONS OFFWORLD ARE DIFFICULT AT THE MOMENT, YOUR MAJESTY.
I'VE MANAGED TO MAKE CONTACT WITH A RESISTANCE CELL OF MON CALAMARI RANGERS, AND HAVE BEEN ACTING AS MILITARY ADVISOR TO THEM. IN TURN, THEY JERRYBUILT THIS COMM FOR ME.
HOWEVER, I HAVE NEED OF YOU HERE ON BASTION AS SOON AS POSSIBLE.
I'M DOING ESSENTIAL WORK HERE, MY LORD. THE RANGERS ARE BECOMING A FINE FIGHTING FORCE, BUT...
I NEED YOU HERE TO TRAIN MORE IMPERIAL KNIGHTS--
--PROGRESS HAS BEEN MADE IN ALLIANCES--BOTH WITH THE JEDI AND ADMIRAL STAZI'S FLEET.
MY REMAINING ON DAC MAY GIVE US A CHANCE FOR AN ALLIANCE WITH THE MON CALAMARI, MY LIEGE.

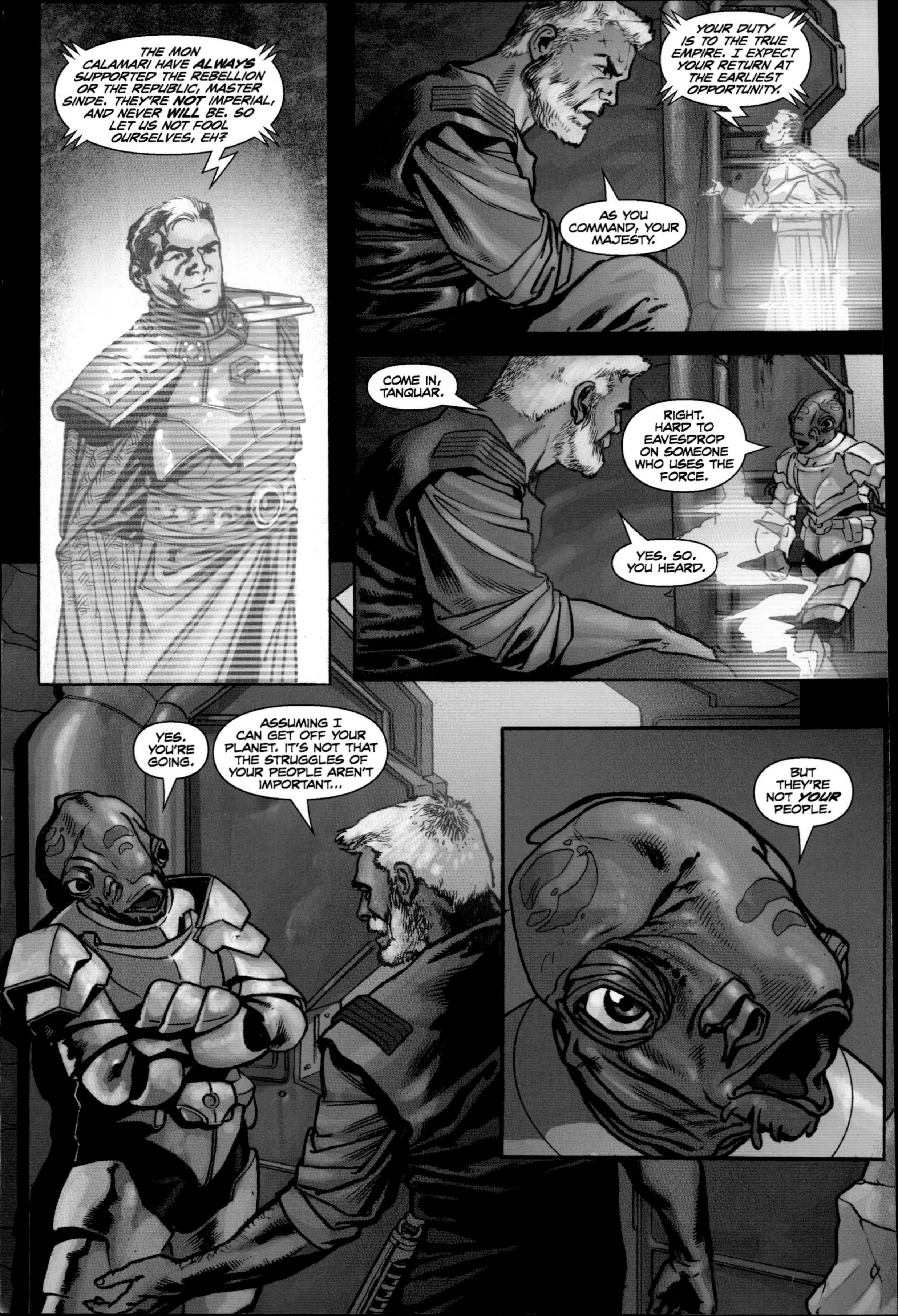
THE MON CALAMARI HAVE ALWAYS SUPPORTED THE REBELLION OR THE REPUBLIC, MASTER SINDE. THEY'RE NOT IMPERIAL, AND NEVER WILL BE. SO LET US NOT FOOL OURSELVES, EH?
YOUR DUTY IS TO THE TRUE EMPIRE. I EXPECT YOUR RETURN AT THE EARLIEST OPPORTUNITY.
AS YOU COMMAND, YOUR MAJESTY.
COME IN, TANQUAR.
RIGHT. HARD TO EAVESDROP ON SOMEONE WHO USES THE FORCE.
YES. SO. YOU HEARD.
YES. YOU'RE GOING.
ASSUMING I CAN GET OFF YOUR PLANET. IT'S NOT THAT THE STRUGGLES OF YOUR PEOPLE AREN'T IMPORTANT...
BUT THEY'RE NOT YOUR PEOPLE.

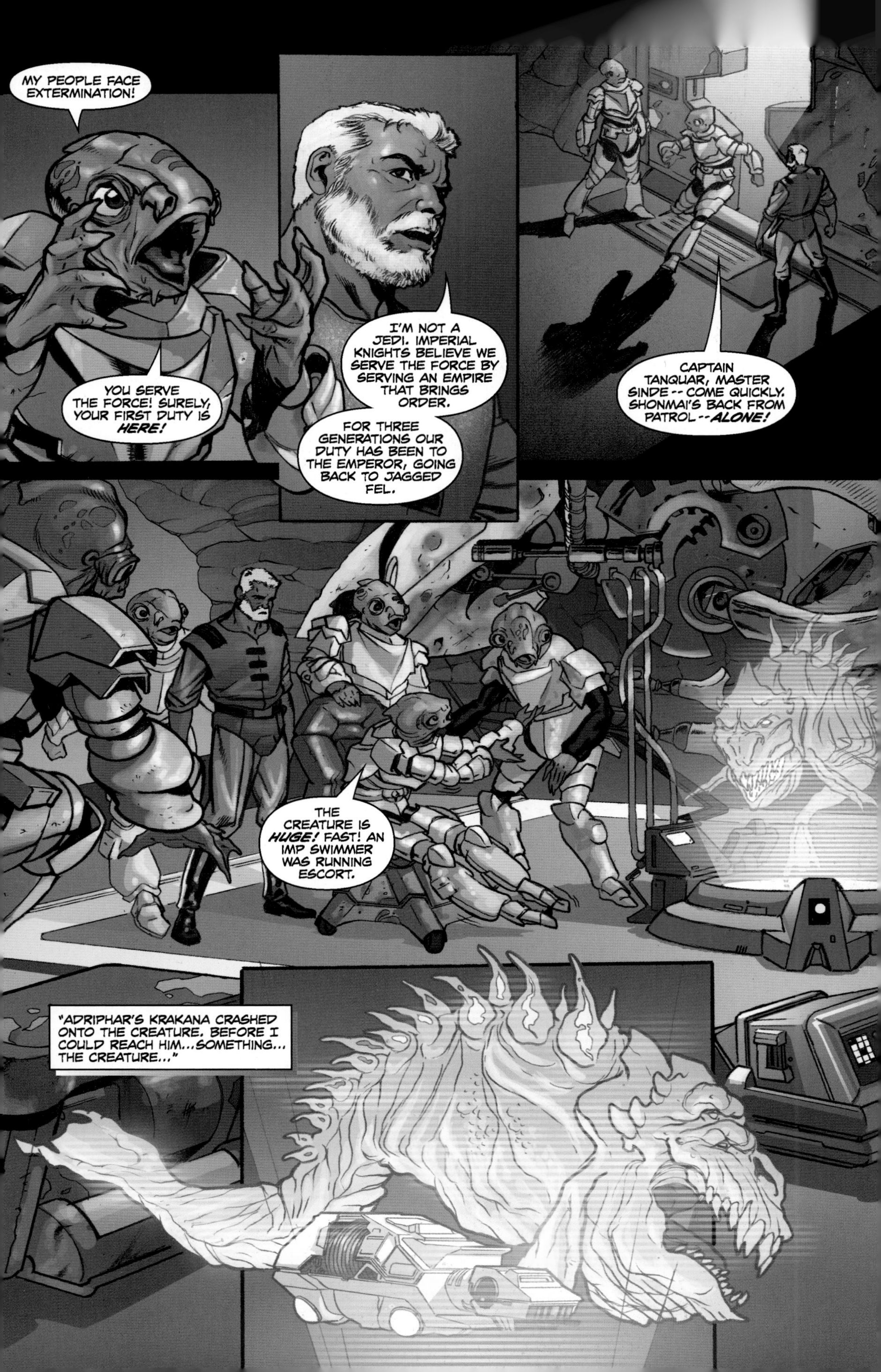
MY PEOPLE FACE EXTERMINATION!
YOU SERVE THE FORCE! SURELY, YOUR FIRST DUTY IS *HERE!*
I'M NOT A JEDI. IMPERIAL KNIGHTS BELIEVE WE SERVE THE FORCE BY SERVING AN EMPIRE THAT BRINGS ORDER.
FOR THREE GENERATIONS OUR DUTY HAS BEEN TO THE EMPEROR, GOING BACK TO JAGGED FEL.
CAPTAIN TANQUAR, MASTER SINDE -- COME QUICKLY. SHONMAI'S BACK FROM PATROL -- *ALONE!*
THE CREATURE IS *HUGE!* FAST! AN IMP SWIMMER WAS RUNNING ESCORT.
"ADRIPHAR'S KRAKANA CRASHED ONTO THE CREATURE. BEFORE I COULD REACH HIM...SOMETHING... THE CREATURE..."

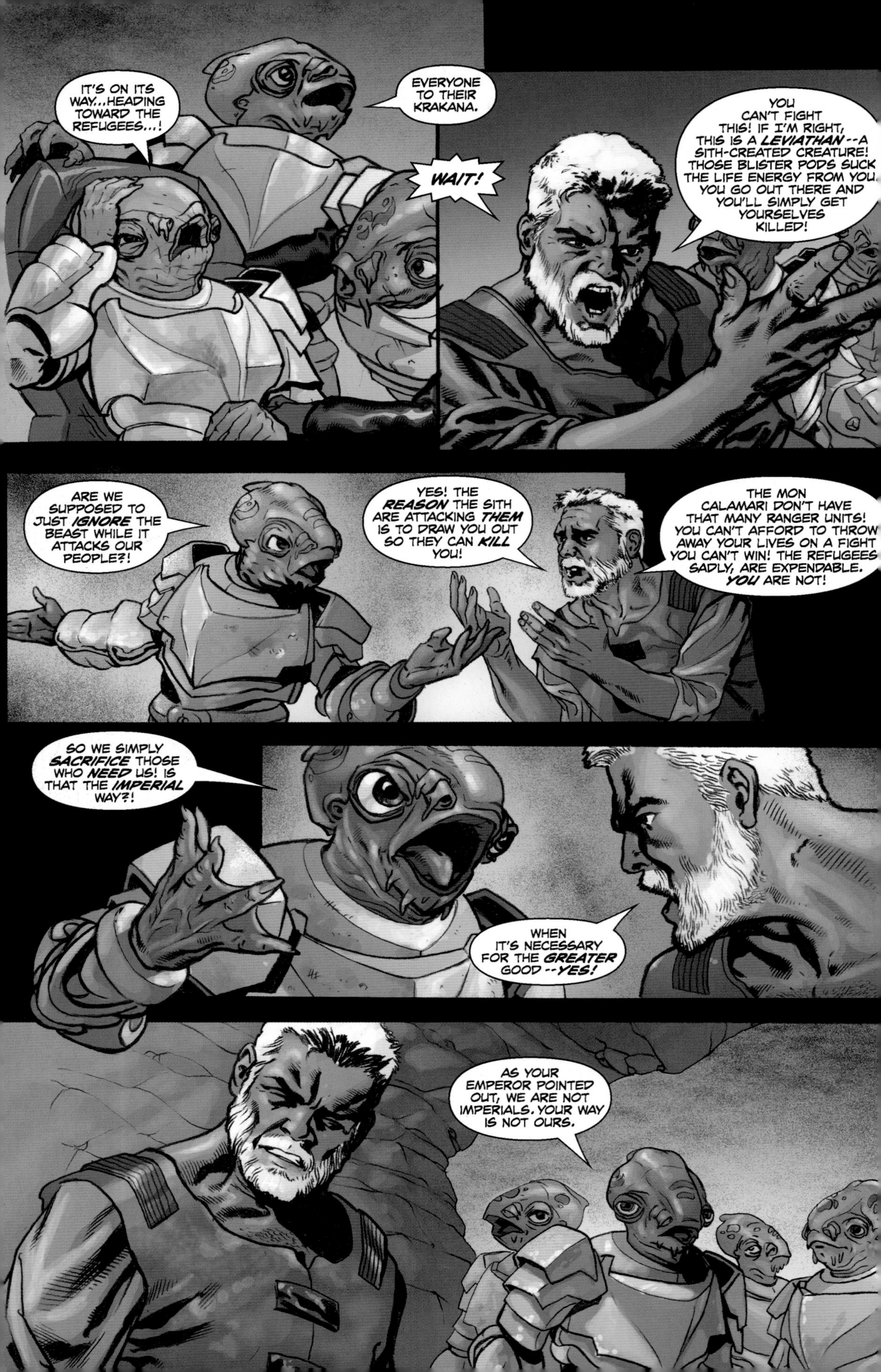
IT'S ON ITS WAY...HEADING TOWARD THE REFUGEES...!
EVERYONE TO THEIR KRAKANA.
WAIT!
YOU CAN'T FIGHT THIS! IF I'M RIGHT, THIS IS A LEVIATHAN--A SITH-CREATED CREATURE! THOSE BLISTER PODS SUCK THE LIFE ENERGY FROM YOU. YOU GO OUT THERE AND YOU'LL SIMPLY GET YOURSELVES KILLED!
ARE WE SUPPOSED TO JUST IGNORE THE BEAST WHILE IT ATTACKS OUR PEOPLE?!
YES! THE REASON THE SITH ARE ATTACKING THEM IS TO DRAW YOU OUT SO THEY CAN KILL YOU!
THE MON CALAMARI DON'T HAVE THAT MANY RANGER UNITS! YOU CAN'T AFFORD TO THROW AWAY YOUR LIVES ON A FIGHT YOU CAN'T WIN! THE REFUGEES SADLY, ARE EXPENDABLE. YOU ARE NOT!
SO WE SIMPLY SACRIFICE THOSE WHO NEED US! IS THAT THE IMPERIAL WAY?!
WHEN IT'S NECESSARY FOR THE GREATER GOOD--YES!
AS YOUR EMPEROR POINTED OUT, WE ARE NOT IMPERIALS. YOUR WAY IS NOT OURS.

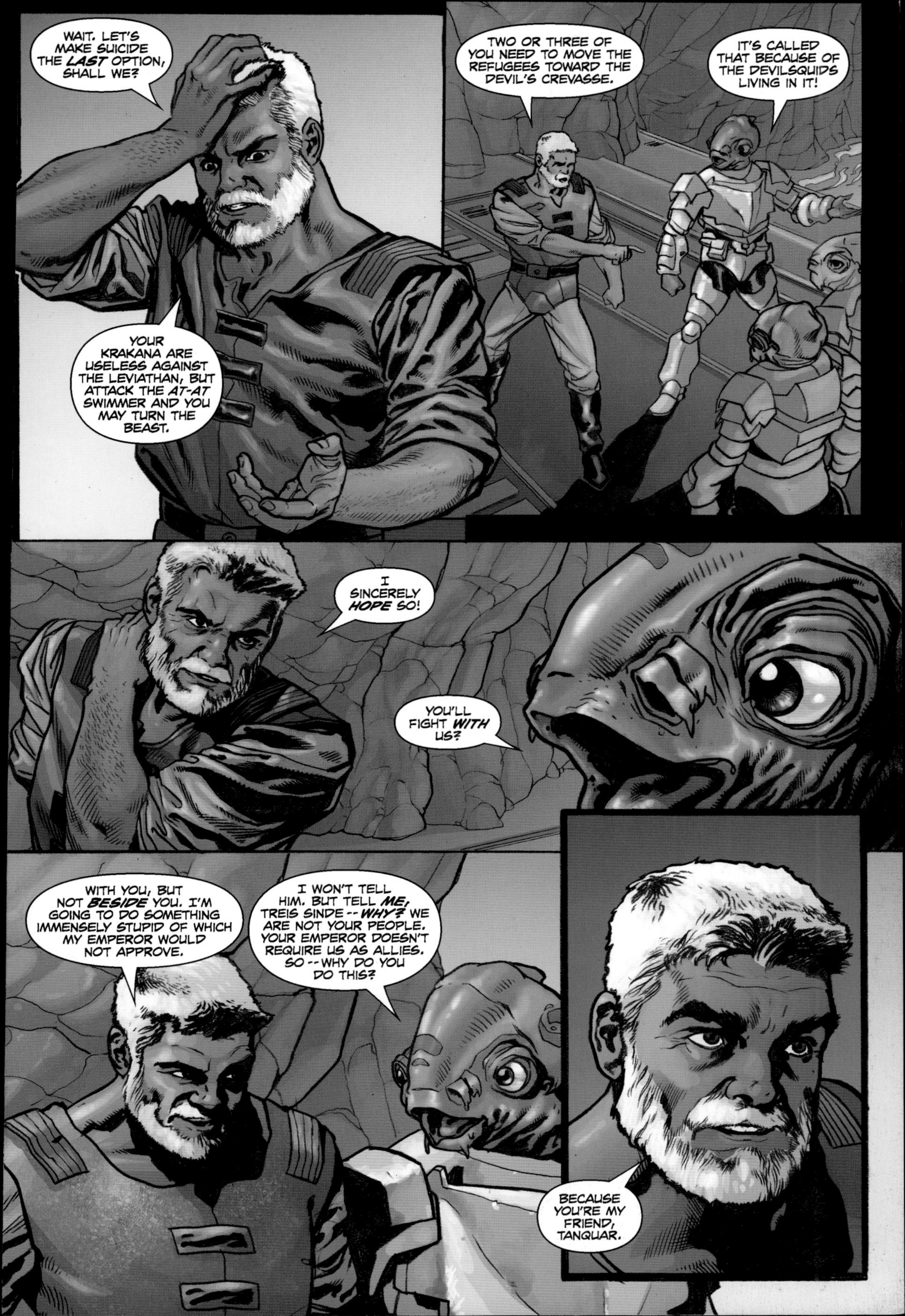
WAIT. LET'S MAKE SUICIDE THE *LAST* OPTION, SHALL WE?
YOUR KRAKANA ARE USELESS AGAINST THE LEVIATHAN, BUT ATTACK THE *AT-AT* SWIMMER AND YOU MAY TURN THE BEAST.
TWO OR THREE OF YOU NEED TO MOVE THE REFUGEES TOWARD THE DEVIL'S CREVASSE.
IT'S CALLED THAT BECAUSE OF THE DEVILSQUIDS LIVING IN IT!
I SINCERELY *HOPE* SO!
YOU'LL FIGHT *WITH* US?
WITH YOU, BUT NOT *BESIDE* YOU. I'M GOING TO DO SOMETHING IMMENSELY STUPID OF WHICH MY EMPEROR WOULD NOT APPROVE.
I WON'T TELL HIM. BUT TELL *ME,* TREIS SINDE -- *WHY?* WE ARE NOT YOUR PEOPLE. YOUR EMPEROR DOESN'T REQUIRE US AS ALLIES. SO -- WHY DO YOU DO THIS?
BECAUSE YOU'RE MY FRIEND, TANQUAR.

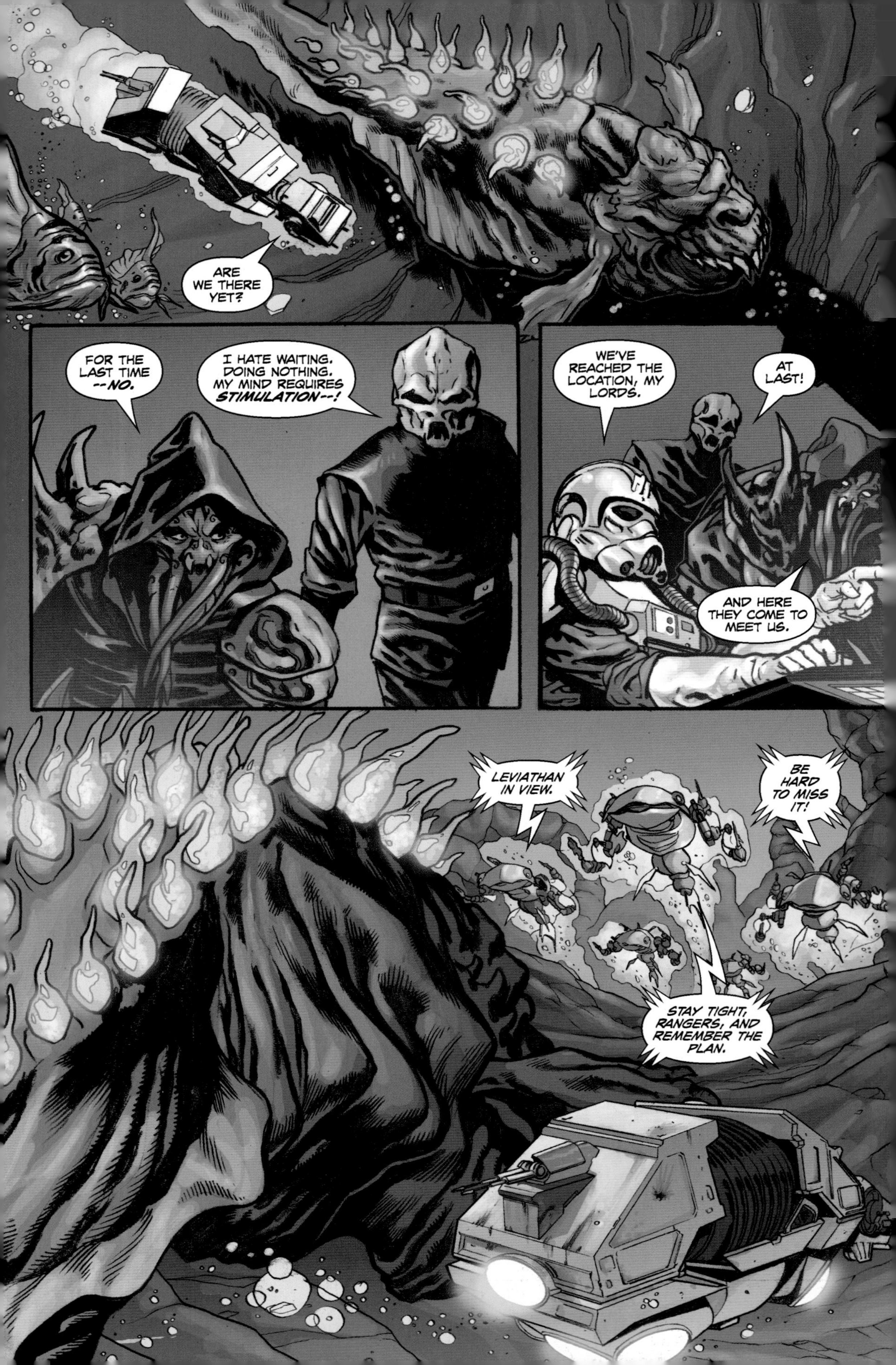
ARE WE THERE YET?
FOR THE LAST TIME --NO.
I HATE WAITING. DOING NOTHING. MY MIND REQUIRES STIMULATION--!
WE'VE REACHED THE LOCATION, MY LORDS.
AT LAST!
AND HERE THEY COME TO MEET US.
LEVIATHAN IN VIEW.
BE HARD TO MISS IT!
STAY TIGHT, RANGERS, AND REMEMBER THE PLAN.

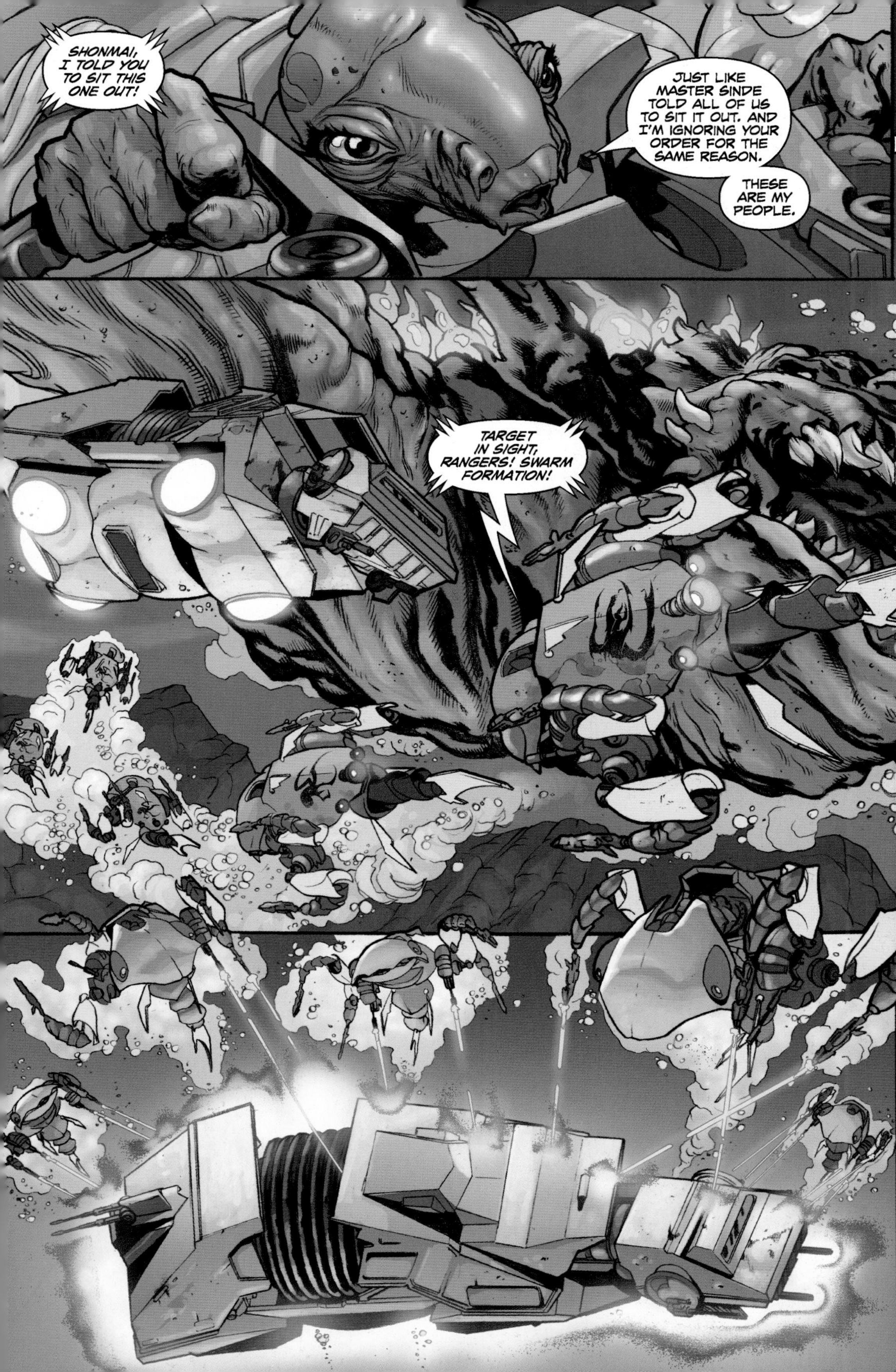
SHONMAI, I TOLD YOU TO SIT THIS ONE OUT!
JUST LIKE MASTER SINDE TOLD ALL OF US TO SIT IT OUT. AND I'M IGNORING YOUR ORDER FOR THE SAME REASON.
THESE ARE MY PEOPLE.
TARGET IN SIGHT, RANGERS! SWARM FORMATION!

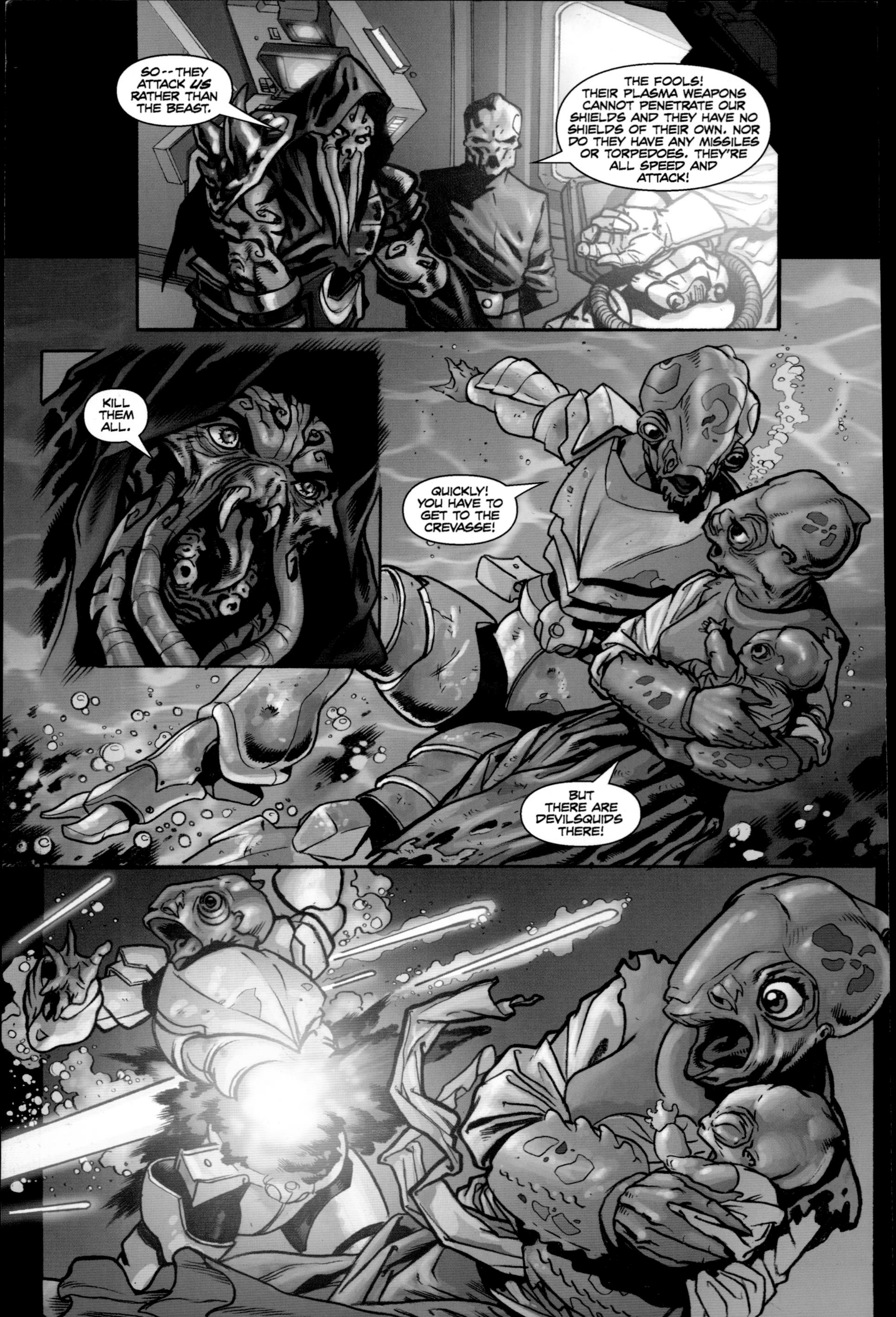
SO--THEY ATTACK US RATHER THAN THE BEAST.
THE FOOLS! THEIR PLASMA WEAPONS CANNOT PENETRATE OUR SHIELDS AND THEY HAVE NO SHIELDS OF THEIR OWN. NOR DO THEY HAVE ANY MISSILES OR TORPEDOES. THEY'RE ALL SPEED AND ATTACK!
KILL THEM ALL.
QUICKLY! YOU HAVE TO GET TO THE CREVASSE!
BUT THERE ARE DEVILSQUIDS THERE!

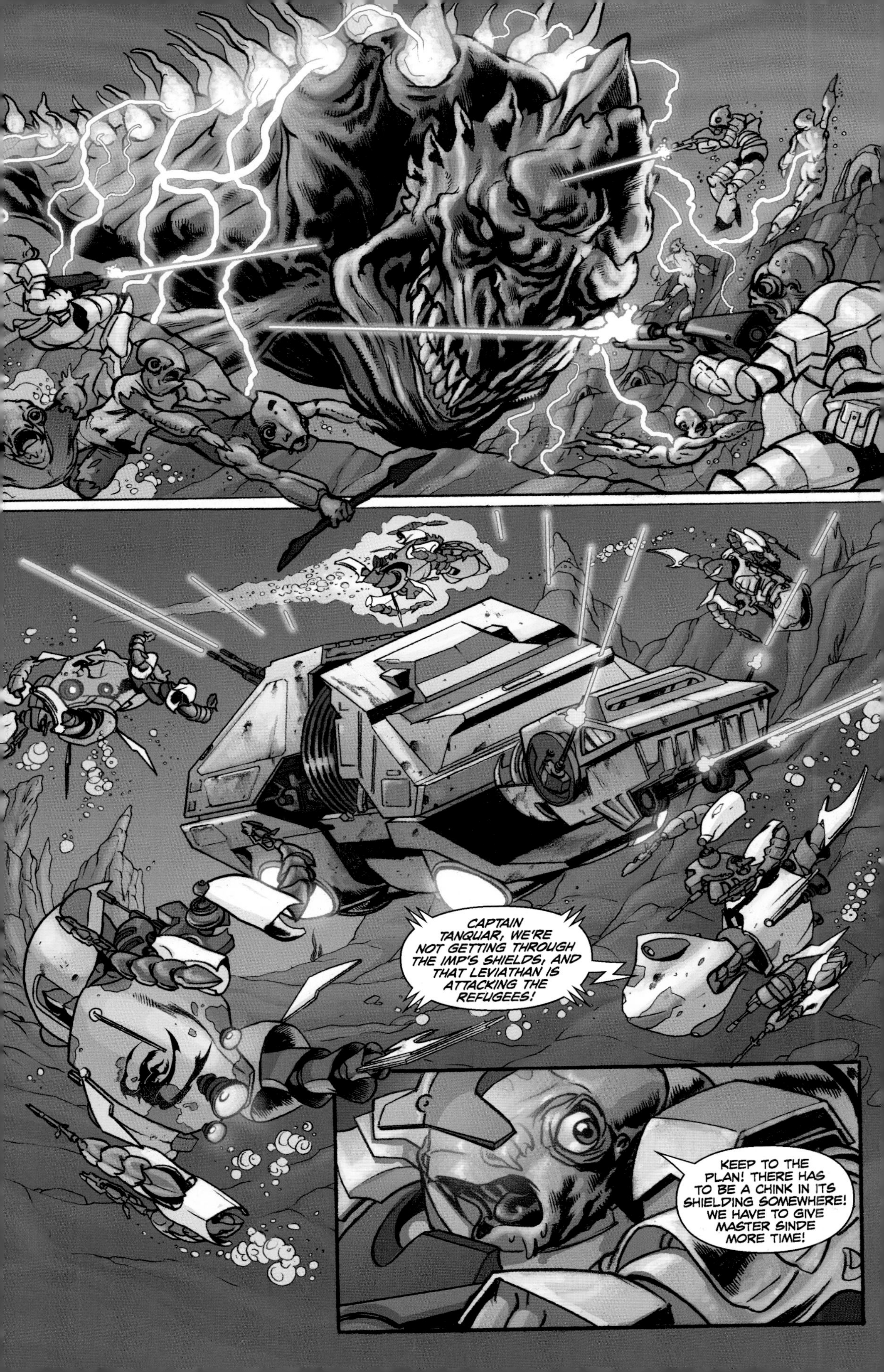
CAPTAIN TANQUAR, WE'RE NOT GETTING THROUGH THE IMP'S SHIELDS, AND THAT LEVIATHAN IS ATTACKING THE REFUGEES!
KEEP TO THE PLAN! THERE HAS TO BE A CHINK IN ITS SHIELDING SOMEWHERE! WE HAVE TO GIVE MASTER SINDE MORE TIME!

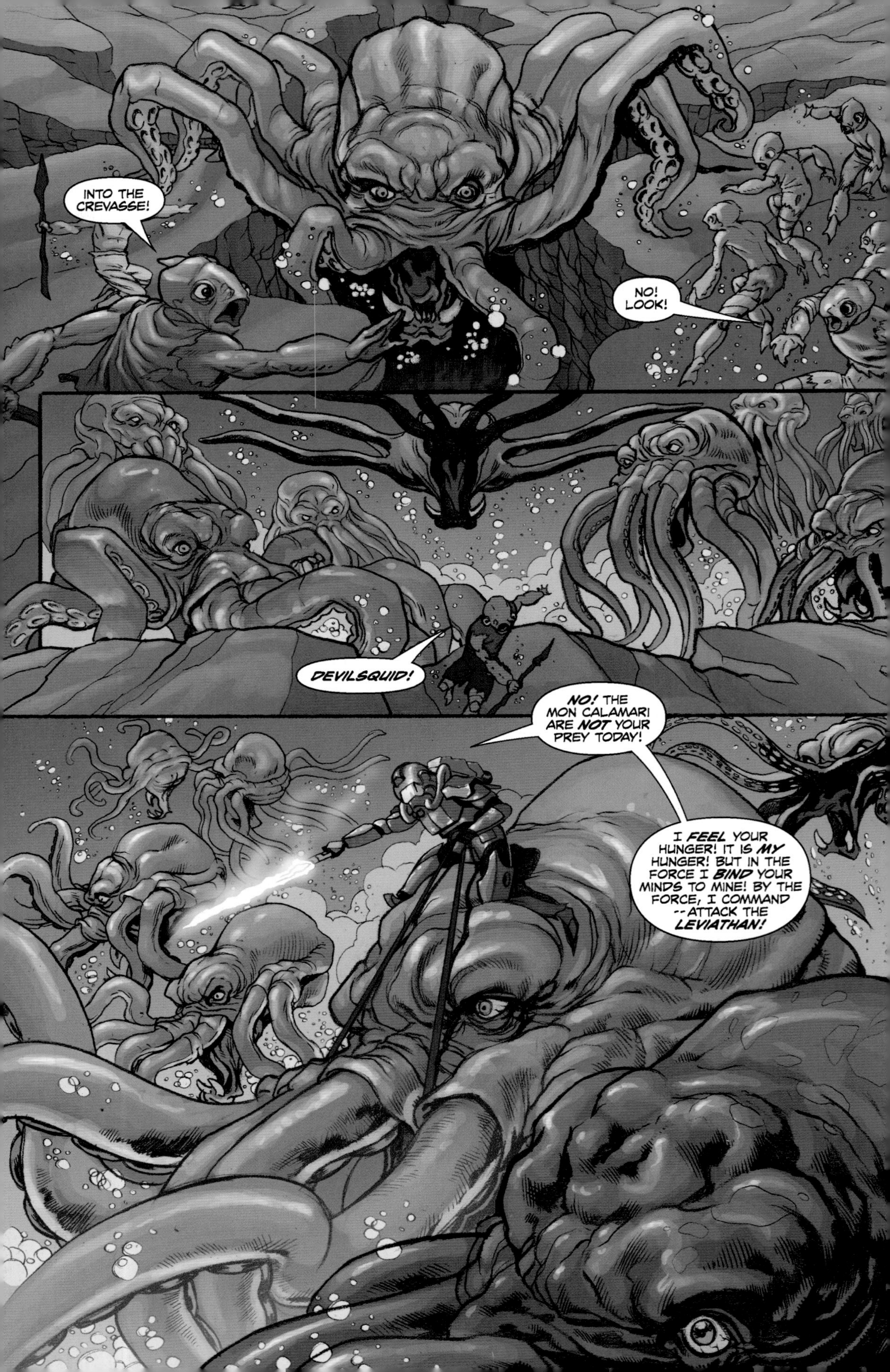
INTO THE CREVASSE!
NO! LOOK!
DEVILSQUID!
NO! THE MON CALAMARI ARE NOT YOUR PREY TODAY!
I FEEL YOUR HUNGER! IT IS MY HUNGER! BUT IN THE FORCE I BIND YOUR MINDS TO MINE! BY THE FORCE, I COMMAND --ATTACK THE LEVIATHAN!

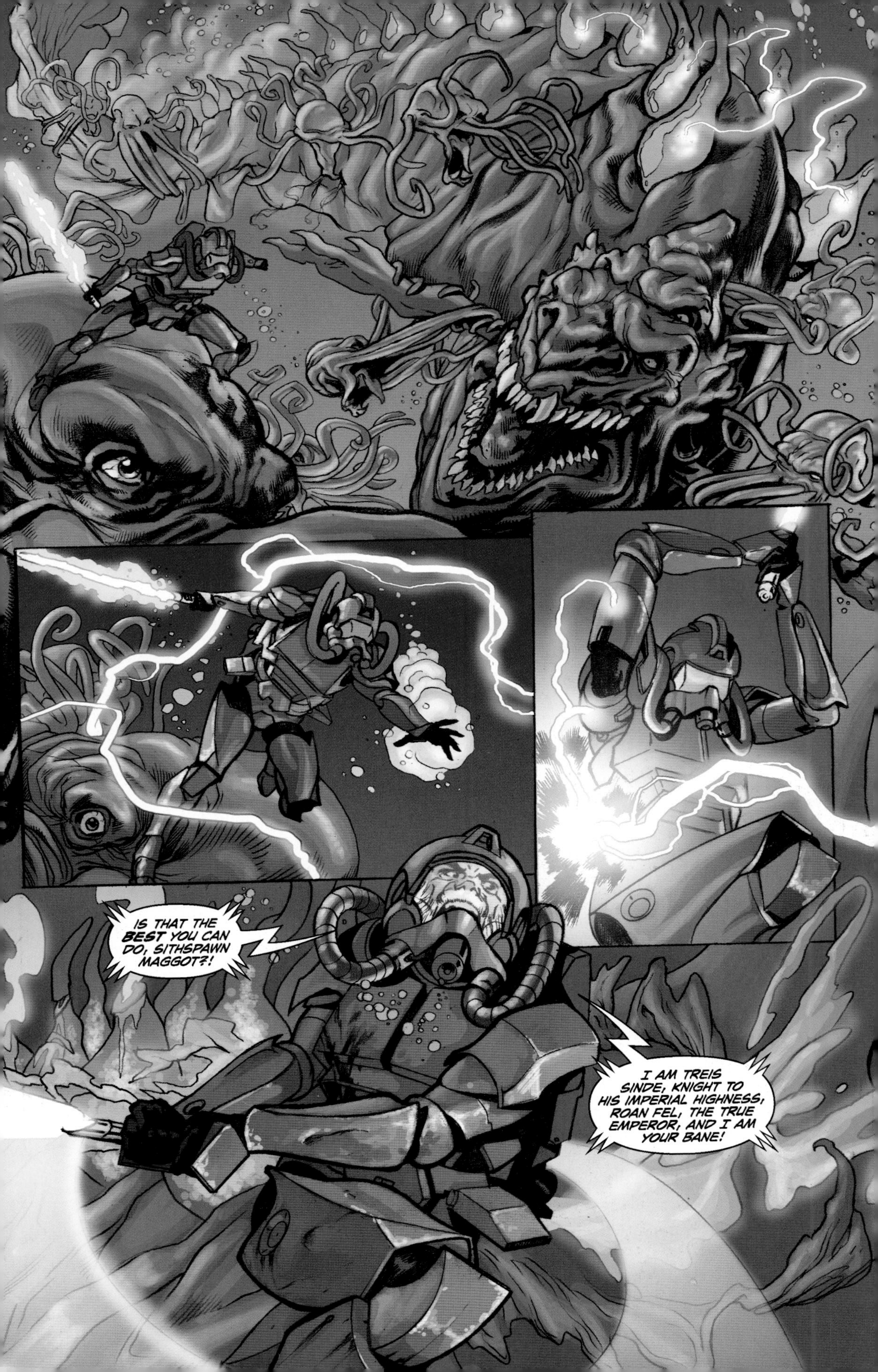
IS THAT THE BEST YOU CAN DO, SITHSPAWN MAGGOT?!
I AM TREIS SINDE, KNIGHT TO HIS IMPERIAL HIGHNESS, ROAN FEL, THE TRUE EMPEROR, AND I AM YOUR BANE!

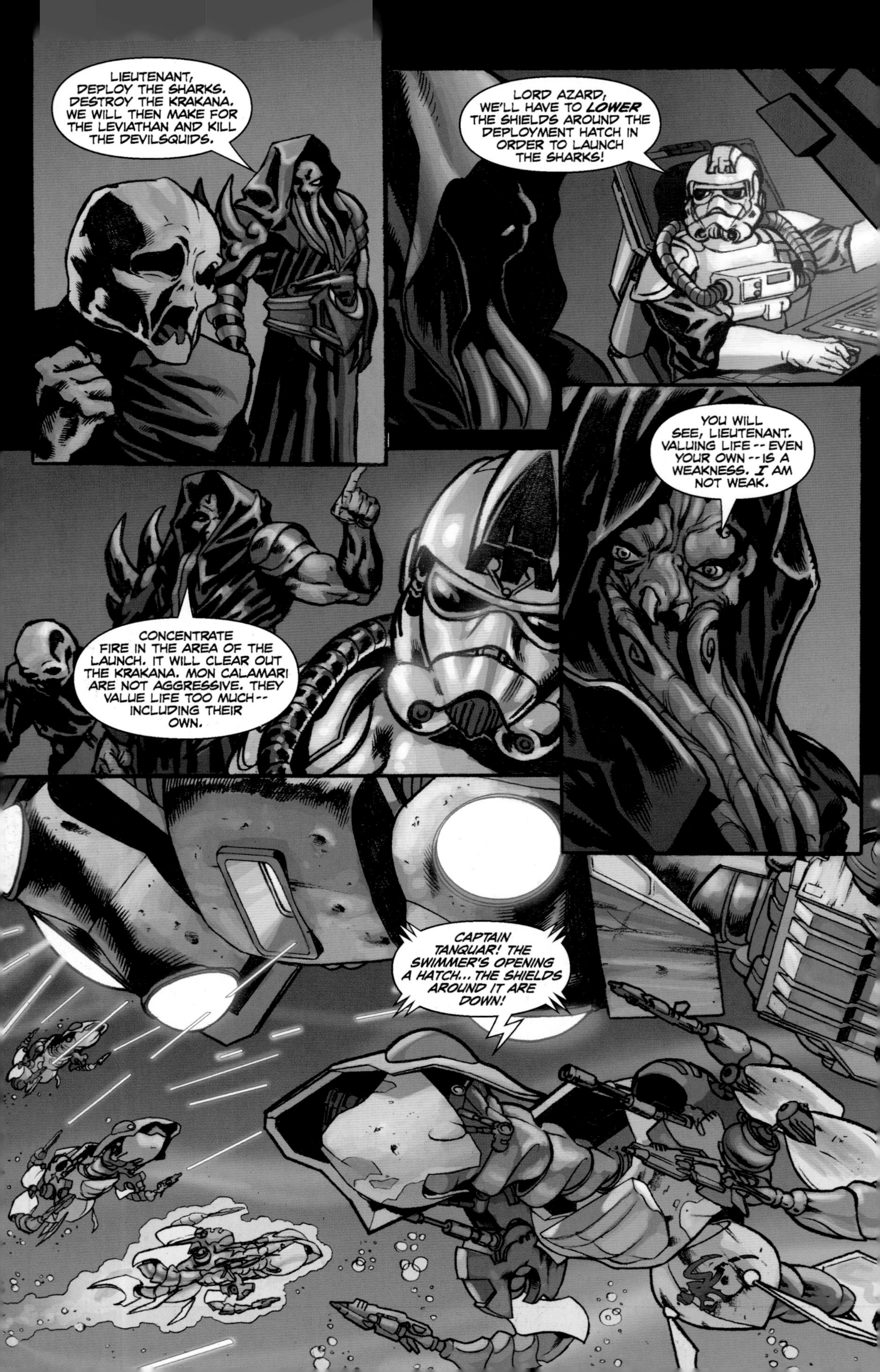
LIEUTENANT, DEPLOY THE SHARKS. DESTROY THE KRAKANA. WE WILL THEN MAKE FOR THE LEVIATHAN AND KILL THE DEVILSQUIDS.
LORD AZARD, WE'LL HAVE TO LOWER THE SHIELDS AROUND THE DEPLOYMENT HATCH IN ORDER TO LAUNCH THE SHARKS!
CONCENTRATE FIRE IN THE AREA OF THE LAUNCH. IT WILL CLEAR OUT THE KRAKANA. MON CALAMARI ARE NOT AGGRESSIVE. THEY VALUE LIFE TOO MUCH-- INCLUDING THEIR OWN.
YOU WILL SEE, LIEUTENANT. VALUING LIFE -- EVEN YOUR OWN -- IS A WEAKNESS. I AM NOT WEAK.
CAPTAIN TANQUAR! THE SWIMMER'S OPENING A HATCH... THE SHIELDS AROUND IT ARE DOWN!

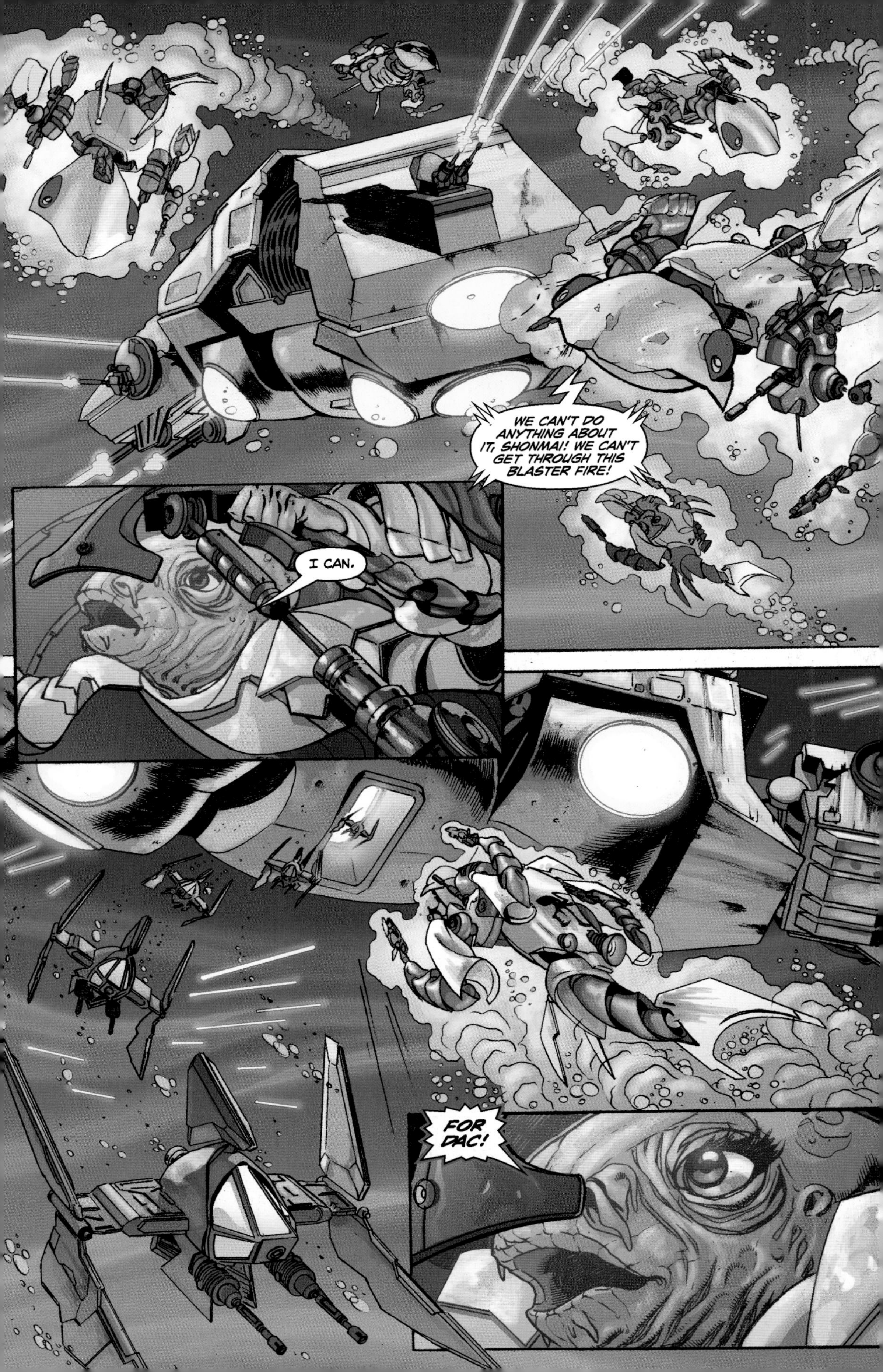
WE CAN'T DO ANYTHING ABOUT IT, SHONMAI! WE CAN'T GET THROUGH THIS BLASTER FIRE!
I CAN.
FOR DAC!

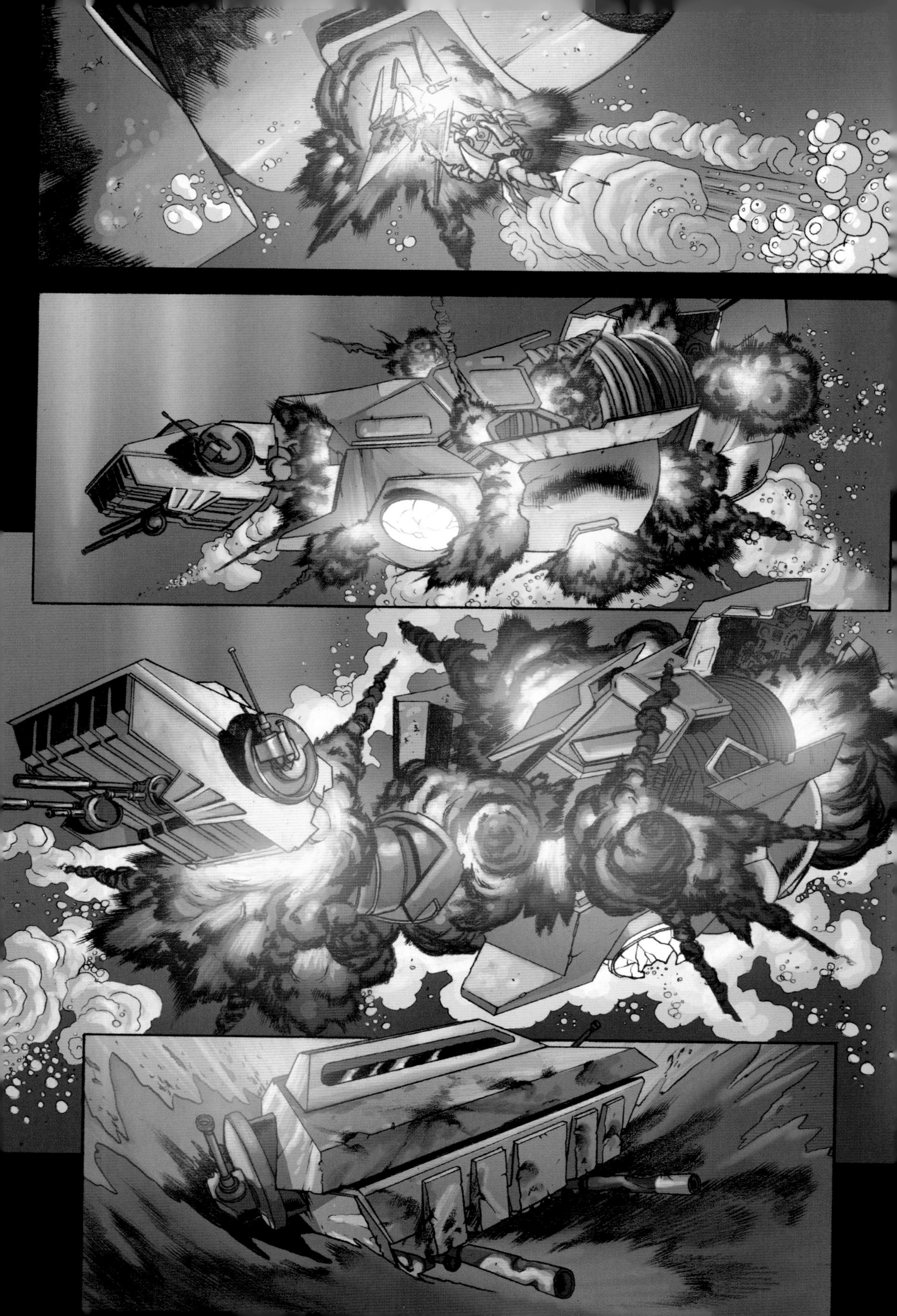

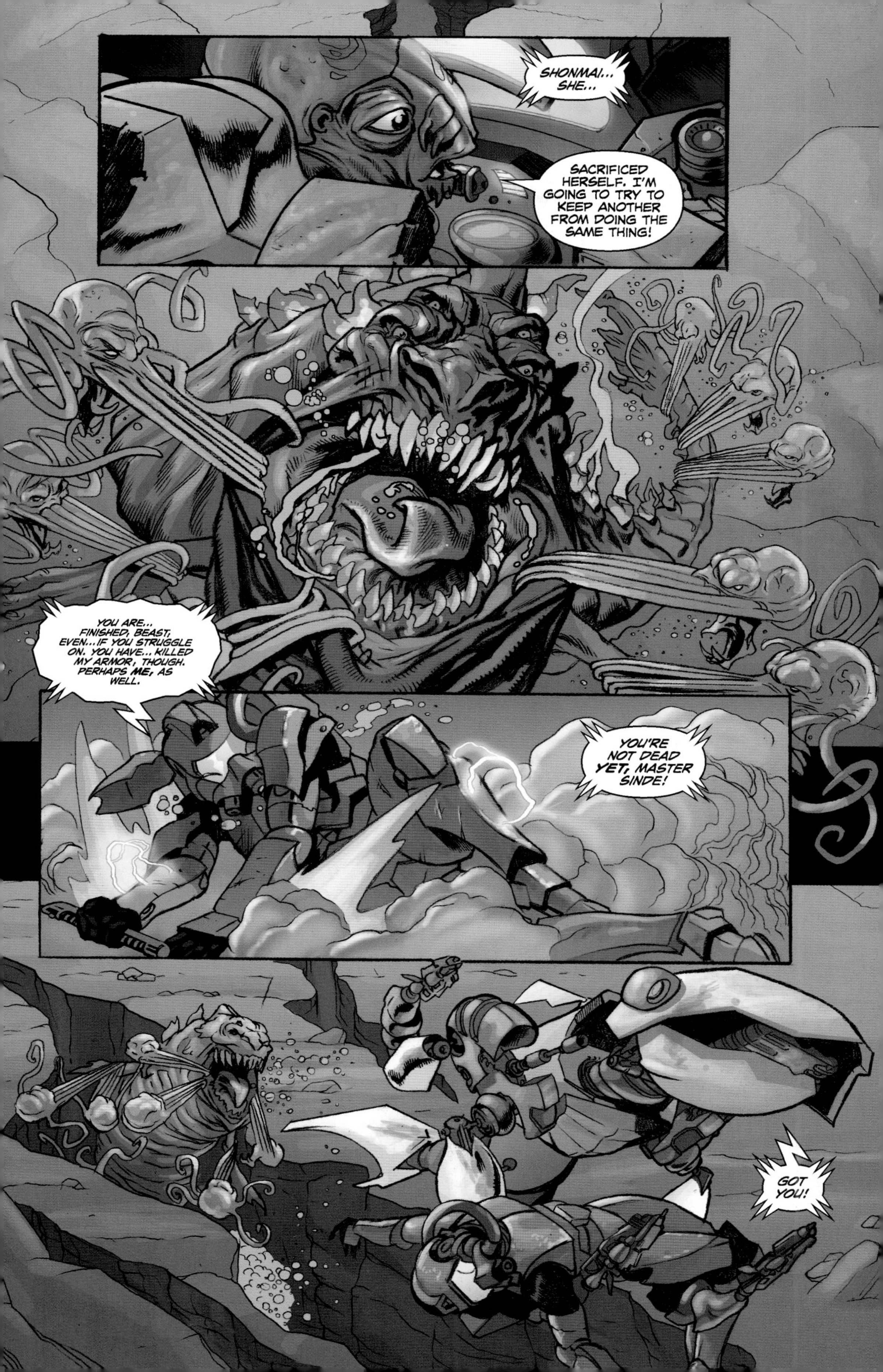
SHONMAI... SHE...
SACRIFICED HERSELF. I'M GOING TO TRY TO KEEP ANOTHER FROM DOING THE SAME THING!
YOU ARE... FINISHED, BEAST, EVEN... IF YOU STRUGGLE ON. YOU HAVE... KILLED MY ARMOR, THOUGH. PERHAPS ME, AS WELL.
YOU'RE NOT DEAD YET, MASTER SINDE!
GOT YOU!

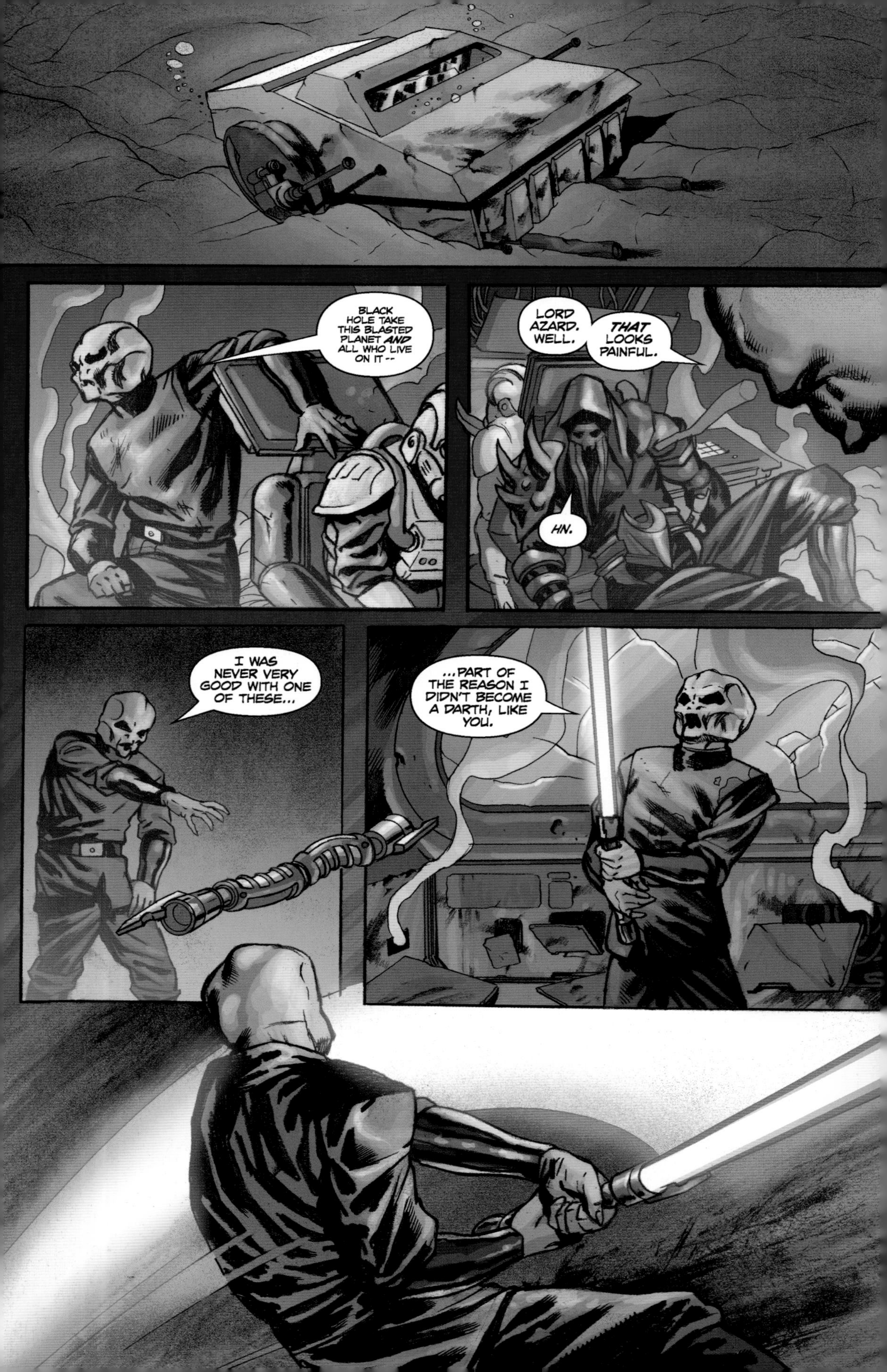
BLACK HOLE TAKE THIS BLASTED PLANET AND ALL WHO LIVE ON IT --
LORD AZARD. WELL.
THAT LOOKS PAINFUL.
HN.
I WAS NEVER VERY GOOD WITH ONE OF THESE...
...PART OF THE REASON I DIDN'T BECOME A DARTH, LIKE YOU.

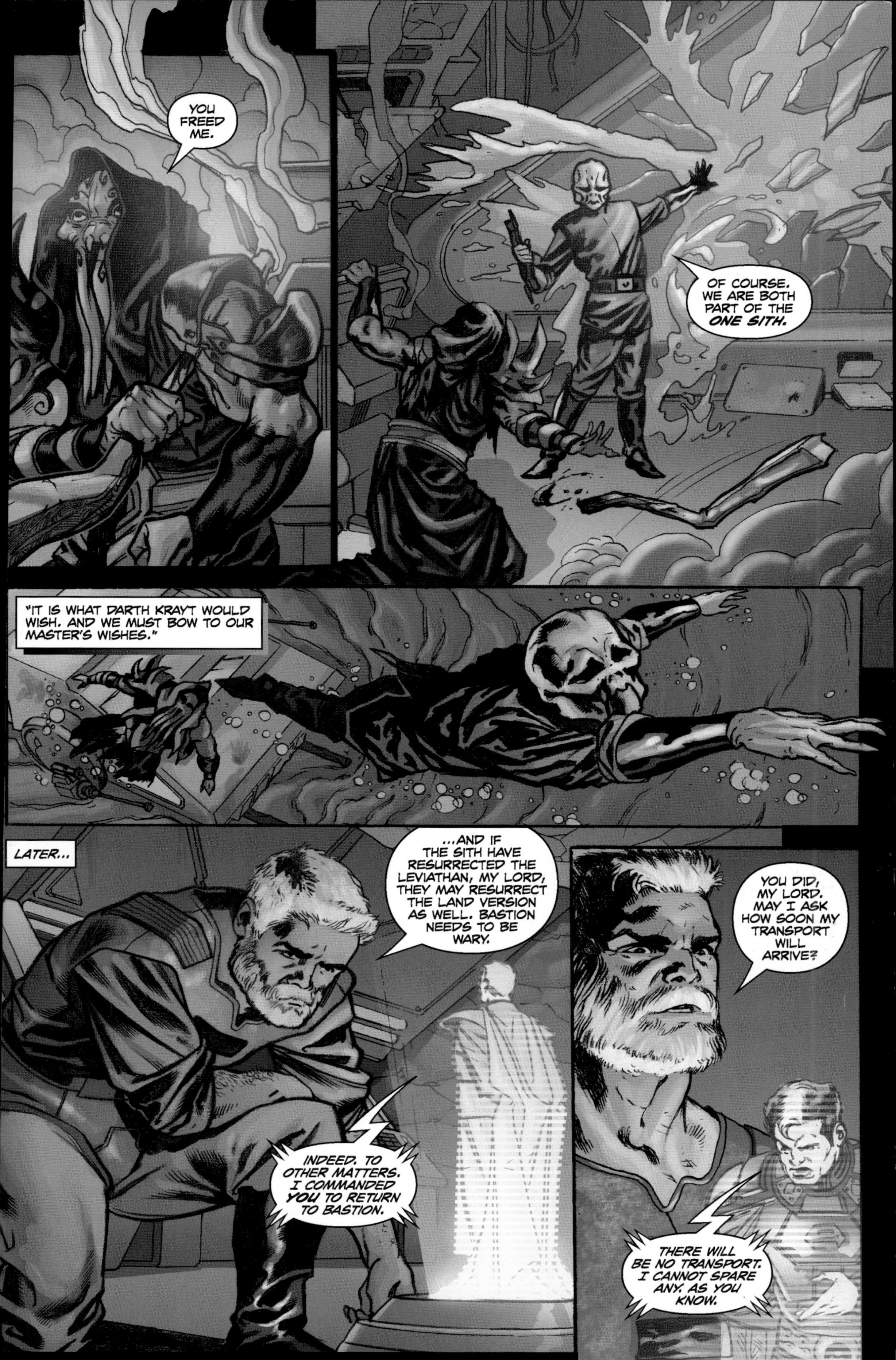
YOU FREED ME.
OF COURSE. WE ARE BOTH PART OF THE ONE SITH.
"IT IS WHAT DARTH KRAY'T WOULD WISH. AND WE MUST BOW TO OUR MASTER'S WISHES."
LATER...
...AND IF THE SITH HAVE RESURRECTED THE LEVIATHAN, MY LORD, THEY MAY RESURRECT THE LAND VERSION AS WELL. BASTION NEEDS TO BE WARY.
INDEED. TO OTHER MATTERS. I COMMANDED YOU TO RETURN TO BASTION.
YOU DID, MY LORD. MAY I ASK HOW SOON MY TRANSPORT WILL ARRIVE?
THERE WILL BE NO TRANSPORT. I CANNOT SPARE ANY. AS YOU KNOW.

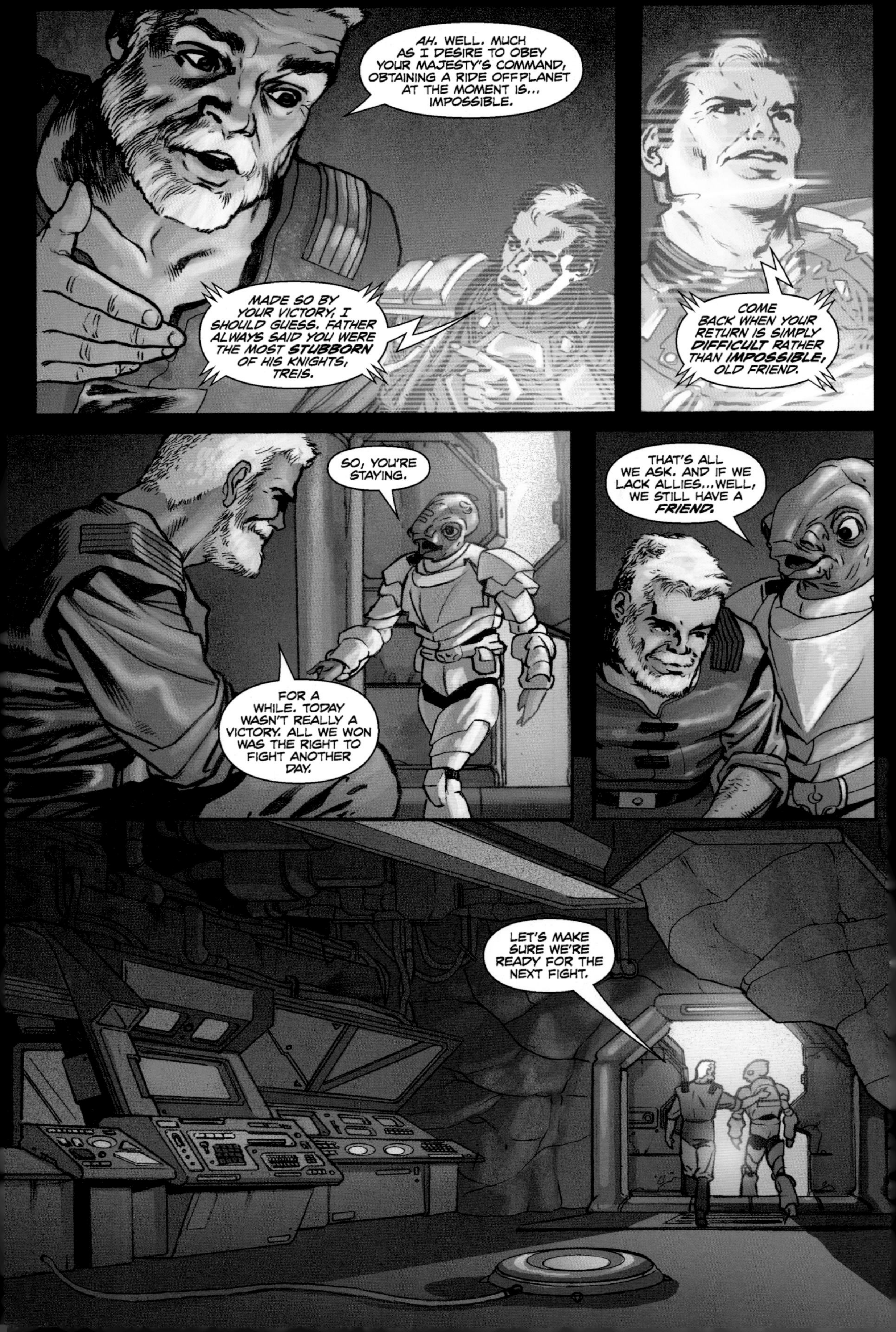
AH. WELL. MUCH AS I DESIRE TO OBEY YOUR MAJESTY'S COMMAND, OBTAINING A RIDE OFFPLANET AT THE MOMENT IS... IMPOSSIBLE.
MADE SO BY YOUR VICTORY, I SHOULD GUESS. FATHER ALWAYS SAID YOU WERE THE MOST STUBBORN OF HIS KNIGHTS, TREIS.
COME BACK WHEN YOUR RETURN IS SIMPLY DIFFICULT RATHER THAN IMPOSSIBLE, OLD FRIEND.
SO, YOU'RE STAYING.
FOR A WHILE. TODAY WASN'T REALLY A VICTORY. ALL WE WON WAS THE RIGHT TO FIGHT ANOTHER DAY.
THAT'S ALL WE ASK. AND IF WE LACK ALLIES...WELL, WE STILL HAVE A FRIEND.
LET'S MAKE SURE WE'RE READY FOR THE NEXT FIGHT.

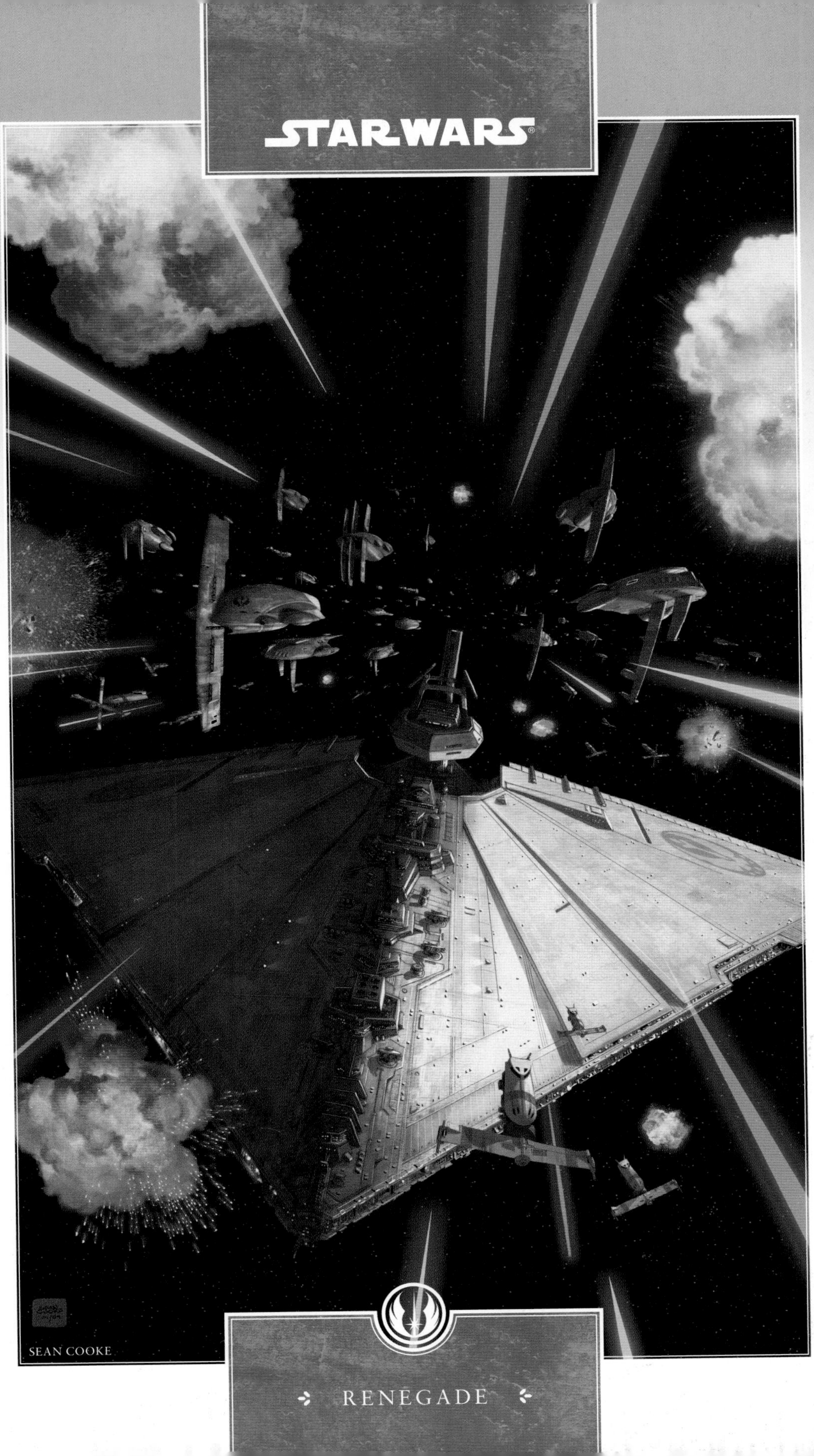
STAR WARS
SEAN COOKE
RENEGADE

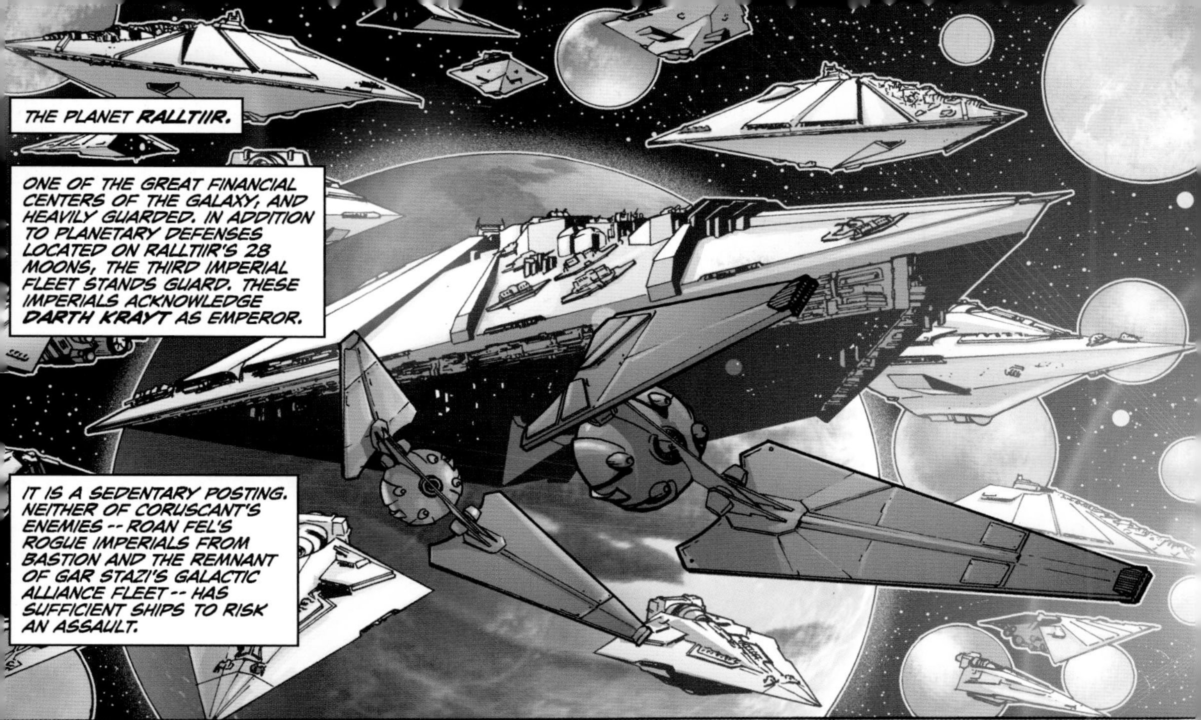
THE PLANET RALLTIIR.
ONE OF THE GREAT FINANCIAL CENTERS OF THE GALAXY, AND HEAVILY GUARDED. IN ADDITION TO PLANETARY DEFENSES LOCATED ON RALLTIIR'S 28 MOONS, THE THIRD IMPERIAL FLEET STANDS GUARD. THESE IMPERIALS ACKNOWLEDGE DARTH KRAYT AS EMPEROR.
IT IS A SEDENTARY POSTING. NEITHER OF CORUSCANT'S ENEMIES -- ROAN FEL'S ROGUE IMPERIALS FROM BASTION AND THE REMNANT OF GAR STAZI'S GALACTIC ALLIANCE FLEET -- HAS SUFFICIENT SHIPS TO RISK AN ASSAULT.
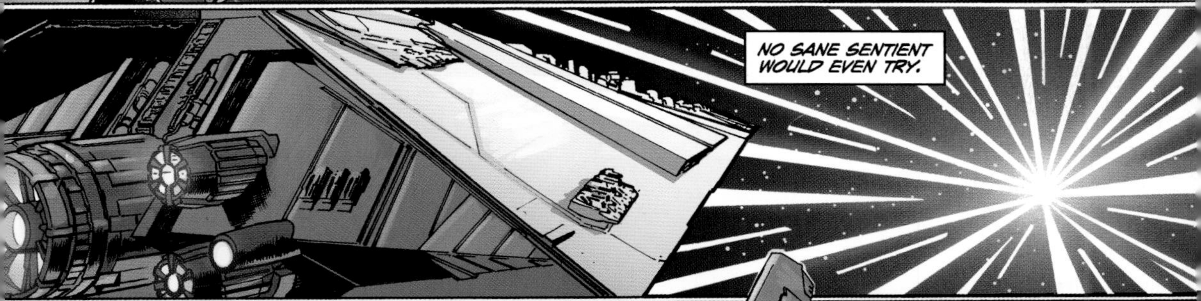
NO SANE SENTIENT WOULD EVEN TRY.
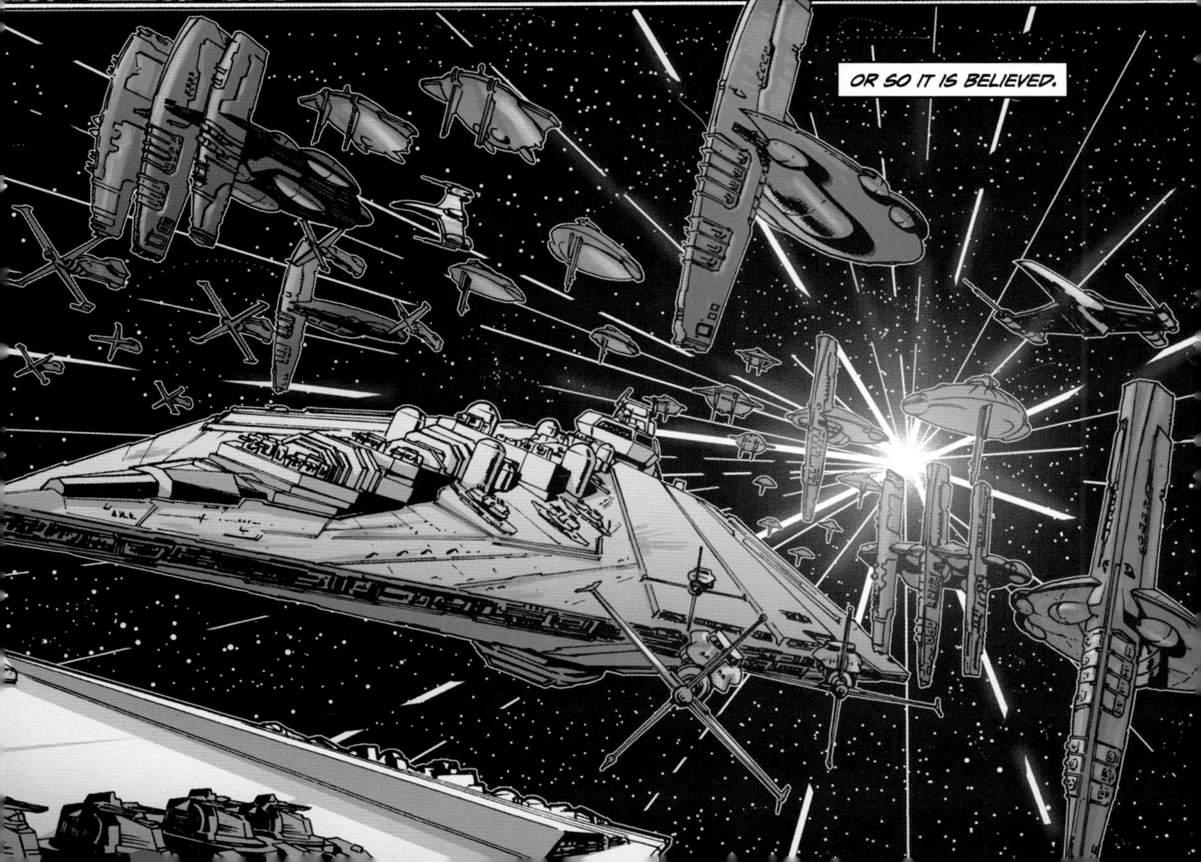
OR SO IT IS BELIEVED.

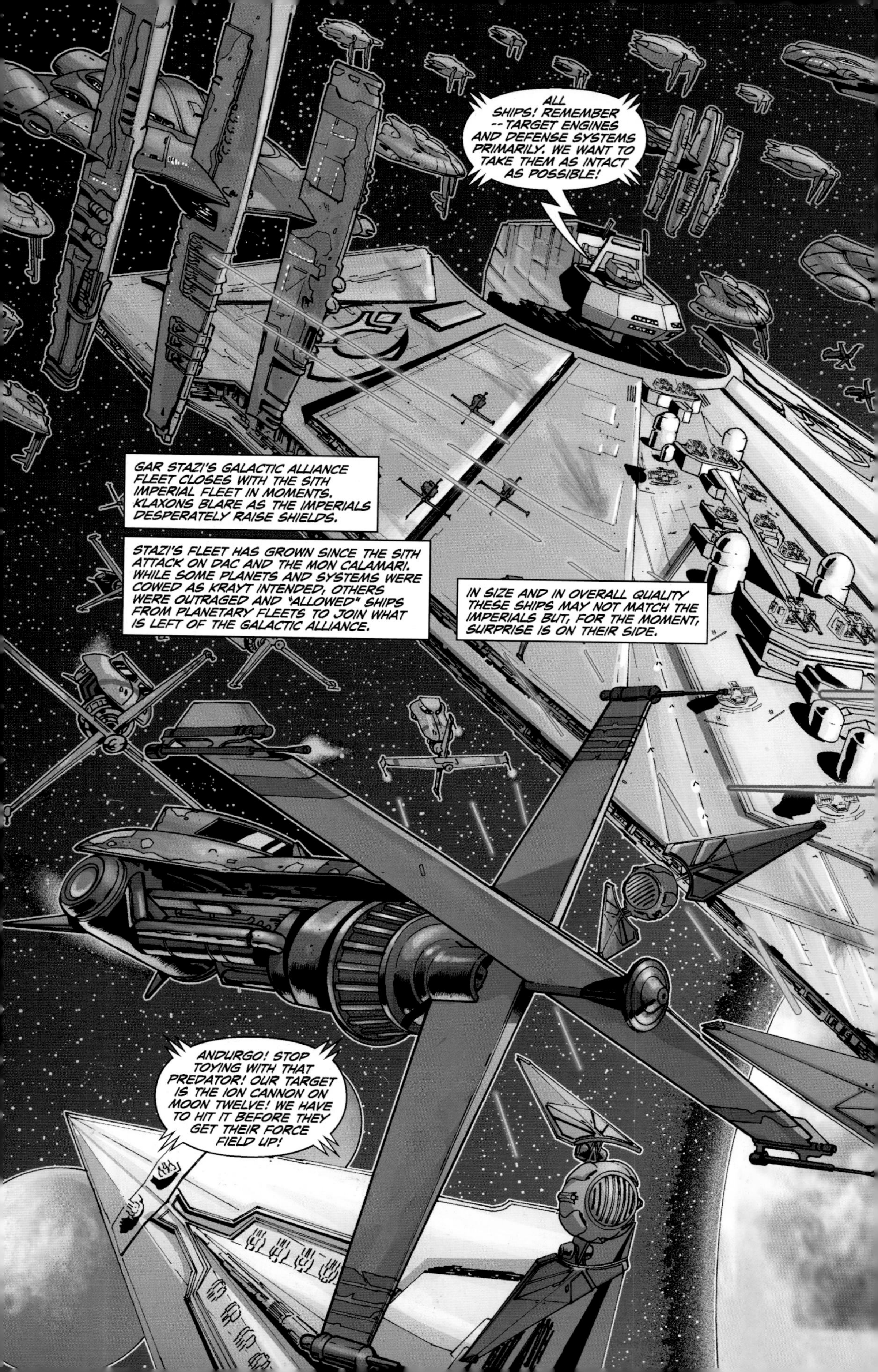
ALL SHIPS! REMEMBER --TARGET ENGINES AND DEFENSE SYSTEMS PRIMARILY. WE WANT TO TAKE THEM AS INTACT AS POSSIBLE!
GAR STAZI'S GALACTIC ALLIANCE FLEET CLOSES WITH THE SITH IMPERIAL FLEET IN MOMENTS. KLAXONS BLARE AS THE IMPERIALS DESPERATELY RAISE SHIELDS.
STAZI'S FLEET HAS GROWN SINCE THE SITH ATTACK ON DAC AND THE MON CALAMARI. WHILE SOME PLANETS AND SYSTEMS WERE COWED AS KRAYT INTENDED, OTHERS WERE OUTRAGED AND "ALLOWED" SHIPS FROM PLANETARY FLEETS TO JOIN WHAT IS LEFT OF THE GALACTIC ALLIANCE.
IN SIZE AND IN OVERALL QUALITY THESE SHIPS MAY NOT MATCH THE IMPERIALS BUT, FOR THE MOMENT, SURPRISE IS ON THEIR SIDE.
ANDURGO! STOP TOYING WITH THAT PREDATOR! OUR TARGET IS THE ION CANNON ON MOON TWELVE! WE HAVE TO HIT IT BEFORE THEY GET THEIR FORCE FIELD UP!

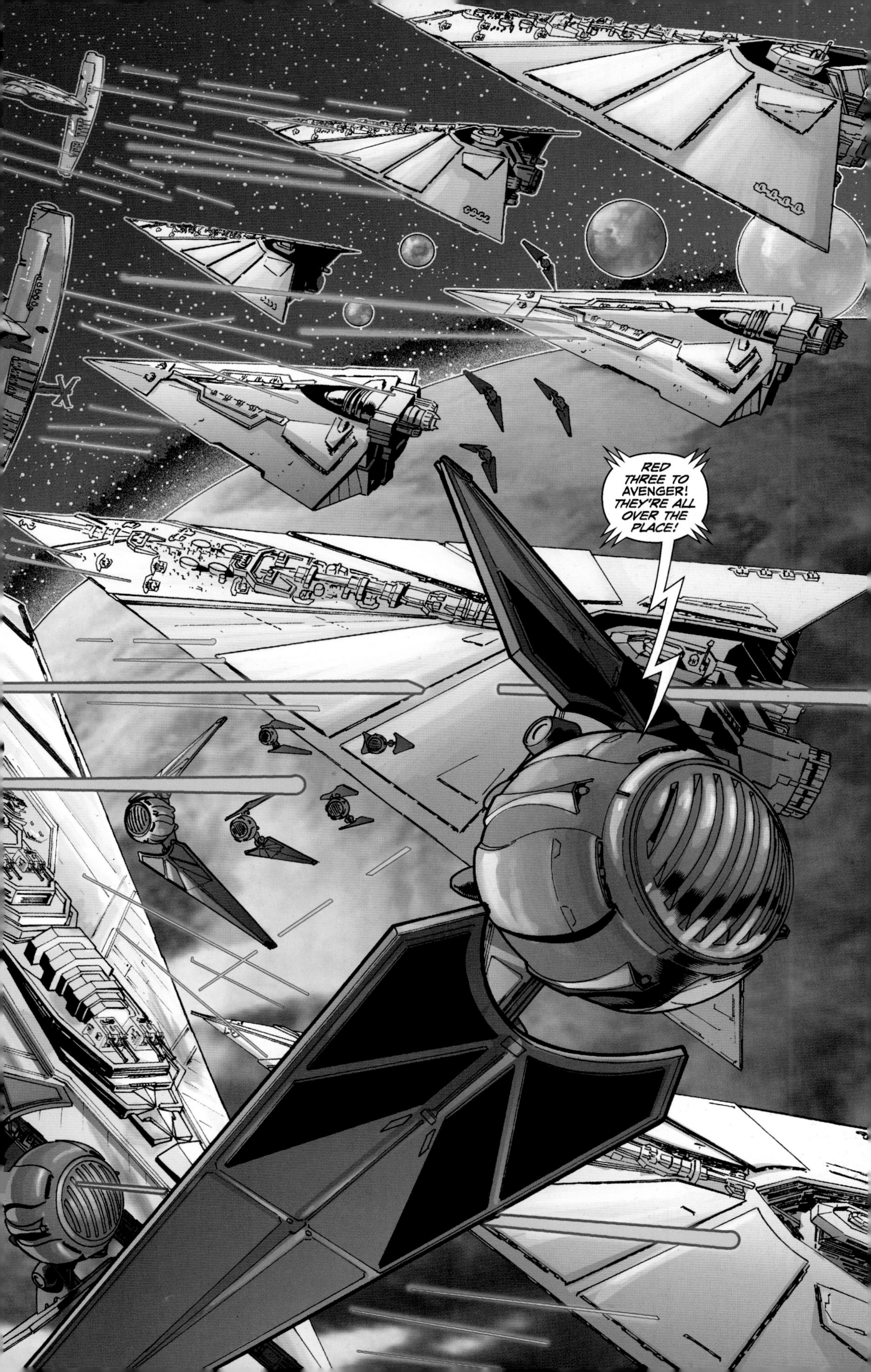
RED THREE TO AVENGER! THEY'RE ALL OVER THE PLACE!

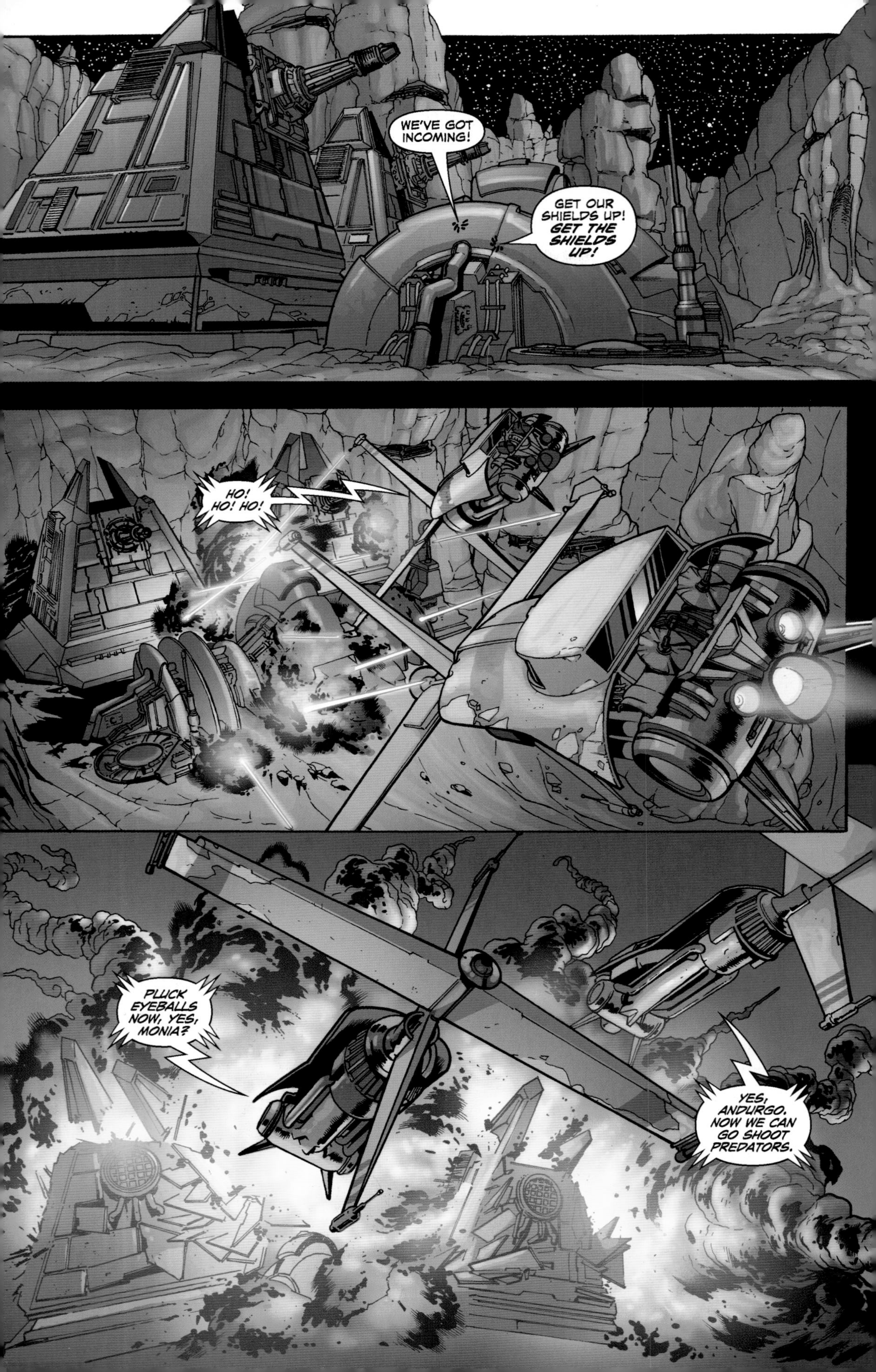
WE'VE GOT INCOMING!
GET OUR SHIELDS UP! GET THE SHIELDS UP!
HO! HO! HO!
PLUCK EYEBALLS NOW, YES, MONIA?
YES, ANDURGO. NOW WE CAN GO SHOOT PREDATORS.

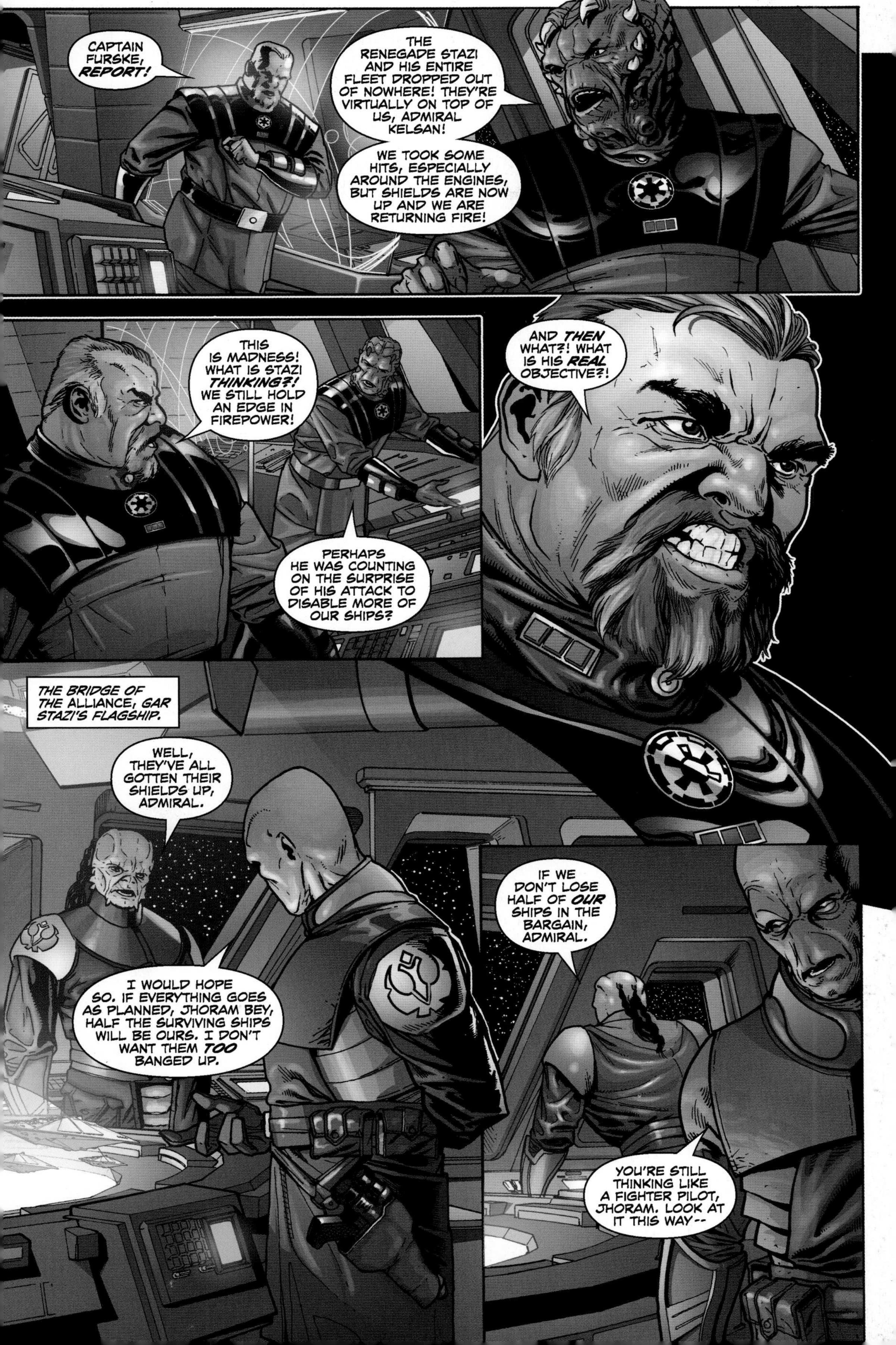
CAPTAIN FURSKE, *REPORT!*
THE RENEGADE STAZI AND HIS ENTIRE FLEET DROPPED OUT OF NOWHERE! THEY'RE VIRTUALLY ON TOP OF US, ADMIRAL KELSAN!
WE TOOK SOME HITS, ESPECIALLY AROUND THE ENGINES, BUT SHIELDS ARE NOW UP AND WE ARE RETURNING FIRE!
THIS IS MADNESS! WHAT IS STAZI *THINKING?!* WE STILL HOLD AN EDGE IN FIREPOWER!
PERHAPS HE WAS COUNTING ON THE SURPRISE OF HIS ATTACK TO DISABLE MORE OF OUR SHIPS?
AND *THEN* WHAT?! WHAT IS HIS *REAL* OBJECTIVE?!
THE BRIDGE OF THE ALLIANCE, GAR STAZI'S FLAGSHIP.
WELL, THEY'VE ALL GOTTEN THEIR SHIELDS UP, ADMIRAL.
I WOULD HOPE SO. IF EVERYTHING GOES AS PLANNED, JHORAM BEY, HALF THE SURVIVING SHIPS WILL BE OURS. I DON'T WANT THEM *TOO* BANGED UP.
IF WE DON'T LOSE HALF OF *OUR* SHIPS IN THE BARGAIN, ADMIRAL.
YOU'RE STILL THINKING LIKE A FIGHTER PILOT, JHORAM. LOOK AT IT THIS WAY--

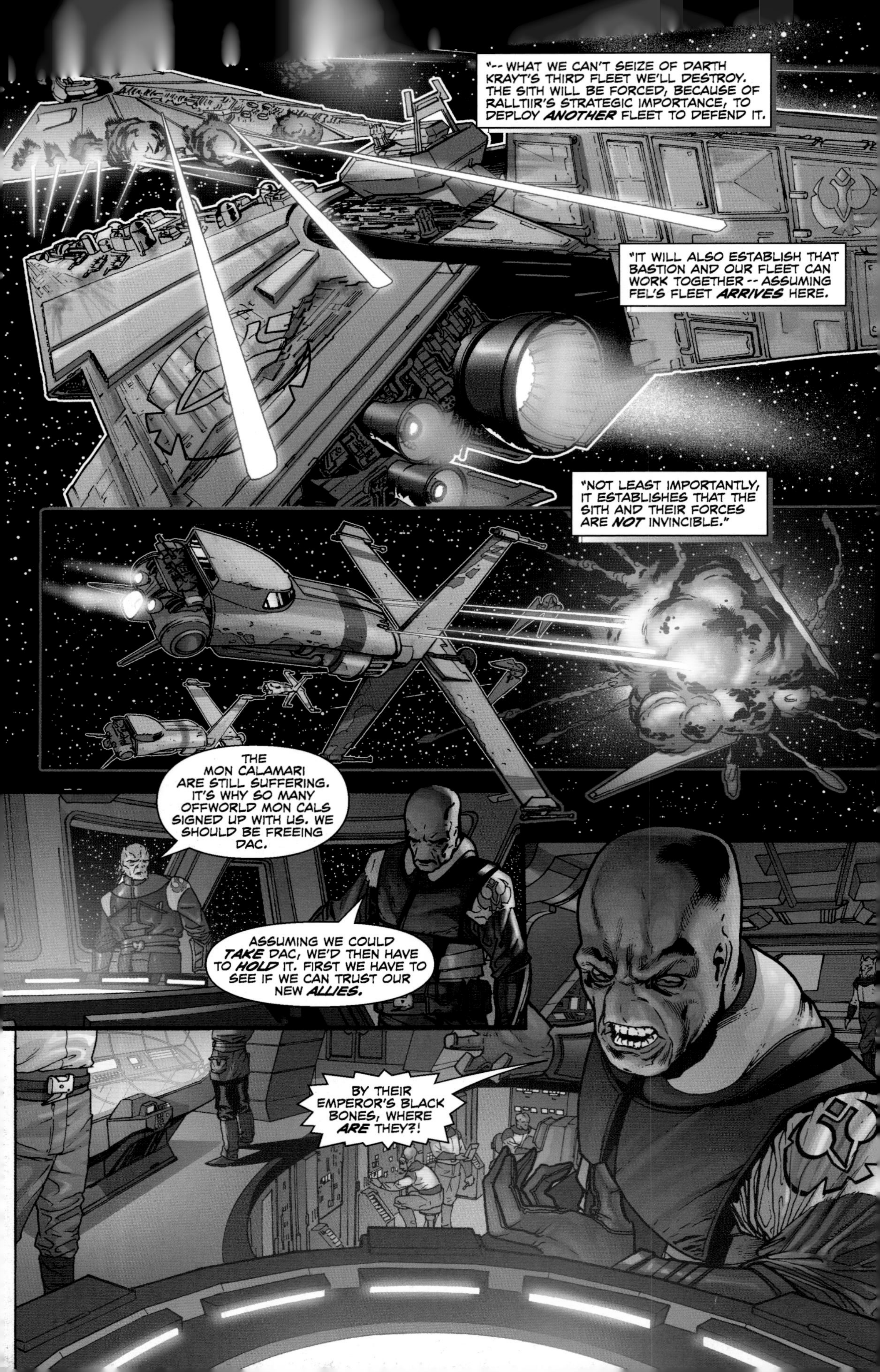
"-- WHAT WE CAN'T SEIZE OF DARTH KRAYT'S THIRD FLEET WE'LL DESTROY. THE SITH WILL BE FORCED, BECAUSE OF RALLTIIR'S STRATEGIC IMPORTANCE, TO DEPLOY ANOTHER FLEET TO DEFEND IT.
"IT WILL ALSO ESTABLISH THAT BASTION AND OUR FLEET CAN WORK TOGETHER -- ASSUMING FEL'S FLEET ARRIVES HERE.
"NOT LEAST IMPORTANTLY, IT ESTABLISHES THAT THE SITH AND THEIR FORCES ARE NOT INVINCIBLE."
THE MON CALAMARI ARE STILL SUFFERING. IT'S WHY SO MANY OFFWORLD MON CALS SIGNED UP WITH US. WE SHOULD BE FREEING DAC.
ASSUMING WE COULD TAKE DAC, WE'D THEN HAVE TO HOLD IT. FIRST WE HAVE TO SEE IF WE CAN TRUST OUR NEW ALLIES.
BY THEIR EMPEROR'S BLACK BONES, WHERE ARE THEY?!

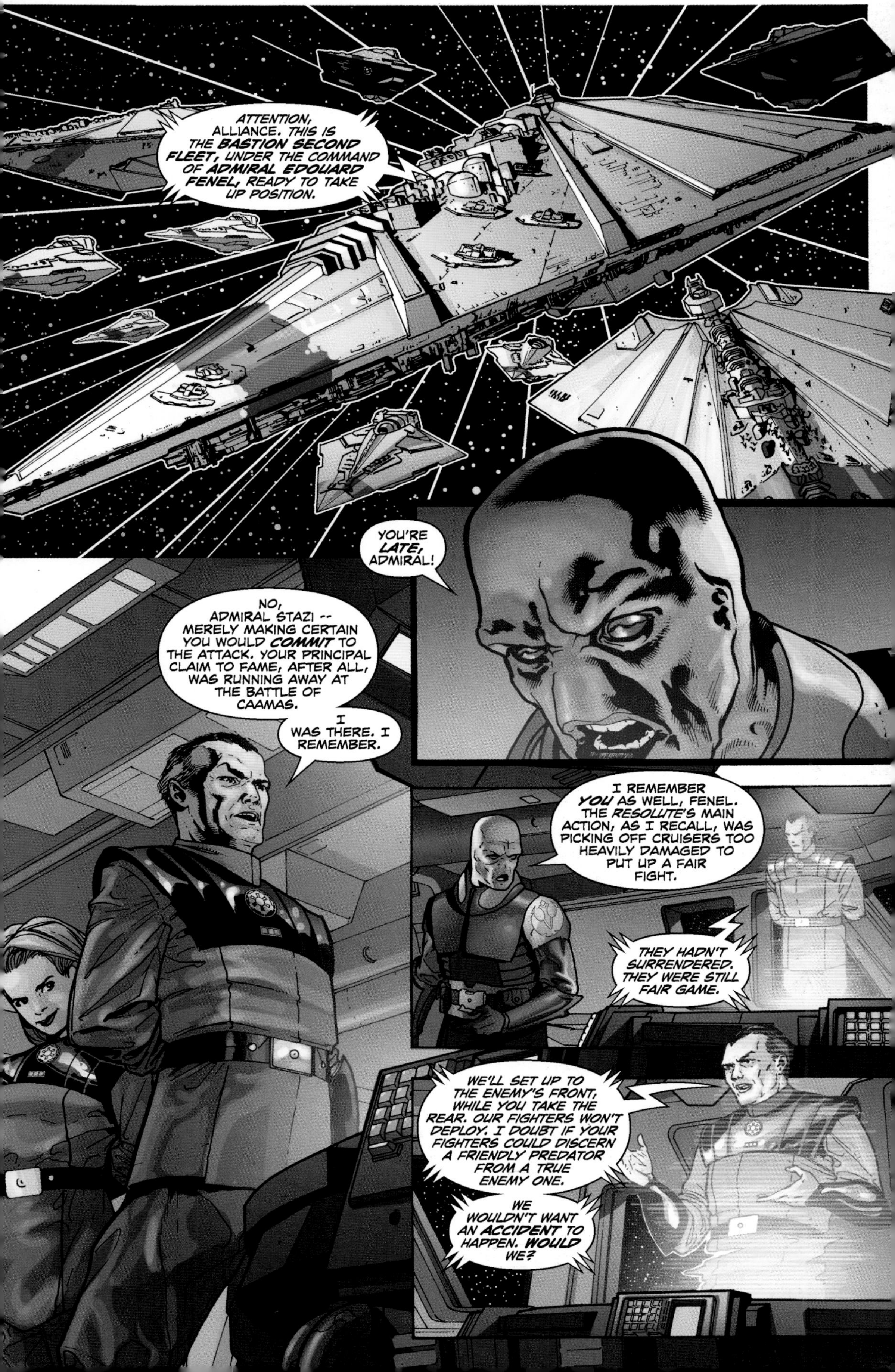
ATTENTION, ALLIANCE. THIS IS THE BASTION SECOND FLEET, UNDER THE COMMAND OF ADMIRAL EDOUARD FENEL, READY TO TAKE UP POSITION.
YOU'RE LATE, ADMIRAL!
NO, ADMIRAL STAZI -- MERELY MAKING CERTAIN YOU WOULD COMMIT TO THE ATTACK. YOUR PRINCIPAL CLAIM TO FAME, AFTER ALL, WAS RUNNING AWAY AT THE BATTLE OF CAAMAS.
I WAS THERE. I REMEMBER.
I REMEMBER YOU AS WELL, FENEL. THE RESOLUTE'S MAIN ACTION, AS I RECALL, WAS PICKING OFF CRUISERS TOO HEAVILY DAMAGED TO PUT UP A FAIR FIGHT.
THEY HADN'T SURRENDERED. THEY WERE STILL FAIR GAME.
WE'LL SET UP TO THE ENEMY'S FRONT, WHILE YOU TAKE THE REAR. OUR FIGHTERS WON'T DEPLOY. I DOUBT IF YOUR FIGHTERS COULD DISCERN A FRIENDLY PREDATOR FROM A TRUE ENEMY ONE.
WE WOULDN'T WANT AN ACCIDENT TO HAPPEN. WOULD WE?

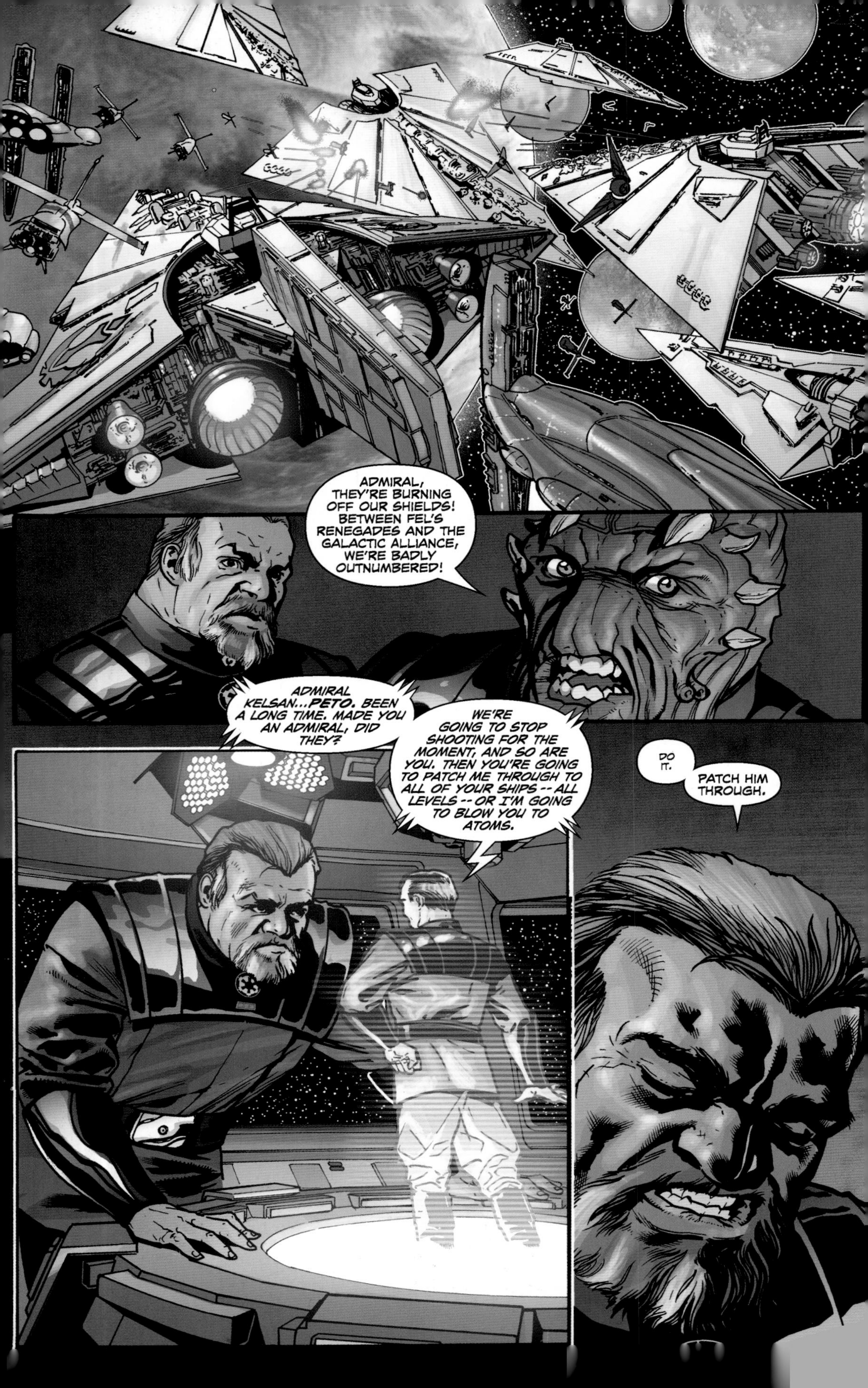
ADMIRAL, THEY'RE BURNING OFF OUR SHIELDS! BETWEEN FEL'S RENEGADES AND THE GALACTIC ALLIANCE, WE'RE BADLY OUTNUMBERED!
ADMIRAL KELSAN...PETO. BEEN A LONG TIME. MADE YOU AN ADMIRAL, DID THEY?
WE'RE GOING TO STOP SHOOTING FOR THE MOMENT, AND SO ARE YOU. THEN YOU'RE GOING TO PATCH ME THROUGH TO ALL OF YOUR SHIPS -- ALL LEVELS -- OR I'M GOING TO BLOW YOU TO ATOMS.
DO IT.
PATCH HIM THROUGH.

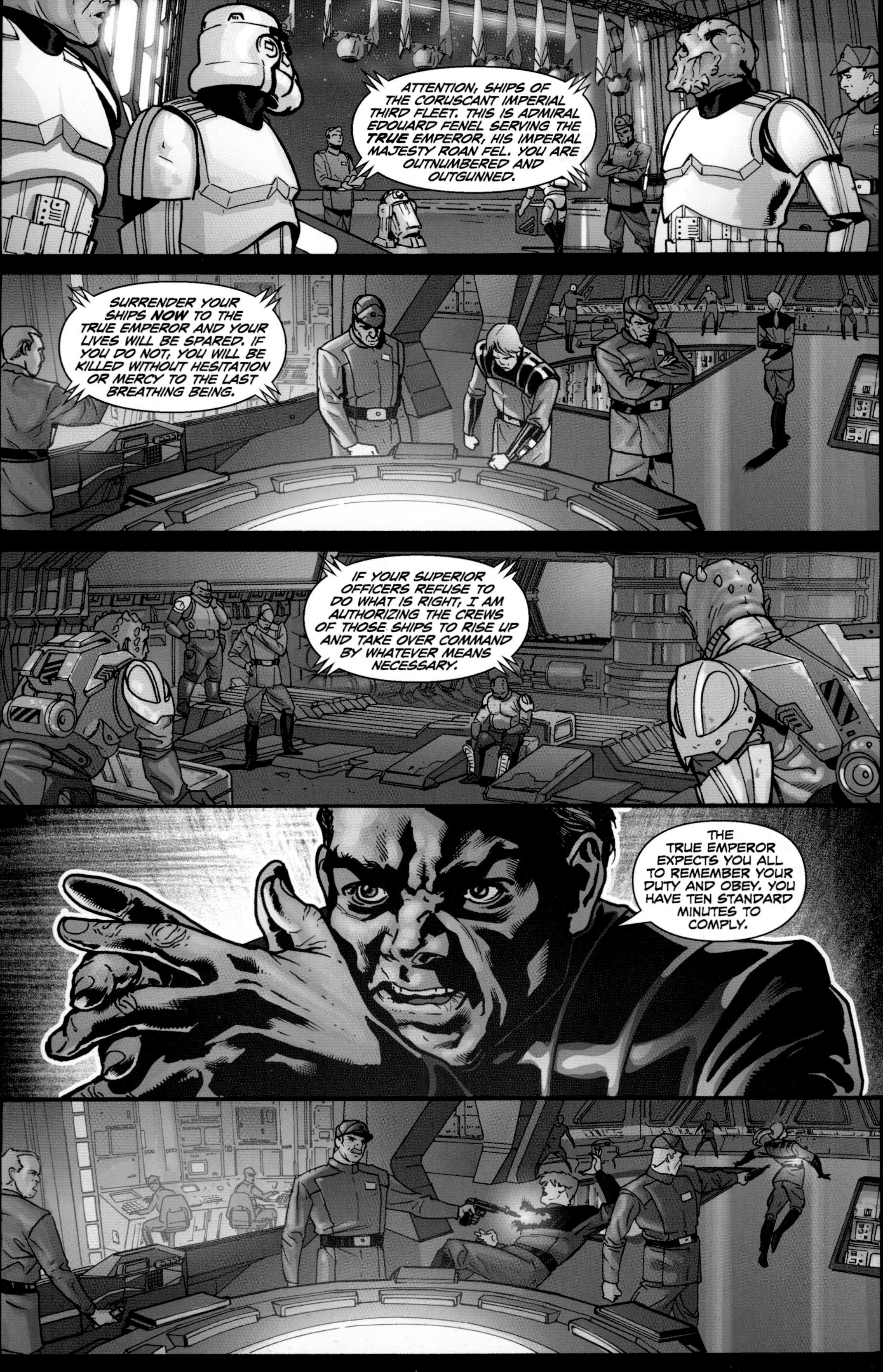
ATTENTION, SHIPS OF THE CORUSCANT IMPERIAL THIRD FLEET. THIS IS ADMIRAL EDOUARD FENEL SERVING THE **TRUE** EMPEROR, HIS IMPERIAL MAJESTY ROAN FEL. YOU ARE OUTNUMBERED AND OUTGUNNED.
SURRENDER YOUR SHIPS **NOW** TO THE TRUE EMPEROR AND YOUR LIVES WILL BE SPARED. IF YOU DO NOT, YOU WILL BE KILLED WITHOUT HESITATION OR MERCY TO THE LAST BREATHING BEING.
IF YOUR SUPERIOR OFFICERS REFUSE TO DO WHAT IS RIGHT, I AM AUTHORIZING THE CREWS OF THOSE SHIPS TO RISE UP AND TAKE OVER COMMAND BY WHATEVER MEANS NECESSARY.
THE TRUE EMPEROR EXPECTS YOU ALL TO REMEMBER YOUR DUTY AND OBEY. YOU HAVE TEN STANDARD MINUTES TO COMPLY.

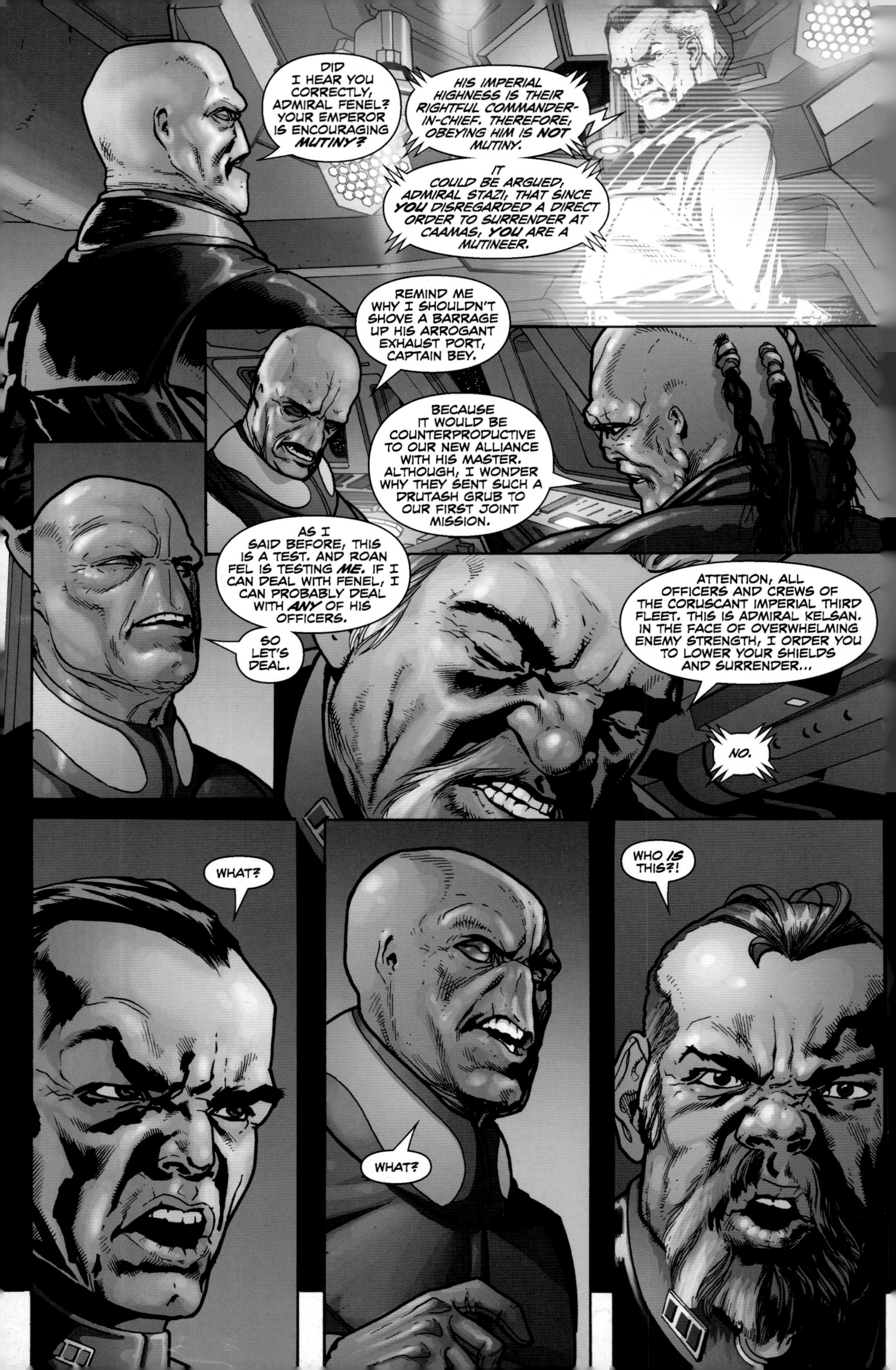
DID I HEAR YOU CORRECTLY, ADMIRAL FENEL? YOUR EMPEROR IS ENCOURAGING MUTINY?
HIS IMPERIAL HIGHNESS IS THEIR RIGHTFUL COMMANDER-IN-CHIEF. THEREFORE, OBEYING HIM IS NOT MUTINY.
IT COULD BE ARGUED, ADMIRAL STAZI, THAT SINCE YOU DISREGARDED A DIRECT ORDER TO SURRENDER AT CAAMAS, YOU ARE A MUTINEER.
REMIND ME WHY I SHOULDN'T SHOVE A BARRAGE UP HIS ARROGANT EXHAUST PORT, CAPTAIN BEY.
BECAUSE IT WOULD BE COUNTERPRODUCTIVE TO OUR NEW ALLIANCE WITH HIS MASTER. ALTHOUGH, I WONDER WHY THEY SENT SUCH A DRUTASH GRUB TO OUR FIRST JOINT MISSION.
AS I SAID BEFORE, THIS IS A TEST. AND ROAN FEL IS TESTING ME. IF I CAN DEAL WITH FENEL, I CAN PROBABLY DEAL WITH ANY OF HIS OFFICERS.
SO LET'S DEAL.
ATTENTION, ALL OFFICERS AND CREWS OF THE CORUSCANT IMPERIAL THIRD FLEET. THIS IS ADMIRAL KELSAN. IN THE FACE OF OVERWHELMING ENEMY STRENGTH, I ORDER YOU TO LOWER YOUR SHIELDS AND SURRENDER...
NO.
WHAT?
WHAT?
WHO IS THIS?!

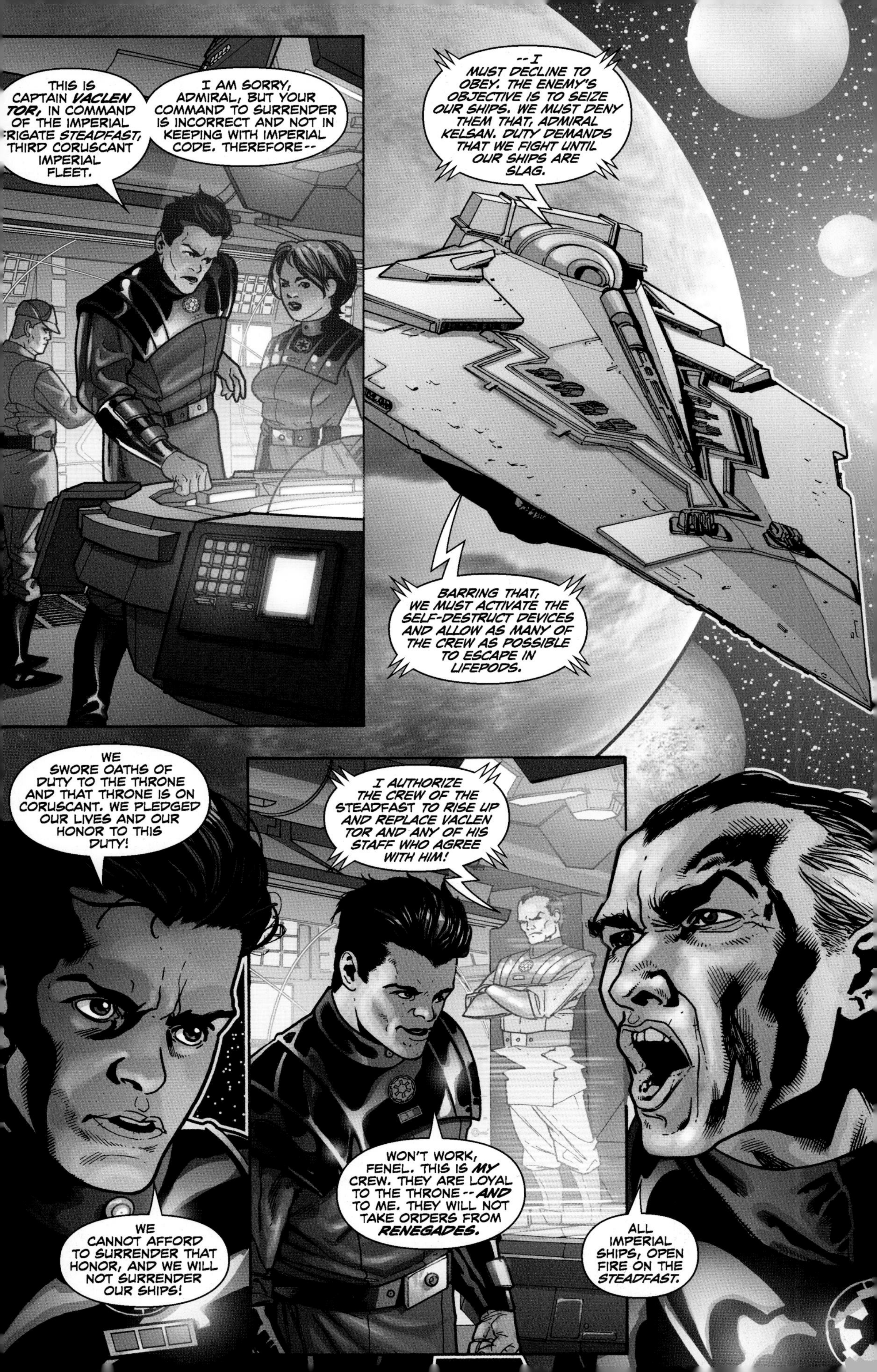
THIS IS CAPTAIN VACLEN TOR, IN COMMAND OF THE IMPERIAL FRIGATE STEADFAST, THIRD CORUSCANT IMPERIAL FLEET.
I AM SORRY, ADMIRAL, BUT YOUR COMMAND TO SURRENDER IS INCORRECT AND NOT IN KEEPING WITH IMPERIAL CODE. THEREFORE--
--I MUST DECLINE TO OBEY. THE ENEMY'S OBJECTIVE IS TO SEIZE OUR SHIPS. WE MUST DENY THEM THAT, ADMIRAL KELSAN. DUTY DEMANDS THAT WE FIGHT UNTIL OUR SHIPS ARE SLAG.
BARRING THAT, WE MUST ACTIVATE THE SELF-DESTRUCT DEVICES AND ALLOW AS MANY OF THE CREW AS POSSIBLE TO ESCAPE IN LIFEPODS.
WE SWORE OATHS OF DUTY TO THE THRONE AND THAT THRONE IS ON CORUSCANT. WE PLEDGED OUR LIVES AND OUR HONOR TO THIS DUTY!
WE CANNOT AFFORD TO SURRENDER THAT HONOR, AND WE WILL NOT SURRENDER OUR SHIPS!
I AUTHORIZE THE CREW OF THE STEADFAST TO RISE UP AND REPLACE VACLEN TOR AND ANY OF HIS STAFF WHO AGREE WITH HIM!
WON'T WORK, FENEL. THIS IS MY CREW. THEY ARE LOYAL TO THE THRONE--AND TO ME. THEY WILL NOT TAKE ORDERS FROM RENEGADES.
ALL IMPERIAL SHIPS, OPEN FIRE ON THE STEADFAST.

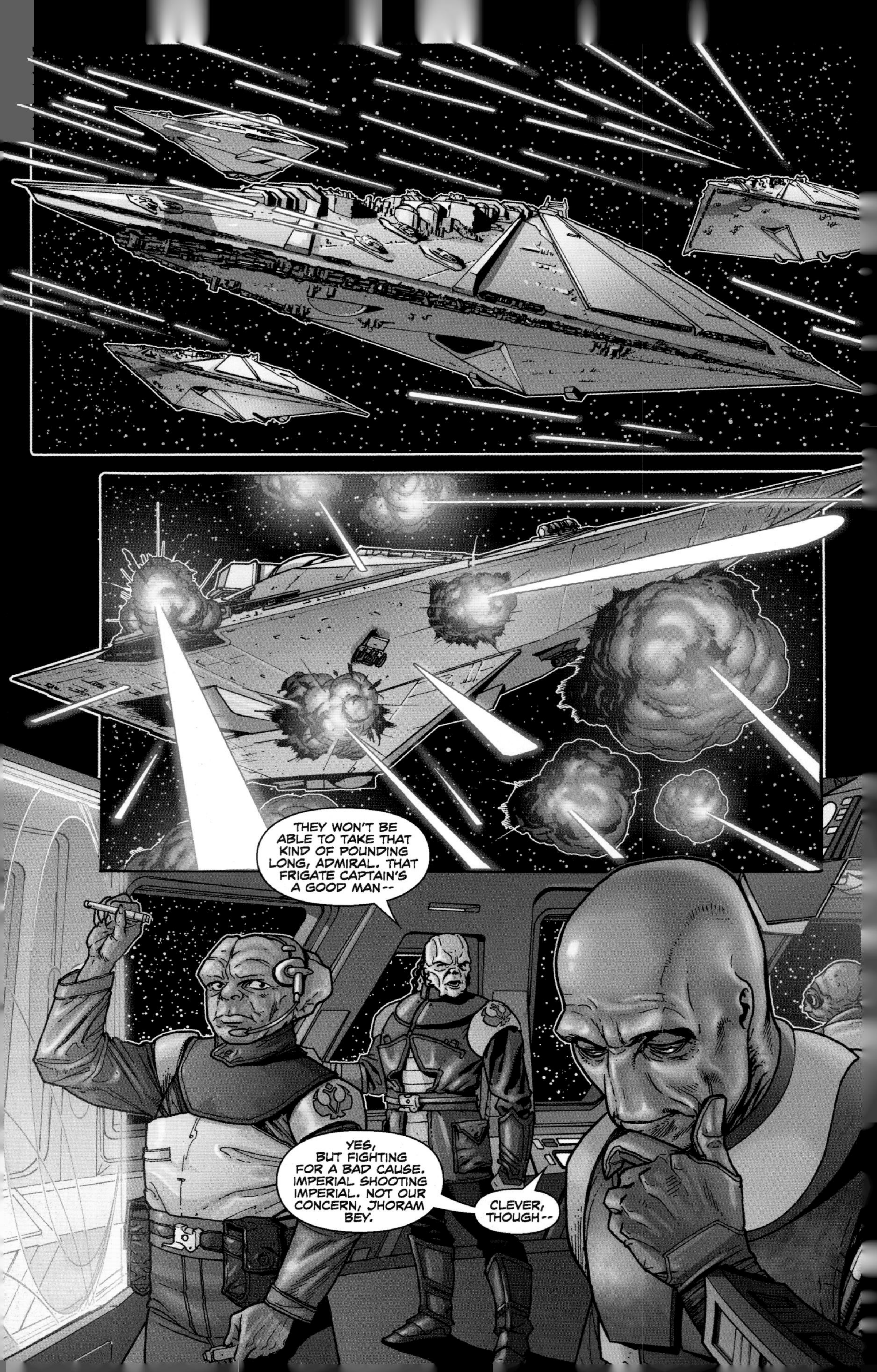
THEY WON'T BE ABLE TO TAKE THAT KIND OF POUNDING LONG, ADMIRAL. THAT FRIGATE CAPTAIN'S A GOOD MAN--
YES, BUT FIGHTING FOR A BAD CAUSE. IMPERIAL SHOOTING IMPERIAL. NOT OUR CONCERN, JHORAM BEY.
CLEVER, THOUGH--

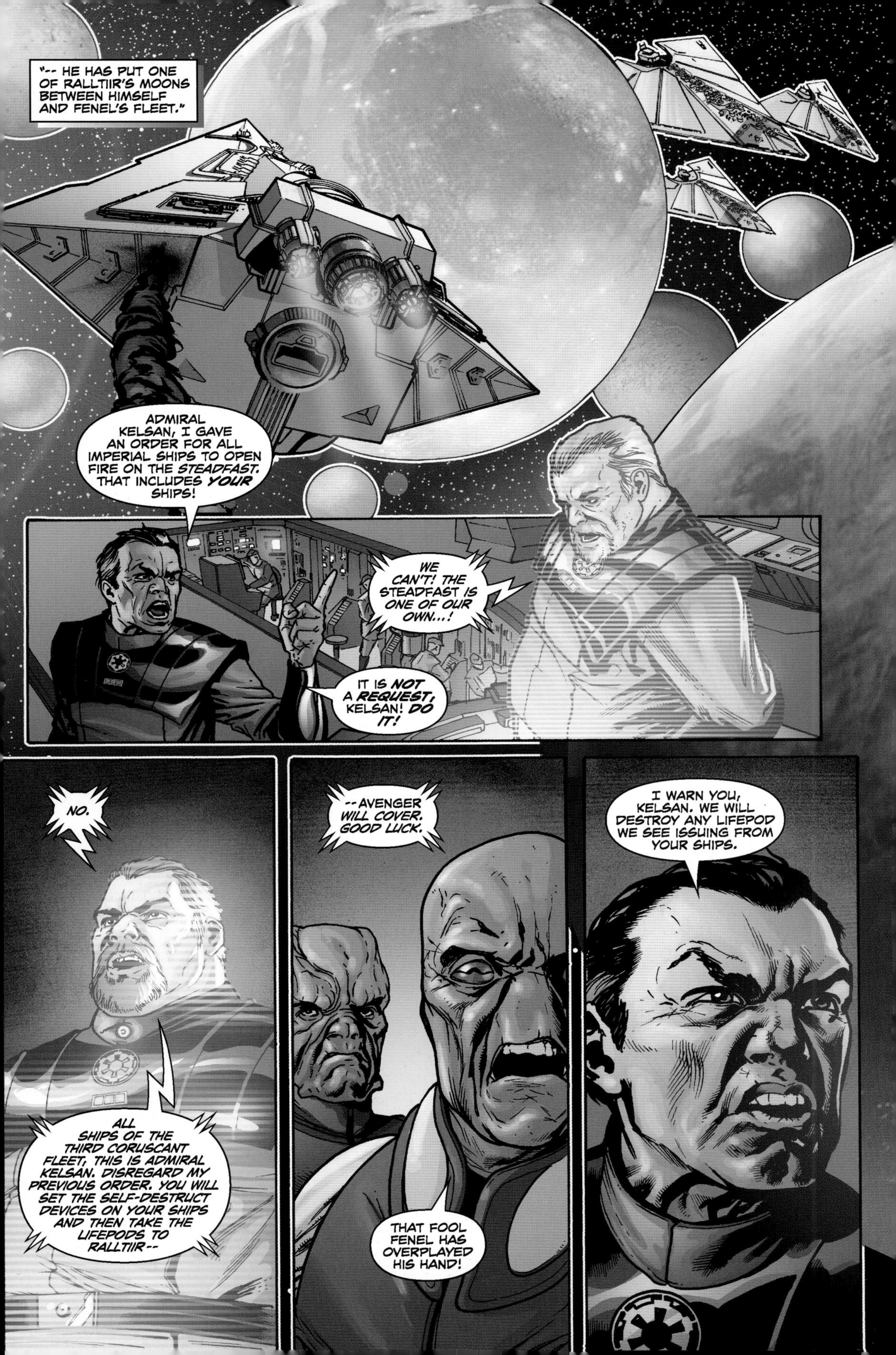
"-- HE HAS PUT ONE OF RALLTIIR'S MOONS BETWEEN HIMSELF AND FENEL'S FLEET."
ADMIRAL KELSAN, I GAVE AN ORDER FOR ALL IMPERIAL SHIPS TO OPEN FIRE ON THE *STEADFAST*. THAT INCLUDES ***YOUR*** SHIPS!
WE CAN'T! THE *STEADFAST* IS ONE OF OUR OWN...!
IT IS ***NOT*** A ***REQUEST,*** KELSAN! ***DO IT!***
NO.
ALL SHIPS OF THE THIRD CORUSCANT FLEET, THIS IS ADMIRAL KELSAN. DISREGARD MY PREVIOUS ORDER. YOU WILL SET THE SELF-DESTRUCT DEVICES ON YOUR SHIPS AND THEN TAKE THE LIFEPODS TO RALLTIIR--
--AVENGER WILL COVER. GOOD LUCK.
THAT FOOL FENEL HAS OVERPLAYED HIS HAND!
I WARN YOU, KELSAN. WE WILL DESTROY ANY LIFEPOD WE SEE ISSUING FROM YOUR SHIPS.

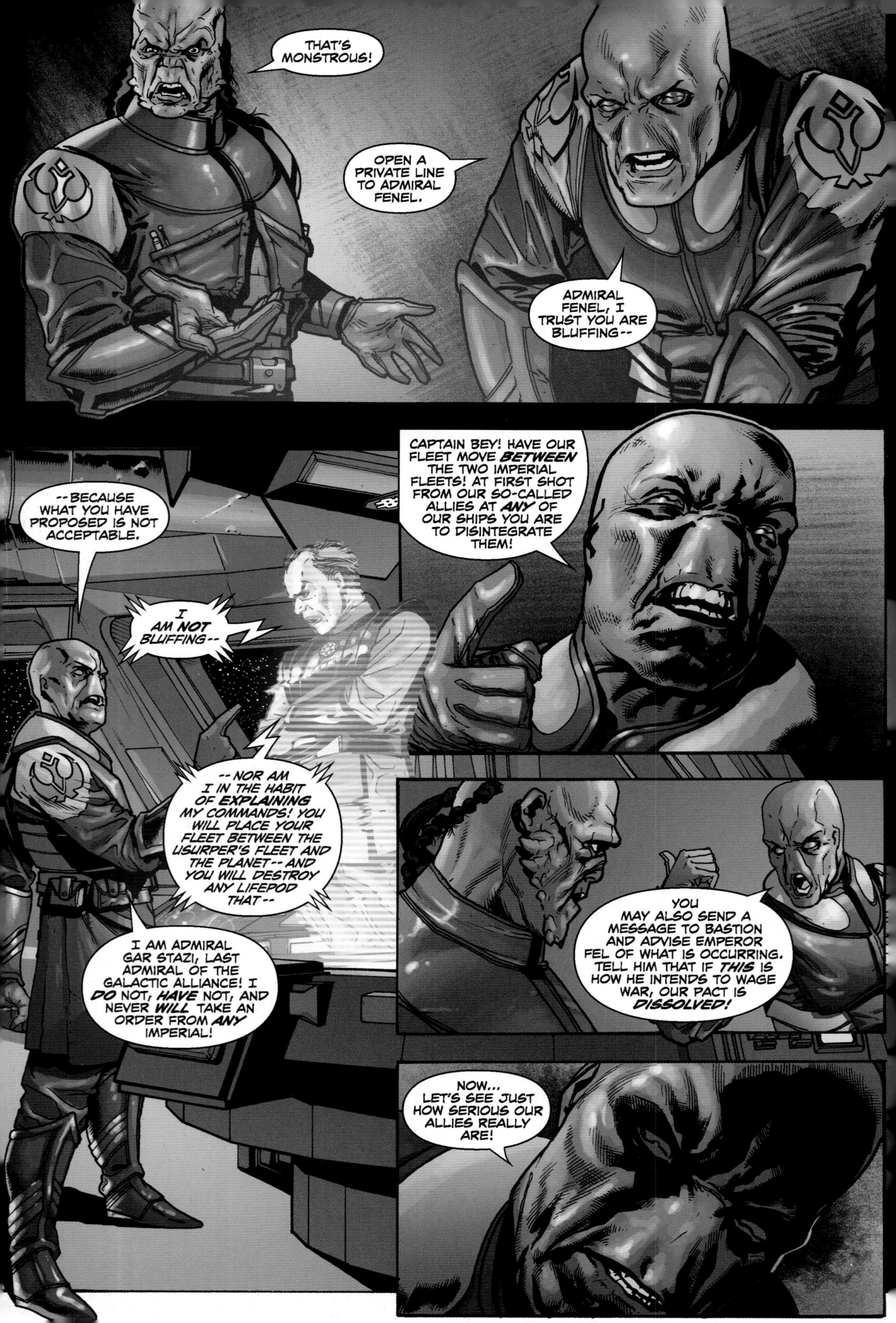
THAT'S MONSTROUS!
OPEN A PRIVATE LINE TO ADMIRAL FENEL.
ADMIRAL FENEL, I TRUST YOU ARE BLUFFING--
--BECAUSE WHAT YOU HAVE PROPOSED IS NOT ACCEPTABLE.
I AM **NOT** BLUFFING--
--NOR AM I IN THE HABIT OF **EXPLAINING** MY COMMANDS! YOU WILL PLACE YOUR FLEET BETWEEN THE USURPER'S FLEET AND THE PLANET--AND YOU WILL DESTROY ANY LIFEPOD THAT--
I AM ADMIRAL GAR STAZI, LAST ADMIRAL OF THE GALACTIC ALLIANCE! I **DO** NOT, **HAVE** NOT, AND NEVER **WILL** TAKE AN ORDER FROM **ANY** IMPERIAL!
CAPTAIN BEY! HAVE OUR FLEET MOVE **BETWEEN** THE TWO IMPERIAL FLEETS! AT FIRST SHOT FROM OUR SO-CALLED ALLIES AT **ANY** OF OUR SHIPS YOU ARE TO DISINTEGRATE THEM!
YOU MAY ALSO SEND A MESSAGE TO BASTION AND ADVISE EMPEROR FEL OF WHAT IS OCCURRING. TELL HIM THAT IF **THIS** IS HOW HE INTENDS TO WAGE WAR, OUR PACT IS **DISSOLVED!**
NOW... LET'S SEE JUST HOW SERIOUS OUR ALLIES REALLY ARE!

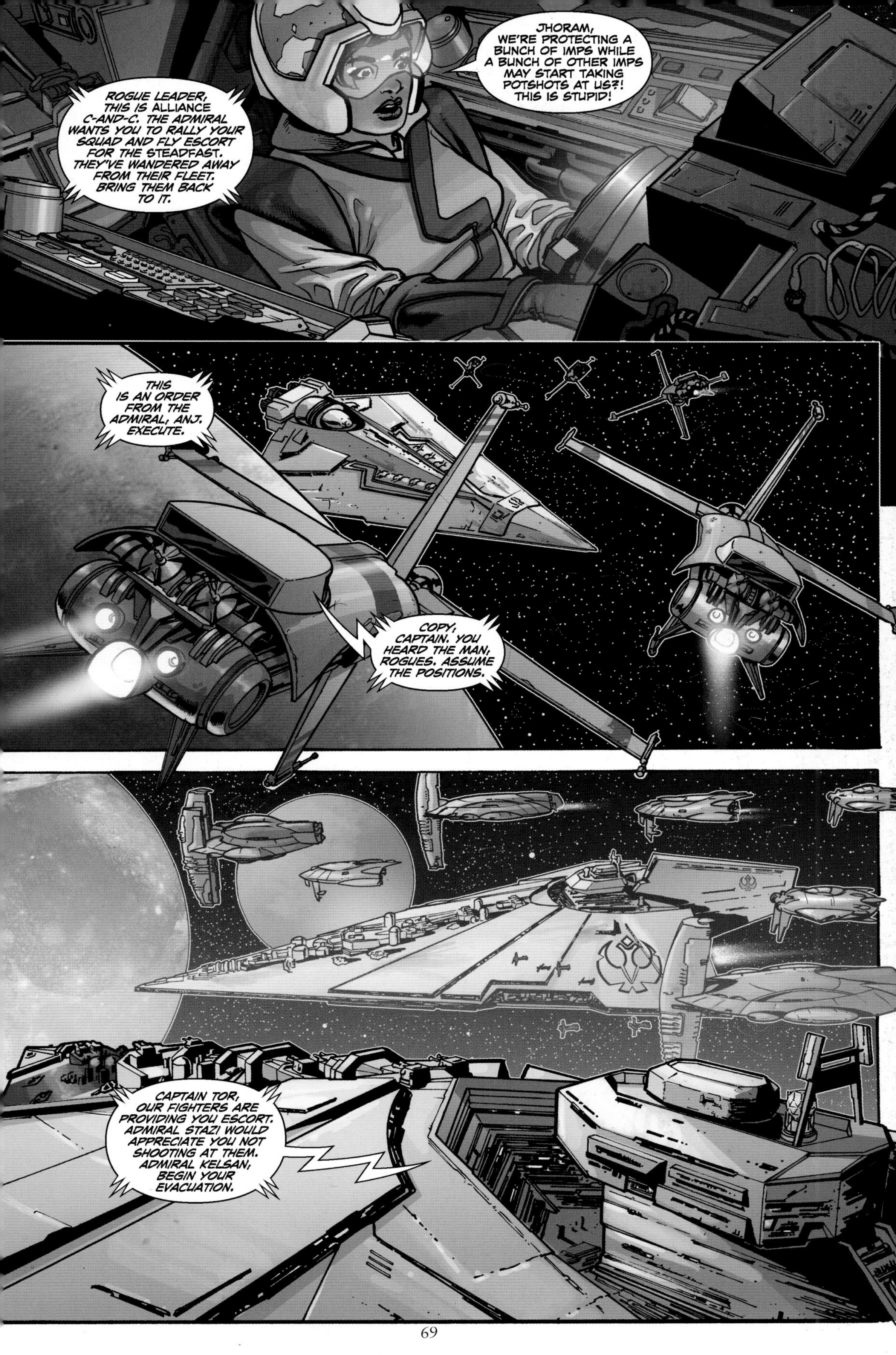
ROGUE LEADER, THIS IS ALLIANCE C-AND-C. THE ADMIRAL WANTS YOU TO RALLY YOUR SQUAD AND FLY ESCORT FOR THE STEADFAST. THEY'VE WANDERED AWAY FROM THEIR FLEET. BRING THEM BACK TO IT.
JHORAM, WE'RE PROTECTING A BUNCH OF IMPS WHILE A BUNCH OF OTHER IMPS MAY START TAKING POTSHOTS AT US?! THIS IS STUPID!
THIS IS AN ORDER FROM THE ADMIRAL, ANJ. EXECUTE.
COPY, CAPTAIN. YOU HEARD THE MAN, ROGUES. ASSUME THE POSITIONS.
CAPTAIN TOR, OUR FIGHTERS ARE PROVIDING YOU ESCORT. ADMIRAL STAZI WOULD APPRECIATE YOU NOT SHOOTING AT THEM. ADMIRAL KELSAN, BEGIN YOUR EVACUATION.

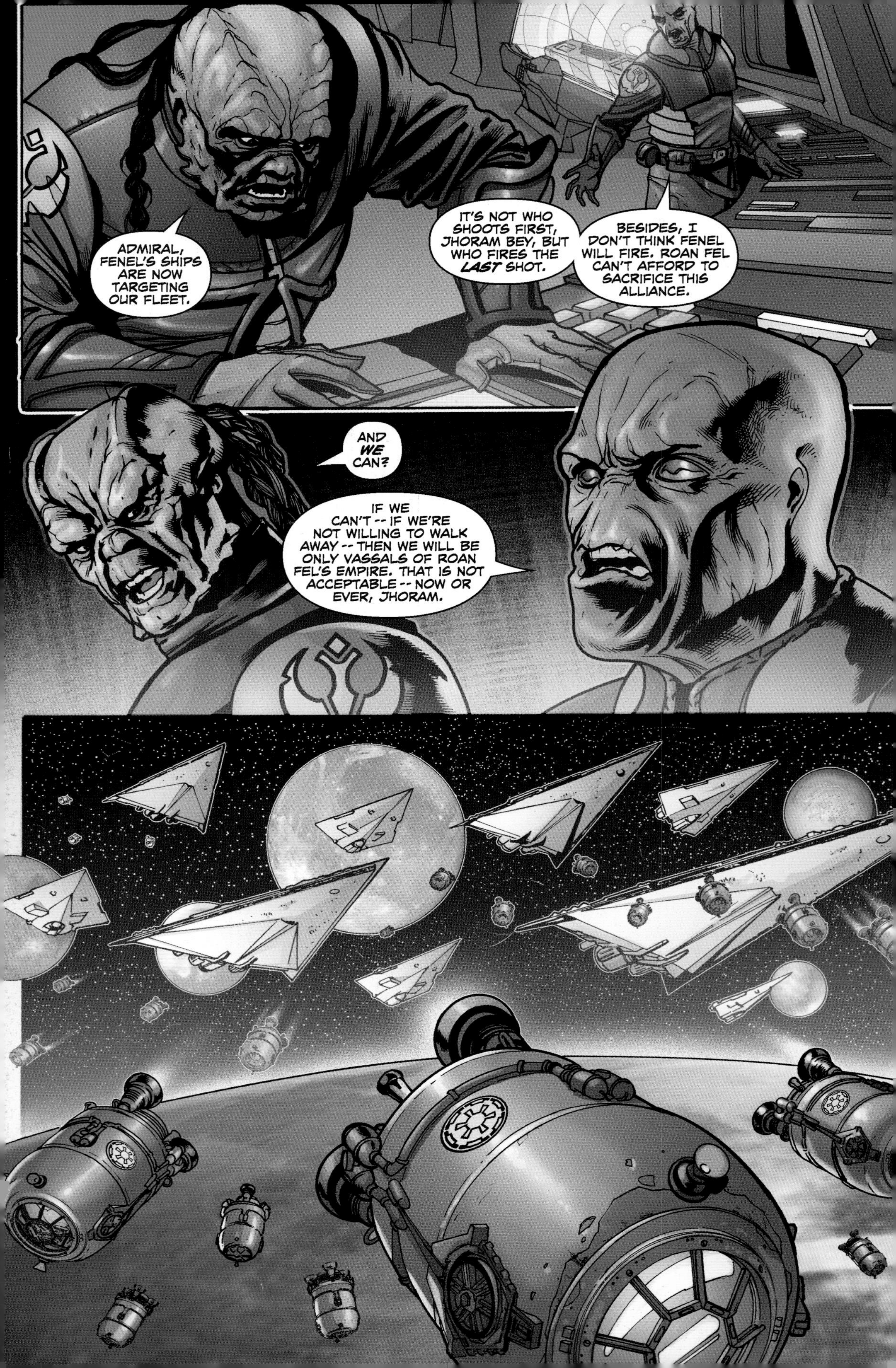
ADMIRAL, FENEL'S SHIPS ARE NOW TARGETING OUR FLEET.
IT'S NOT WHO SHOOTS FIRST, JHORAM BEY, BUT WHO FIRES THE *LAST* SHOT.
BESIDES, I DON'T THINK FENEL WILL FIRE. ROAN FEL CAN'T AFFORD TO SACRIFICE THIS ALLIANCE.
AND *WE* CAN?
IF WE CAN'T -- IF WE'RE NOT WILLING TO WALK AWAY -- THEN WE WILL BE ONLY VASSALS OF ROAN FEL'S EMPIRE. THAT IS NOT ACCEPTABLE -- NOW OR EVER, JHORAM.

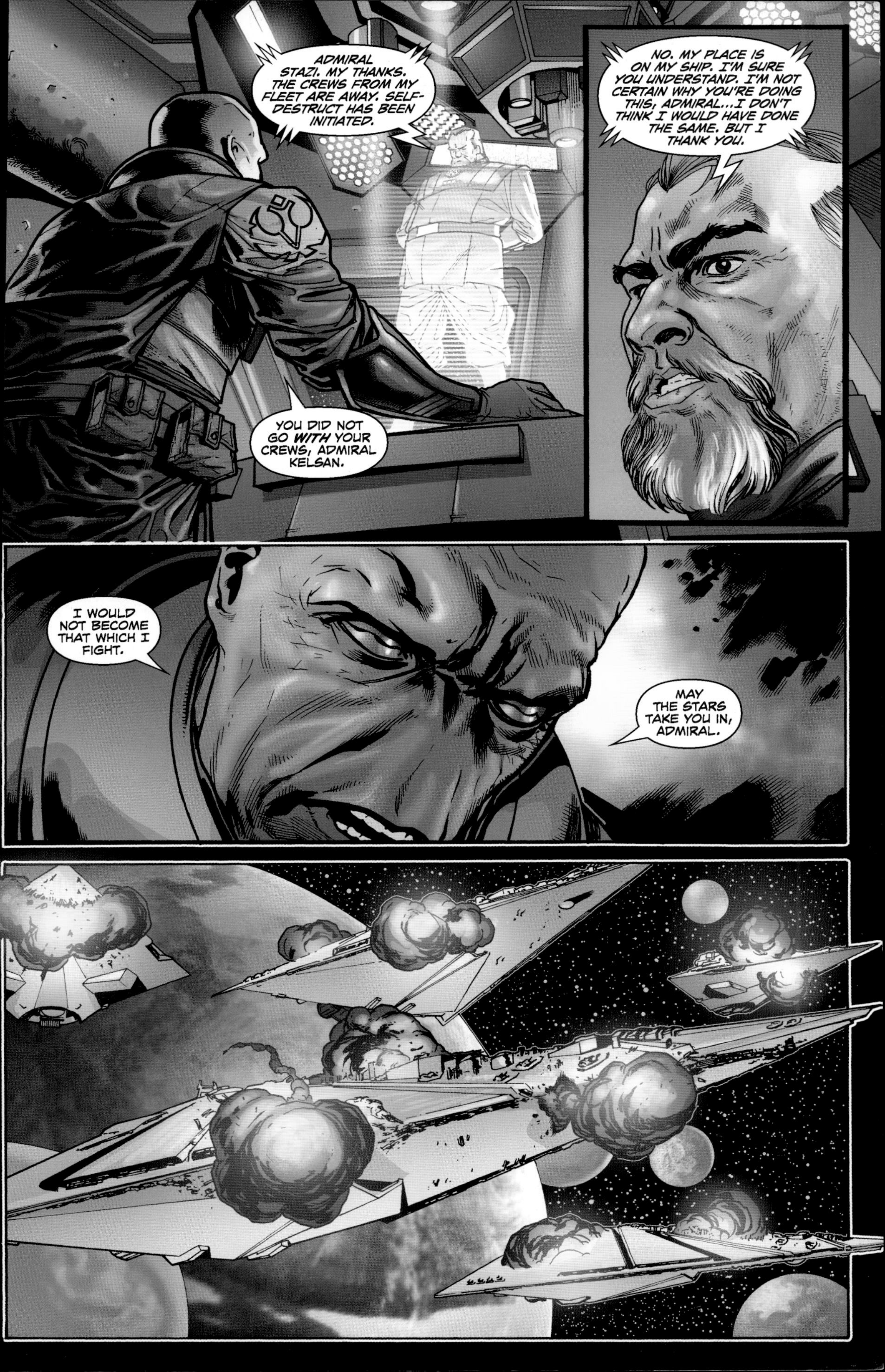
ADMIRAL STAZI. MY THANKS. THE CREWS FROM MY FLEET ARE AWAY. SELF-DESTRUCT HAS BEEN INITIATED.
YOU DID NOT GO WITH YOUR CREWS, ADMIRAL KELSAN.
NO. MY PLACE IS ON MY SHIP. I'M SURE YOU UNDERSTAND. I'M NOT CERTAIN WHY YOU'RE DOING THIS, ADMIRAL...I DON'T THINK I WOULD HAVE DONE THE SAME. BUT I THANK YOU.
I WOULD NOT BECOME THAT WHICH I FIGHT.
MAY THE STARS TAKE YOU IN, ADMIRAL.

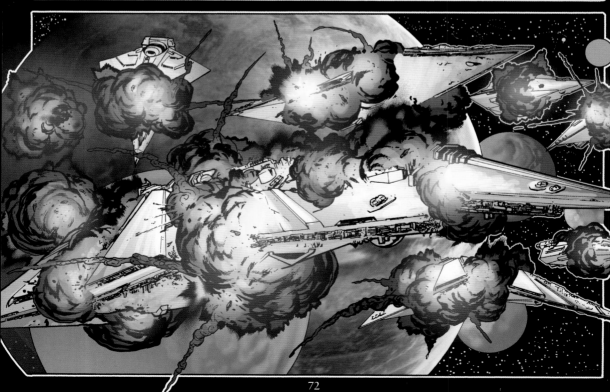

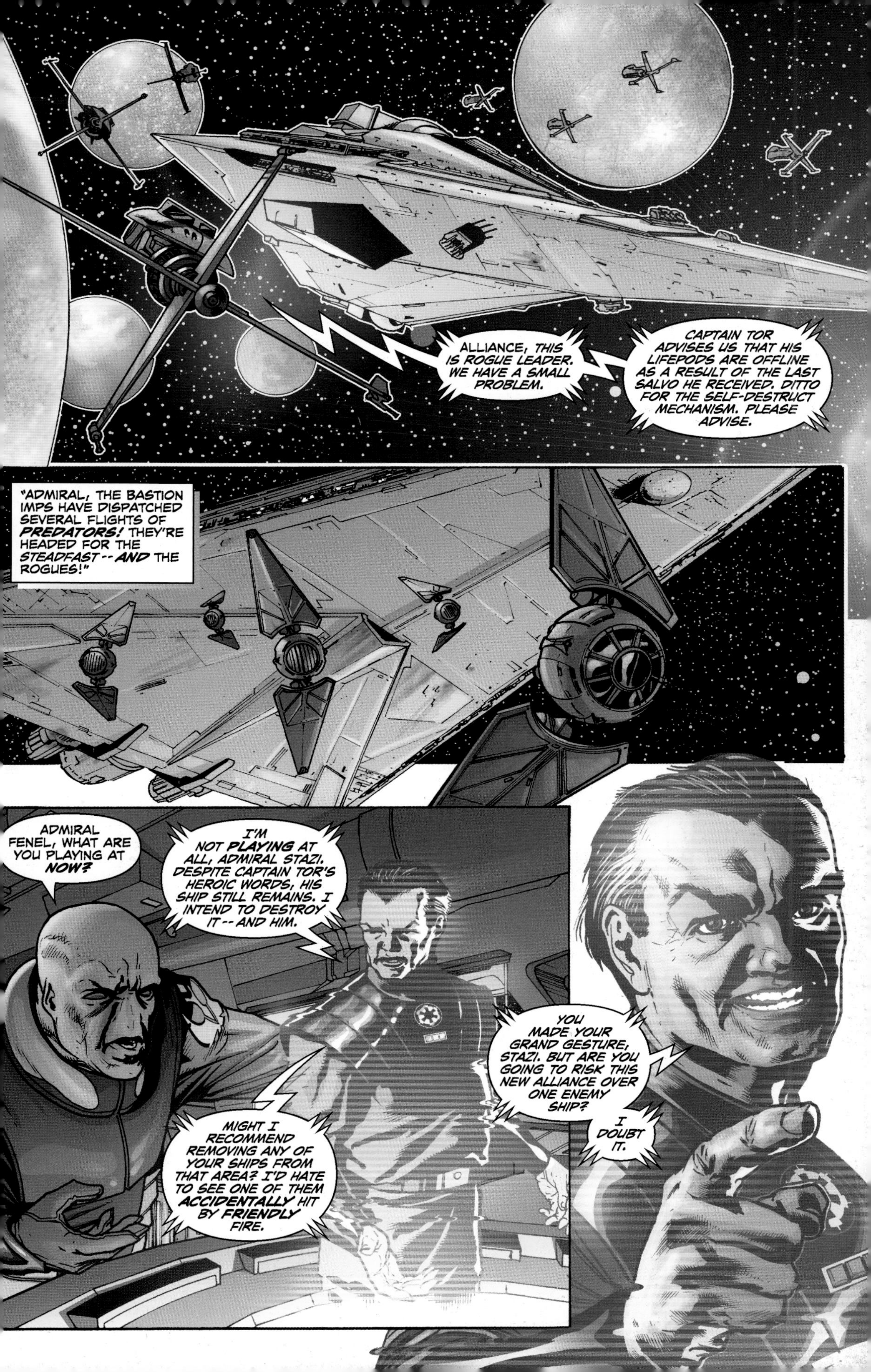
ALLIANCE, THIS IS ROGUE LEADER. WE HAVE A SMALL PROBLEM.
CAPTAIN TOR ADVISES US THAT HIS LIFEPODS ARE OFFLINE AS A RESULT OF THE LAST SALVO HE RECEIVED. DITTO FOR THE SELF-DESTRUCT MECHANISM. PLEASE ADVISE.
"ADMIRAL, THE BASTION IMPS HAVE DISPATCHED SEVERAL FLIGHTS OF PREDATORS! THEY'RE HEADED FOR THE STEADFAST--AND THE ROGUES!"
ADMIRAL FENEL, WHAT ARE YOU PLAYING AT NOW?
I'M NOT PLAYING AT ALL, ADMIRAL STAZI. DESPITE CAPTAIN TOR'S HEROIC WORDS, HIS SHIP STILL REMAINS. I INTEND TO DESTROY IT--AND HIM.
YOU MADE YOUR GRAND GESTURE, STAZI. BUT ARE YOU GOING TO RISK THIS NEW ALLIANCE OVER ONE ENEMY SHIP?
I DOUBT IT.
MIGHT I RECOMMEND REMOVING ANY OF YOUR SHIPS FROM THAT AREA? I'D HATE TO SEE ONE OF THEM ACCIDENTALLY HIT BY FRIENDLY FIRE.

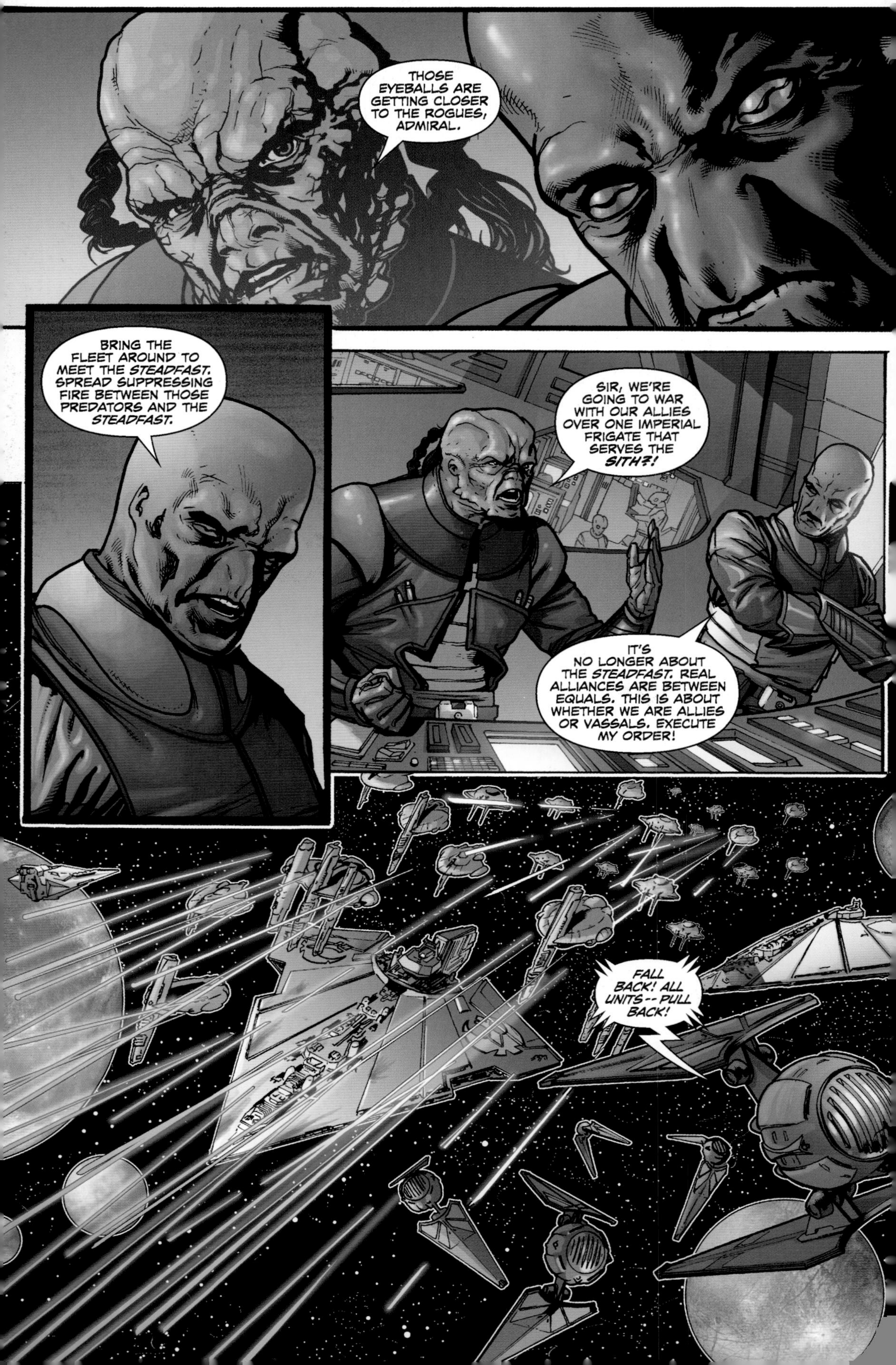
THOSE EYEBALLS ARE GETTING CLOSER TO THE ROGUES, ADMIRAL.
BRING THE FLEET AROUND TO MEET THE *STEADFAST*. SPREAD SUPPRESSING FIRE BETWEEN THOSE PREDATORS AND THE *STEADFAST*.
SIR, WE'RE GOING TO WAR WITH OUR ALLIES OVER ONE IMPERIAL FRIGATE THAT SERVES THE *SITH*?!
IT'S NO LONGER ABOUT THE *STEADFAST*. REAL ALLIANCES ARE BETWEEN EQUALS. THIS IS ABOUT WHETHER WE ARE ALLIES OR VASSALS. EXECUTE MY ORDER!
FALL BACK! ALL UNITS--PULL BACK!

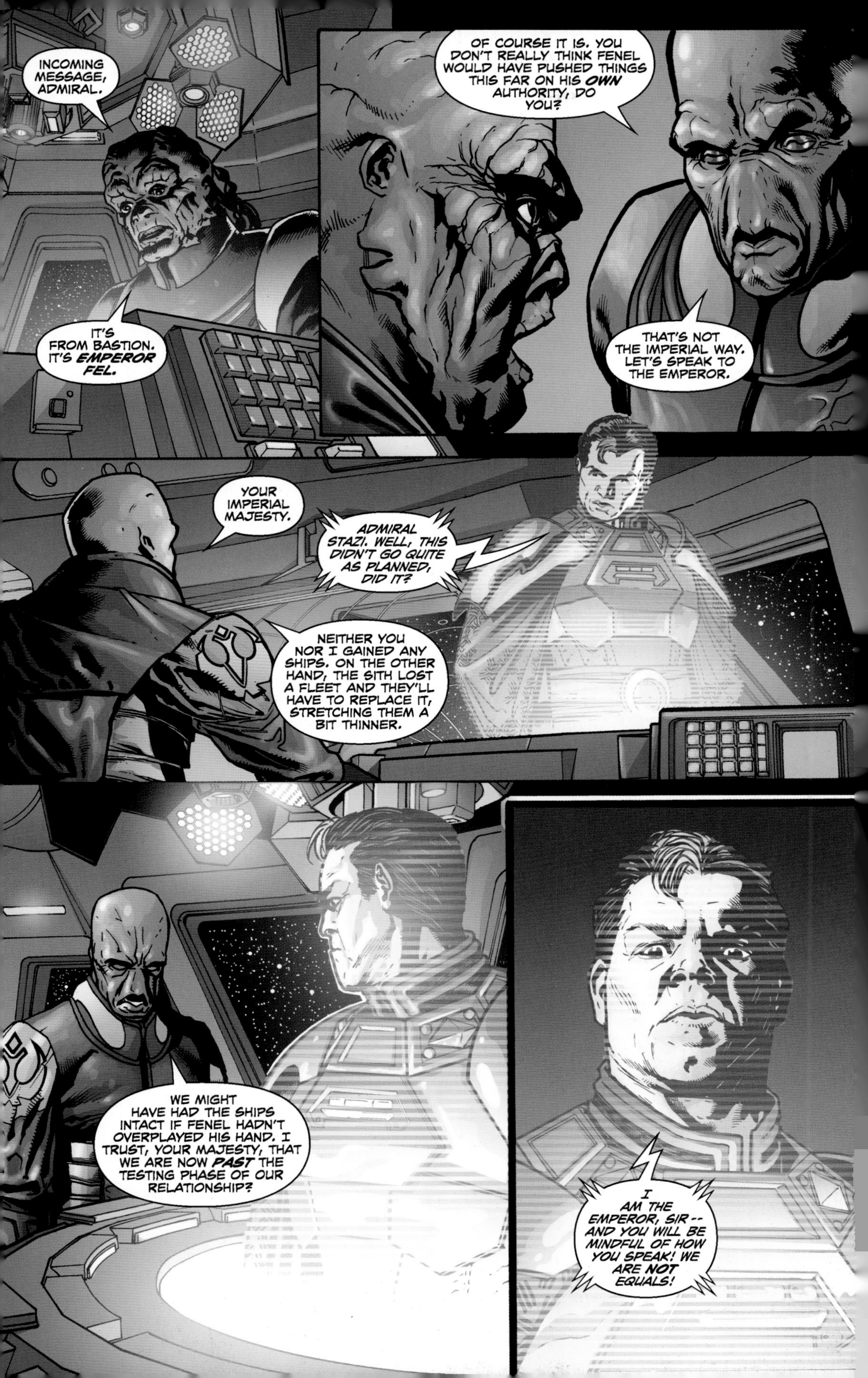
INCOMING MESSAGE, ADMIRAL.
IT'S FROM BASTION. IT'S *EMPEROR FEL.*
OF COURSE IT IS. YOU DON'T REALLY THINK FENEL WOULD HAVE PUSHED THINGS THIS FAR ON HIS *OWN* AUTHORITY, DO YOU?
THAT'S NOT THE IMPERIAL WAY. LET'S SPEAK TO THE EMPEROR.
YOUR IMPERIAL MAJESTY.
ADMIRAL STAZI. WELL, THIS DIDN'T GO QUITE AS PLANNED, DID IT?
NEITHER YOU NOR I GAINED ANY SHIPS. ON THE OTHER HAND, THE SITH LOST A FLEET AND THEY'LL HAVE TO REPLACE IT, STRETCHING THEM A BIT THINNER.
WE MIGHT HAVE HAD THE SHIPS INTACT IF FENEL HADN'T OVERPLAYED HIS HAND. I TRUST, YOUR MAJESTY, THAT WE ARE NOW *PAST* THE TESTING PHASE OF OUR RELATIONSHIP?
I AM THE EMPEROR, SIR -- AND YOU WILL BE MINDFUL OF HOW YOU SPEAK! WE ARE ***NOT*** *EQUALS!*

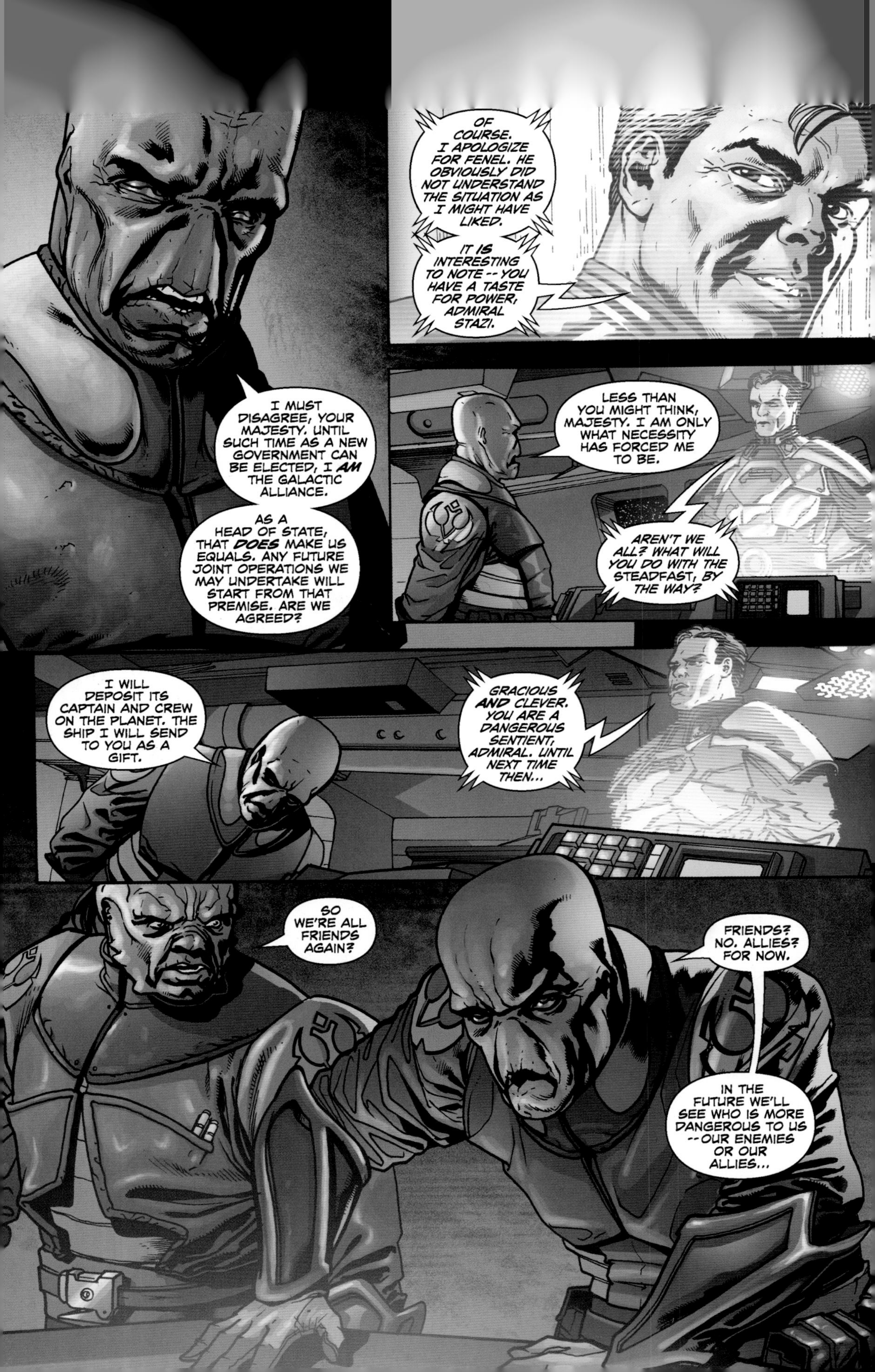
OF COURSE. I APOLOGIZE FOR FENEL. HE OBVIOUSLY DID NOT UNDERSTAND THE SITUATION AS I MIGHT HAVE LIKED.
IT IS INTERESTING TO NOTE -- YOU HAVE A TASTE FOR POWER, ADMIRAL STAZI.
I MUST DISAGREE, YOUR MAJESTY. UNTIL SUCH TIME AS A NEW GOVERNMENT CAN BE ELECTED, I AM THE GALACTIC ALLIANCE.
AS A HEAD OF STATE, THAT DOES MAKE US EQUALS. ANY FUTURE JOINT OPERATIONS WE MAY UNDERTAKE WILL START FROM THAT PREMISE. ARE WE AGREED?
LESS THAN YOU MIGHT THINK, MAJESTY. I AM ONLY WHAT NECESSITY HAS FORCED ME TO BE.
AREN'T WE ALL? WHAT WILL YOU DO WITH THE STEADFAST, BY THE WAY?
I WILL DEPOSIT ITS CAPTAIN AND CREW ON THE PLANET. THE SHIP I WILL SEND TO YOU AS A GIFT.
GRACIOUS AND CLEVER. YOU ARE A DANGEROUS SENTIENT, ADMIRAL. UNTIL NEXT TIME THEN...
SO WE'RE ALL FRIENDS AGAIN?
FRIENDS? NO. ALLIES? FOR NOW.
IN THE FUTURE WE'LL SEE WHO IS MORE DANGEROUS TO US --OUR ENEMIES OR OUR ALLIES...

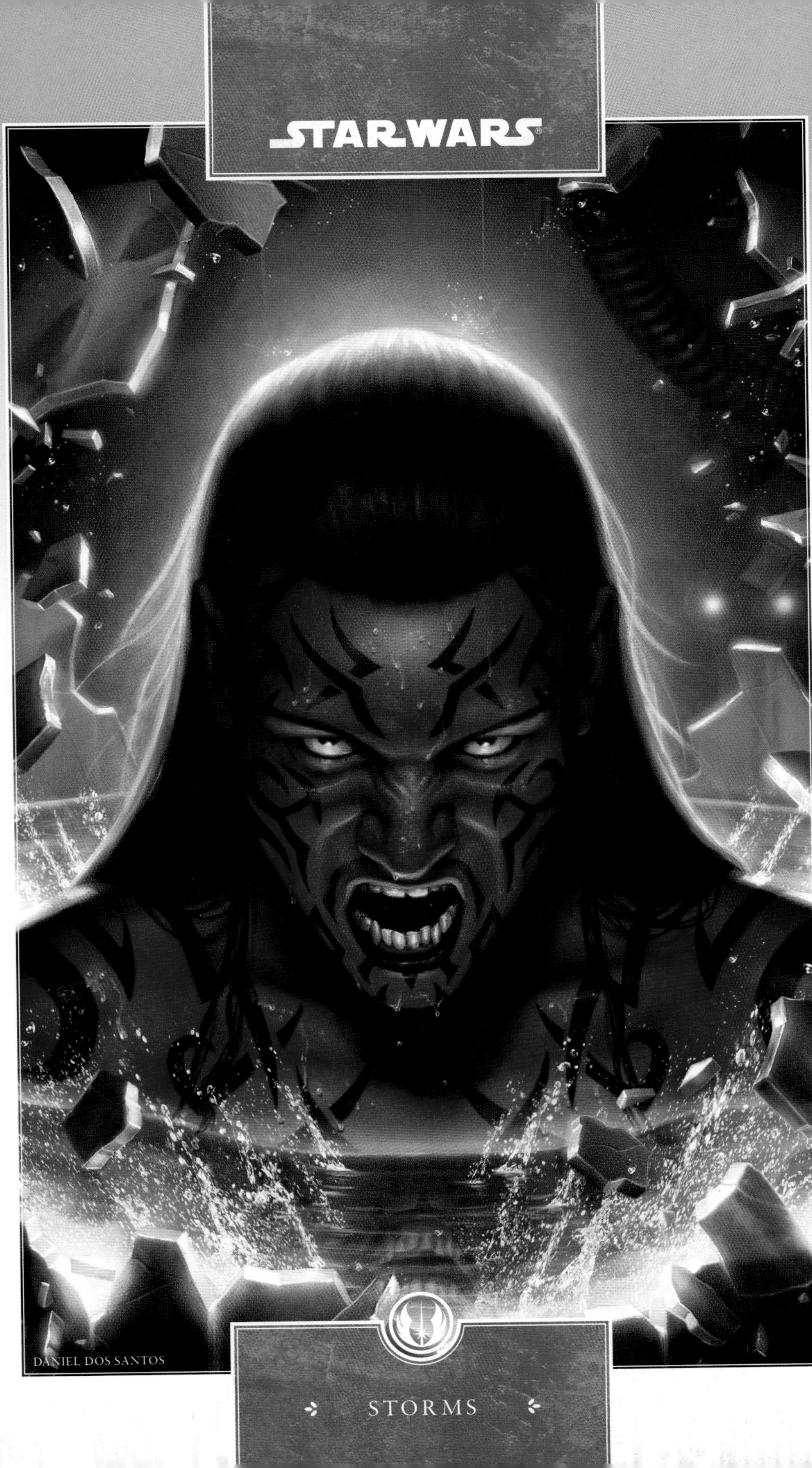
STAR WARS
DANIEL DOS SANTOS
STORMS

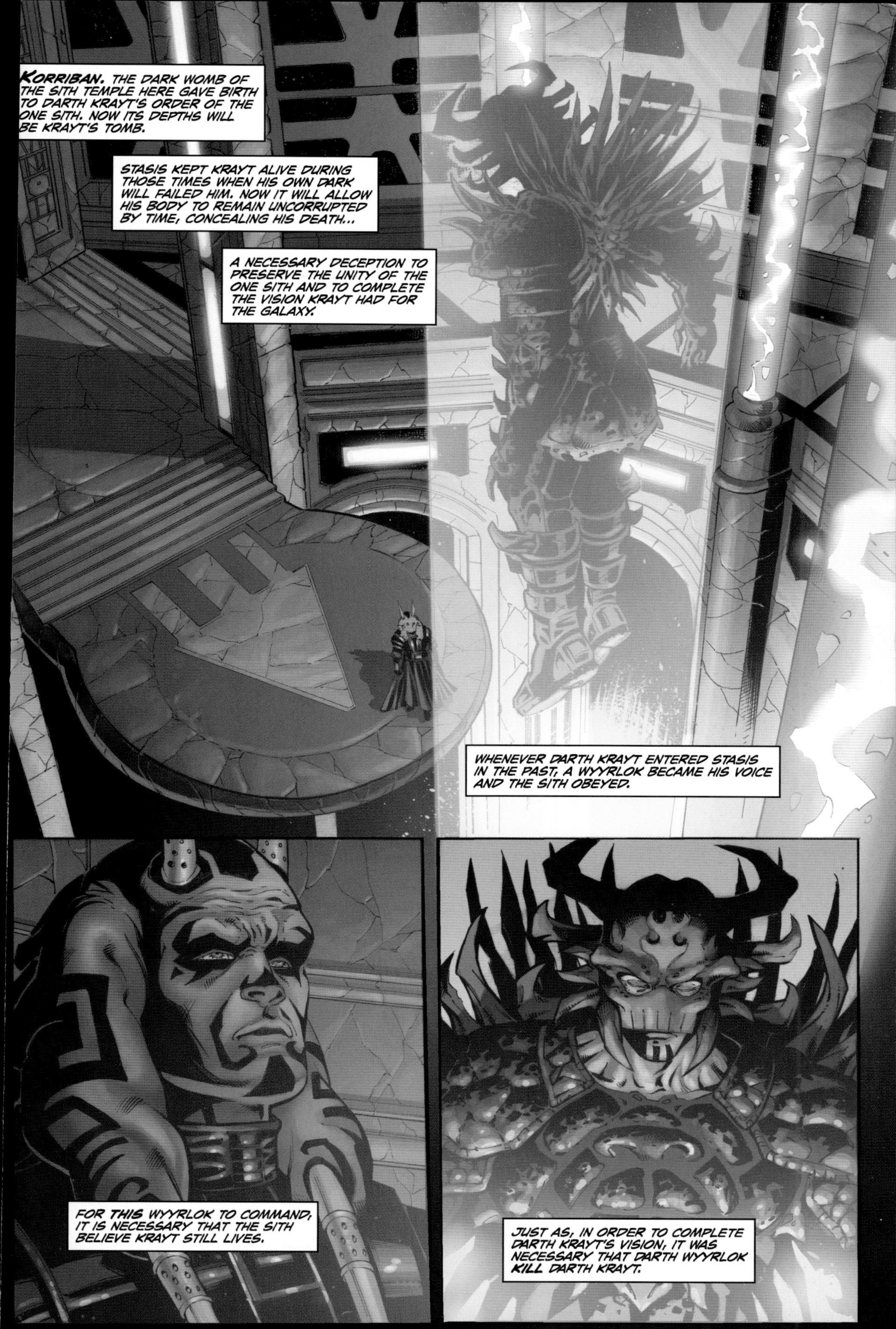
KORRIBAN. THE DARK WOMB OF THE SITH TEMPLE HERE GAVE BIRTH TO DARTH KRAYT'S ORDER OF THE ONE SITH. NOW ITS DEPTHS WILL BE KRAYT'S TOMB.
STASIS KEPT KRAYT ALIVE DURING THOSE TIMES WHEN HIS OWN DARK WILL FAILED HIM. NOW IT WILL ALLOW HIS BODY TO REMAIN UNCORRUPTED BY TIME, CONCEALING HIS DEATH...
A NECESSARY DECEPTION TO PRESERVE THE UNITY OF THE ONE SITH AND TO COMPLETE THE VISION KRAYT HAD FOR THE GALAXY.
WHENEVER DARTH KRAYT ENTERED STASIS IN THE PAST, A WYYRLOK BECAME HIS VOICE AND THE SITH OBEYED.
FOR THIS WYYRLOK TO COMMAND, IT IS NECESSARY THAT THE SITH BELIEVE KRAYT STILL LIVES.
JUST AS, IN ORDER TO COMPLETE DARTH KRAYT'S VISION, IT WAS NECESSARY THAT DARTH WYYRLOK KILL DARTH KRAYT.

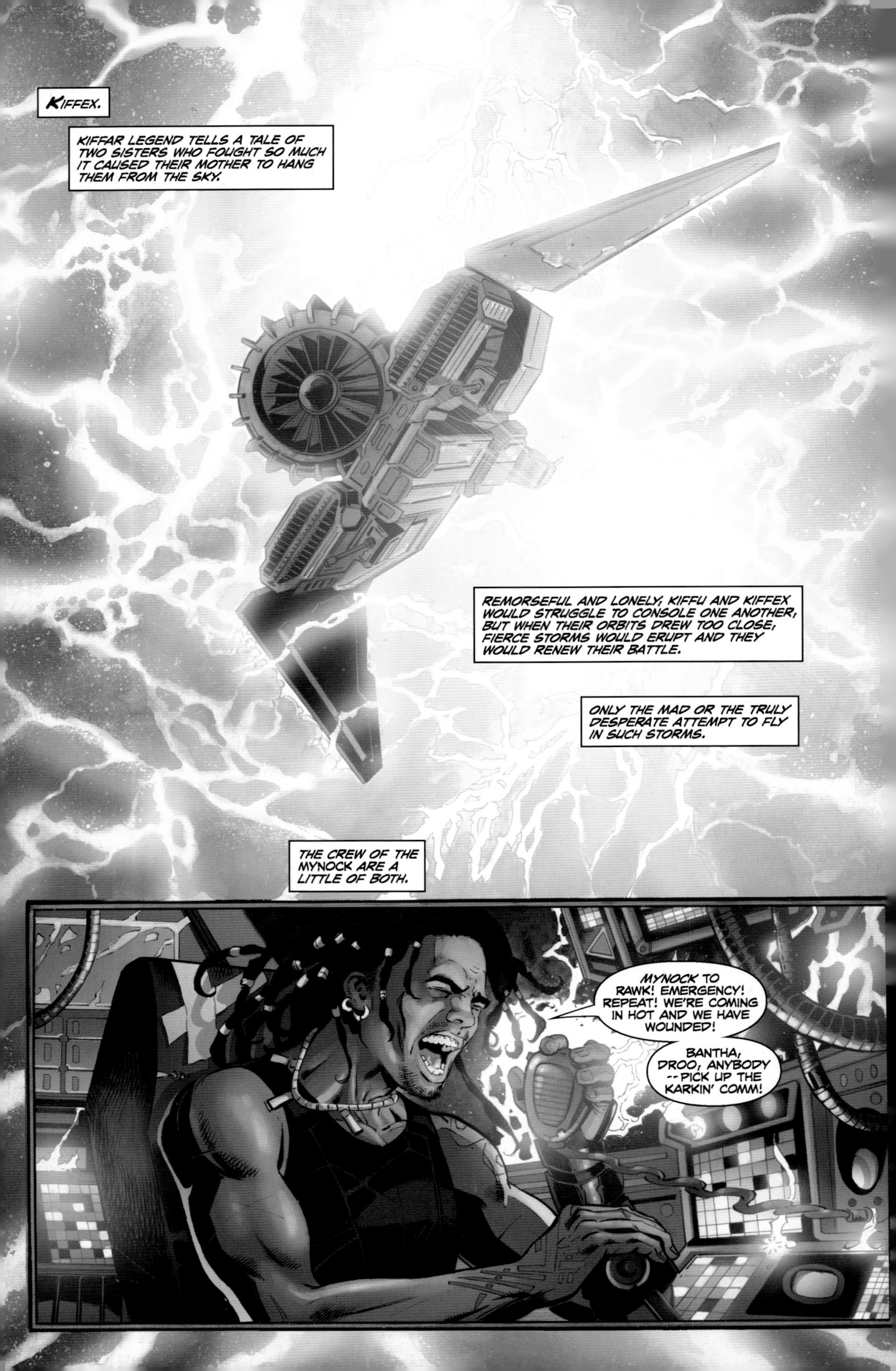
KIFFEX.
KIFFAR LEGEND TELLS A TALE OF TWO SISTERS WHO FOUGHT SO MUCH IT CAUSED THEIR MOTHER TO HANG THEM FROM THE SKY.
REMORSEFUL AND LONELY, KIFFU AND KIFFEX WOULD STRUGGLE TO CONSOLE ONE ANOTHER, BUT WHEN THEIR ORBITS DREW TOO CLOSE, FIERCE STORMS WOULD ERUPT AND THEY WOULD RENEW THEIR BATTLE.
ONLY THE MAD OR THE TRULY DESPERATE ATTEMPT TO FLY IN SUCH STORMS.
THE CREW OF THE MYNOCK ARE A LITTLE OF BOTH.
MYNOCK TO RAWK! EMERGENCY! REPEAT! WE'RE COMING IN HOT AND WE HAVE WOUNDED!
BANTHA, DROO, ANYBODY --PICK UP THE KARKIN' COMM!

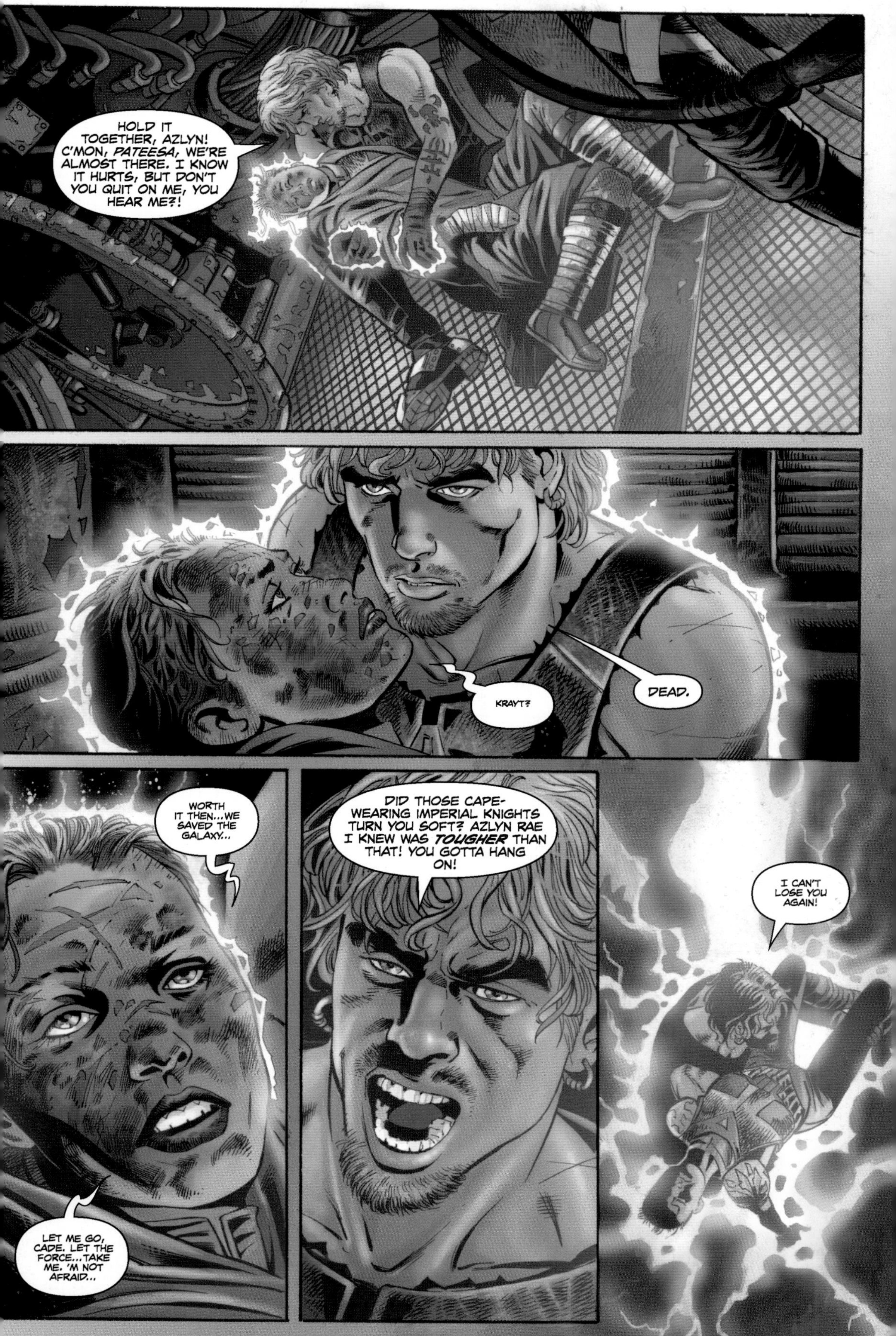
HOLD IT TOGETHER, AZLYN! C'MON, PATEESA, WE'RE ALMOST THERE. I KNOW IT HURTS, BUT DON'T YOU QUIT ON ME, YOU HEAR ME?!
KRAYT?
DEAD.
WORTH IT THEN...WE SAVED THE GALAXY...
LET ME GO, CADE. LET THE FORCE...TAKE ME. 'M NOT AFRAID...
DID THOSE CAPE-WEARING IMPERIAL KNIGHTS TURN YOU SOFT? AZLYN RAE I KNEW WAS TOUGHER THAN THAT! YOU GOTTA HANG ON!
I CAN'T LOSE YOU AGAIN!

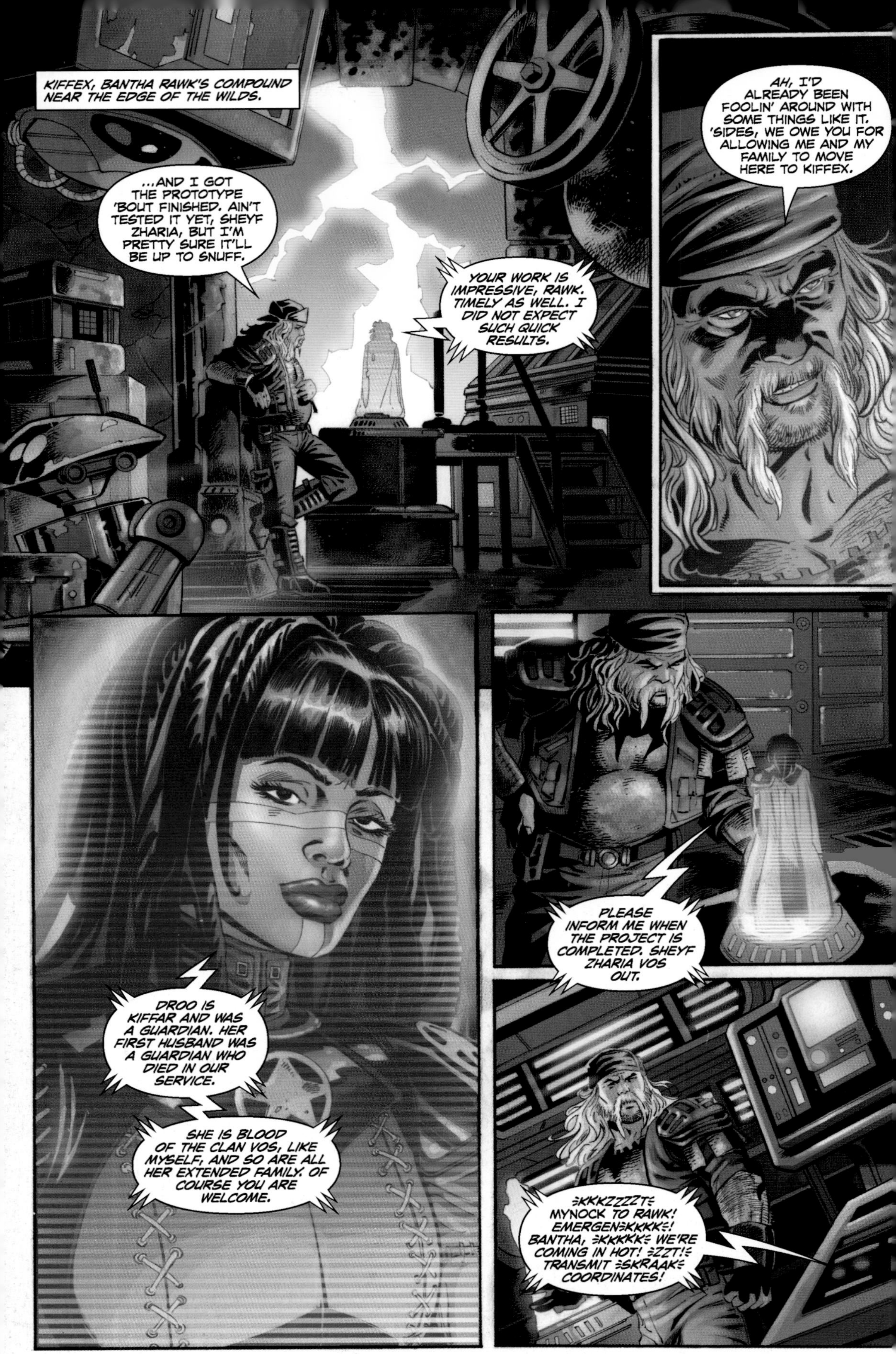
KIFFEX, BANTHA RAWK'S COMPOUND NEAR THE EDGE OF THE WILDS.
...AND I GOT THE PROTOTYPE 'BOUT FINISHED. AIN'T TESTED IT YET, SHEYF ZHARIA, BUT I'M PRETTY SURE IT'LL BE UP TO SNUFF.
YOUR WORK IS IMPRESSIVE, RAWK. TIMELY AS WELL. I DID NOT EXPECT SUCH QUICK RESULTS.
AH, I'D ALREADY BEEN FOOLIN' AROUND WITH SOME THINGS LIKE IT. 'SIDES, WE OWE YOU FOR ALLOWING ME AND MY FAMILY TO MOVE HERE TO KIFFEX.
DROO IS KIFFAR AND WAS A GUARDIAN. HER FIRST HUSBAND WAS A GUARDIAN WHO DIED IN OUR SERVICE.
SHE IS BLOOD OF THE CLAN VOS, LIKE MYSELF, AND SO ARE ALL HER EXTENDED FAMILY. OF COURSE YOU ARE WELCOME.
PLEASE INFORM ME WHEN THE PROJECT IS COMPLETED. SHEYF ZHARIA VOS OUT.
=KKKZZZZT= MYNOCK TO RAWK! EMERGEN=KKKK=! BANTHA, =KKKKK= WE'RE COMING IN HOT! =ZZT!= TRANSMIT =SKRAAK= COORDINATES!

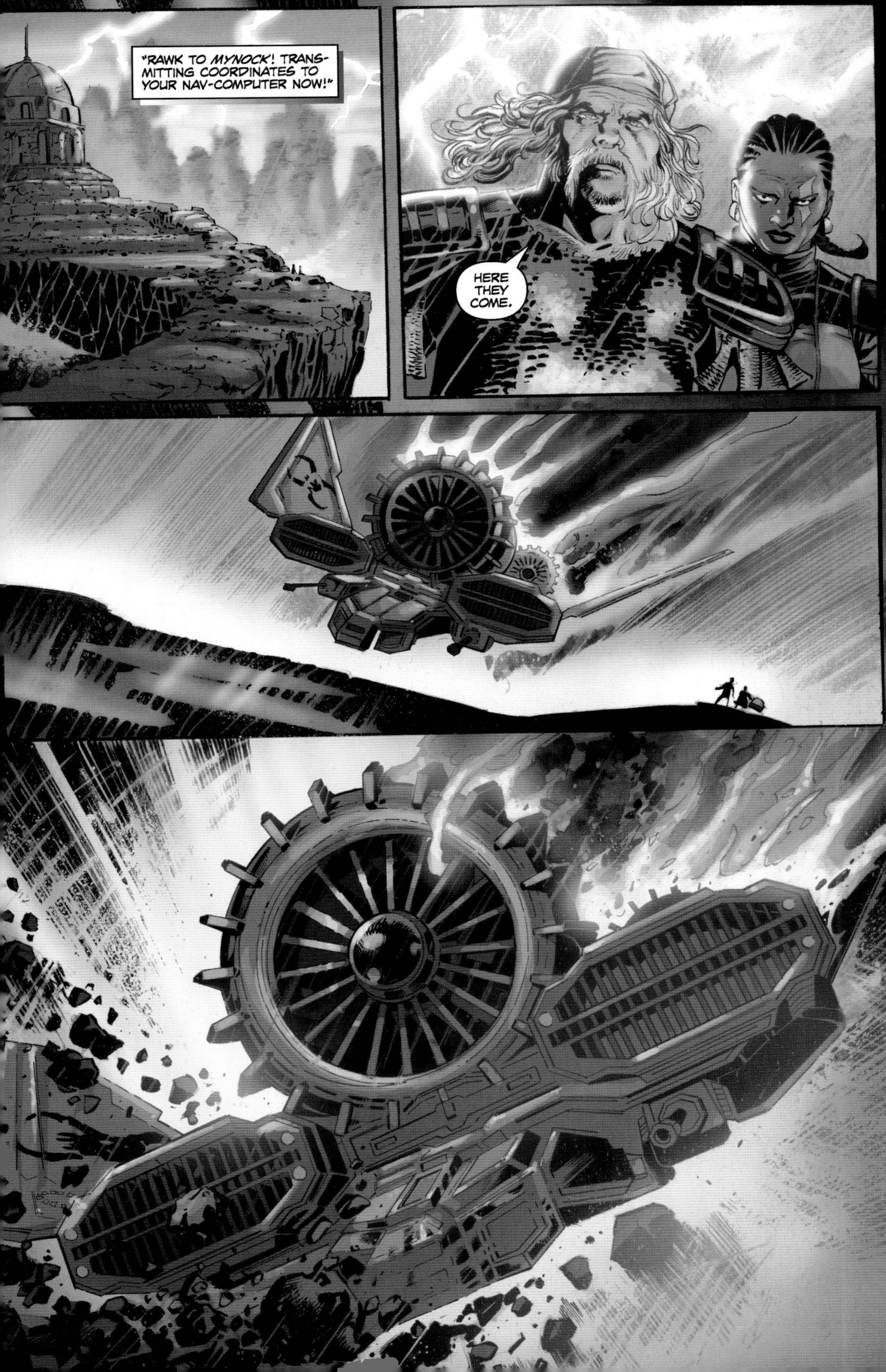
"RAWK TO *MYNOCK*! TRANSMITTING COORDINATES TO YOUR NAV-COMPUTER NOW!"
HERE THEY COME.

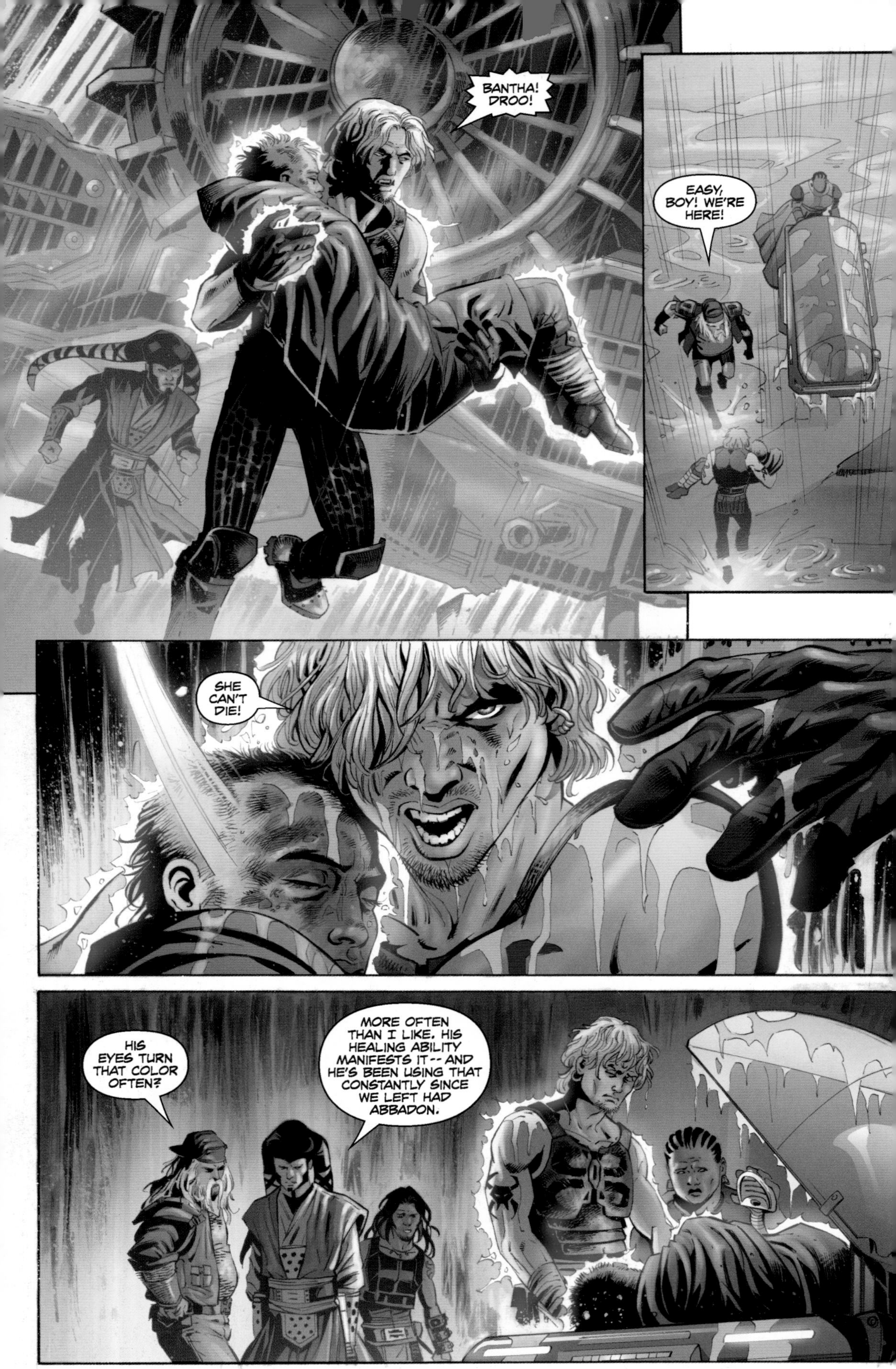
BANTHA! DROO!
EASY, BOY! WE'RE HERE!
SHE CAN'T DIE!
HIS EYES TURN THAT COLOR OFTEN?
MORE OFTEN THAN I LIKE. HIS HEALING ABILITY MANIFESTS IT-- AND HE'S BEEN USING THAT CONSTANTLY SINCE WE LEFT HAD ABBADON.

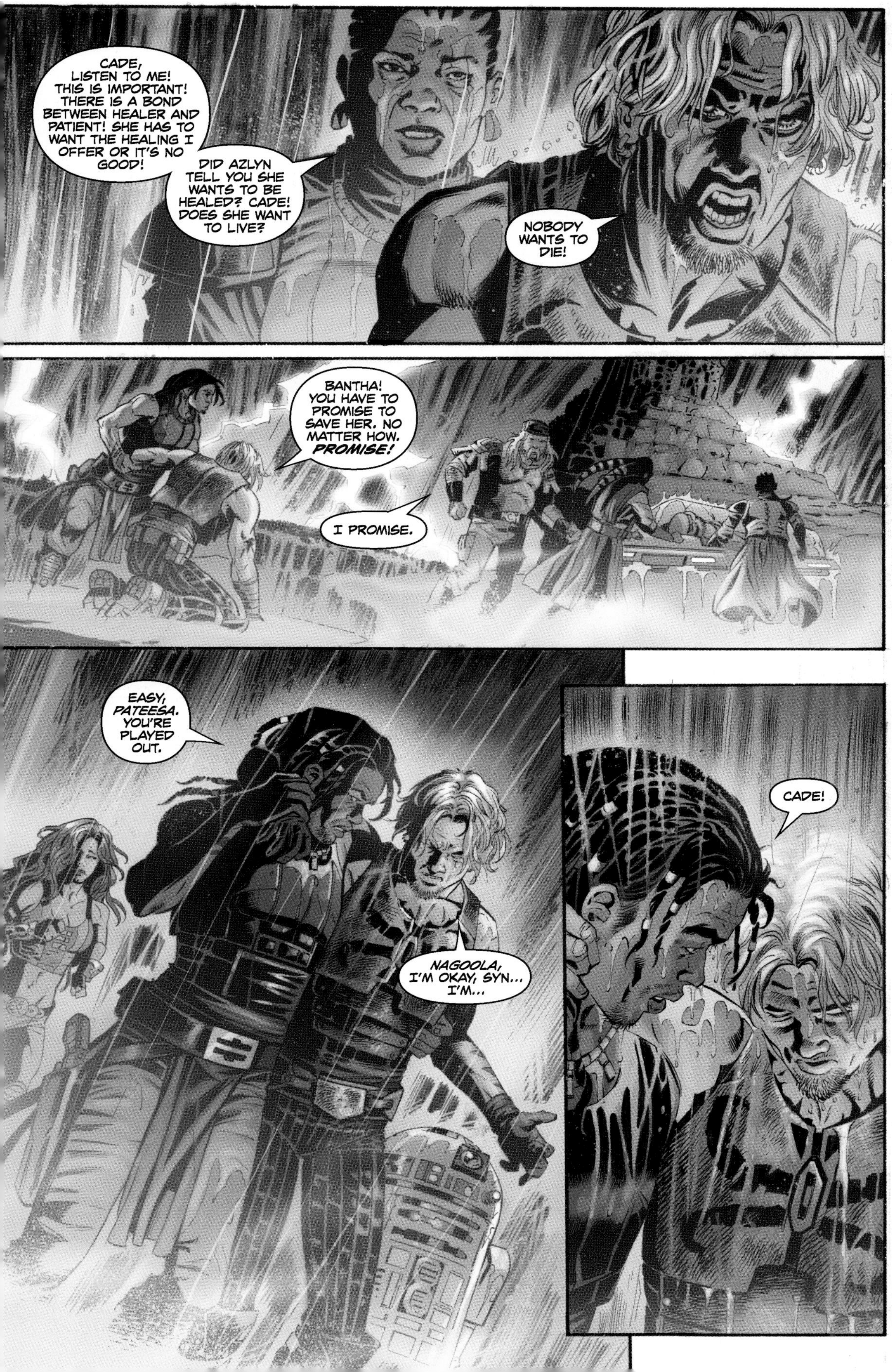
CADE, LISTEN TO ME! THIS IS IMPORTANT! THERE IS A BOND BETWEEN HEALER AND PATIENT! SHE HAS TO WANT THE HEALING I OFFER OR IT'S NO GOOD!
DID AZLYN TELL YOU SHE WANTS TO BE HEALED? CADE! DOES SHE WANT TO LIVE?
NOBODY WANTS TO DIE!
BANTHA! YOU HAVE TO PROMISE TO SAVE HER. NO MATTER HOW. *PROMISE!*
I PROMISE.
EASY, *PATEESA*. YOU'RE PLAYED OUT.
NAGOOLA, I'M OKAY, SYN... I'M...
CADE!

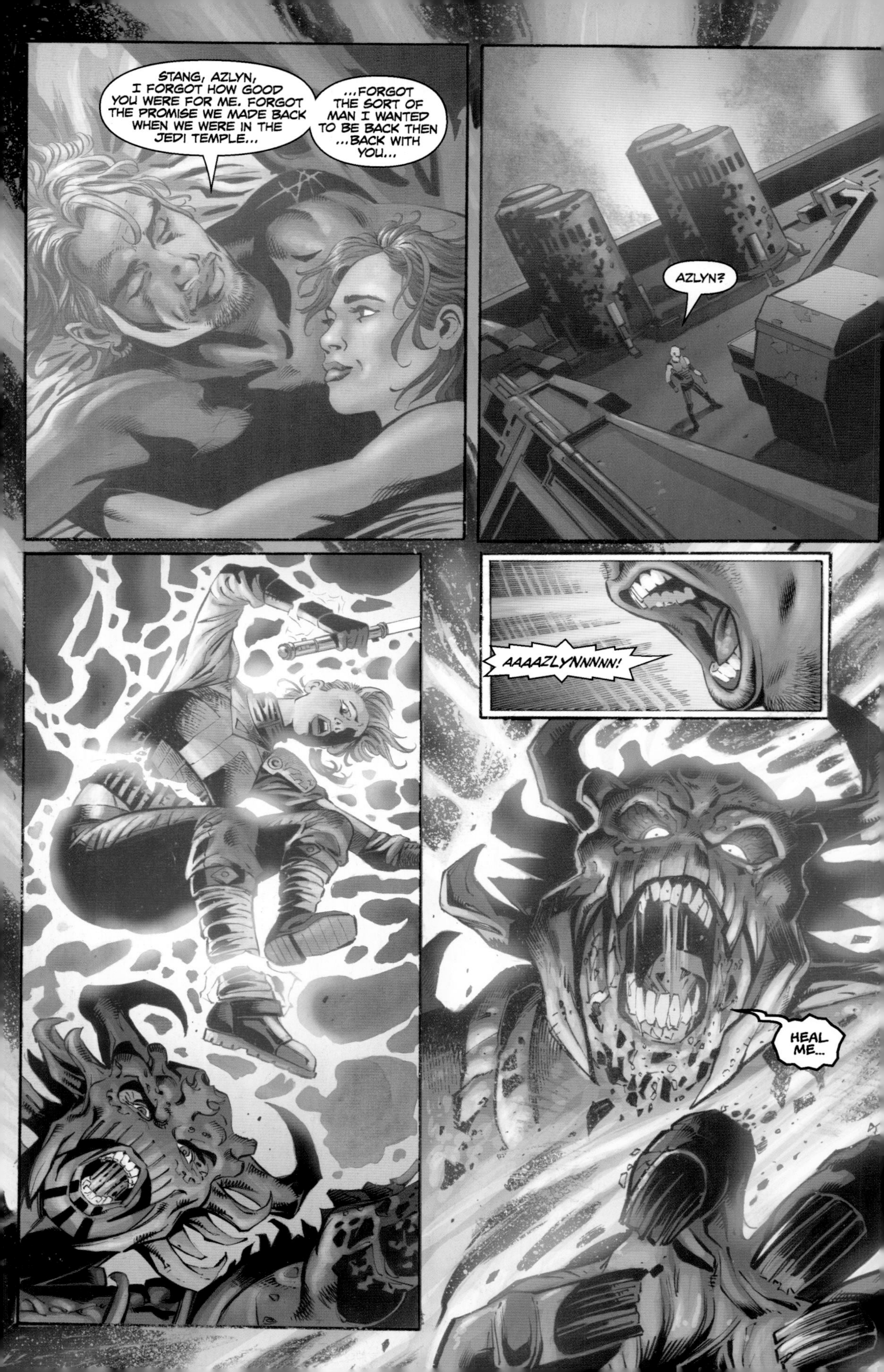
STANG, AZLYN, I FORGOT HOW GOOD YOU WERE FOR ME. FORGOT THE PROMISE WE MADE BACK WHEN WE WERE IN THE JEDI TEMPLE...
...FORGOT THE SORT OF MAN I WANTED TO BE BACK THEN ...BACK WITH YOU...
AZLYN?
AAAAZLYNNNNN!
HEAL ME...

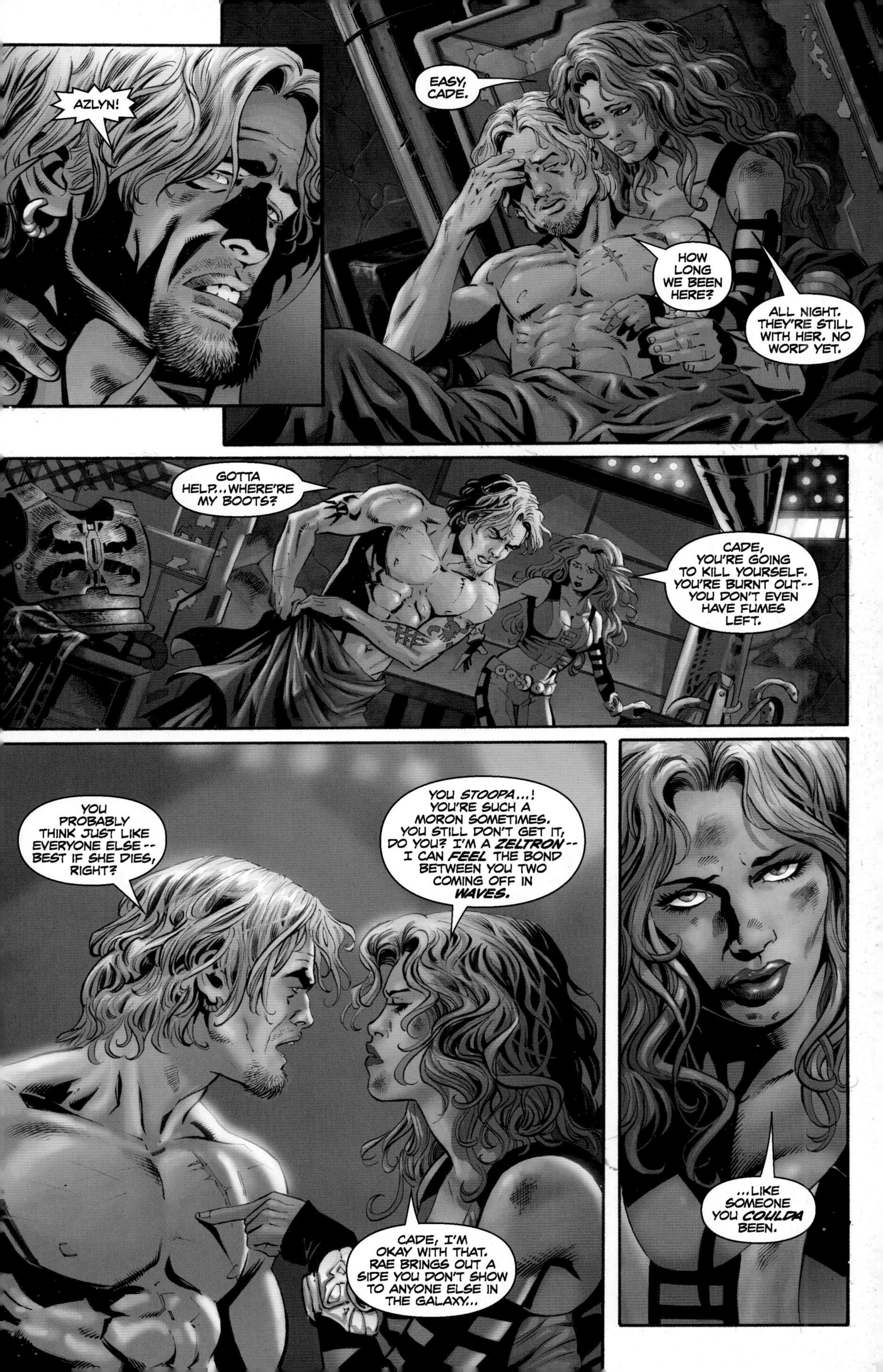
AZLYN!
EASY, CADE.
HOW LONG WE BEEN HERE?
ALL NIGHT. THEY'RE STILL WITH HER. NO WORD YET.
GOTTA HELP...WHERE'RE MY BOOTS?
CADE, YOU'RE GOING TO KILL YOURSELF. YOU'RE BURNT OUT-- YOU DON'T EVEN HAVE FUMES LEFT.
YOU PROBABLY THINK JUST LIKE EVERYONE ELSE-- BEST IF SHE DIES, RIGHT?
YOU *STOOPA*...! YOU'RE SUCH A MORON SOMETIMES. YOU STILL DON'T GET IT, DO YOU? I'M A *ZELTRON*-- I CAN *FEEL* THE BOND BETWEEN YOU TWO COMING OFF IN ***WAVES.***
CADE, I'M OKAY WITH THAT. RAE BRINGS OUT A SIDE YOU DON'T SHOW TO ANYONE ELSE IN THE GALAXY...
...LIKE SOMEONE YOU *COULDA* BEEN.

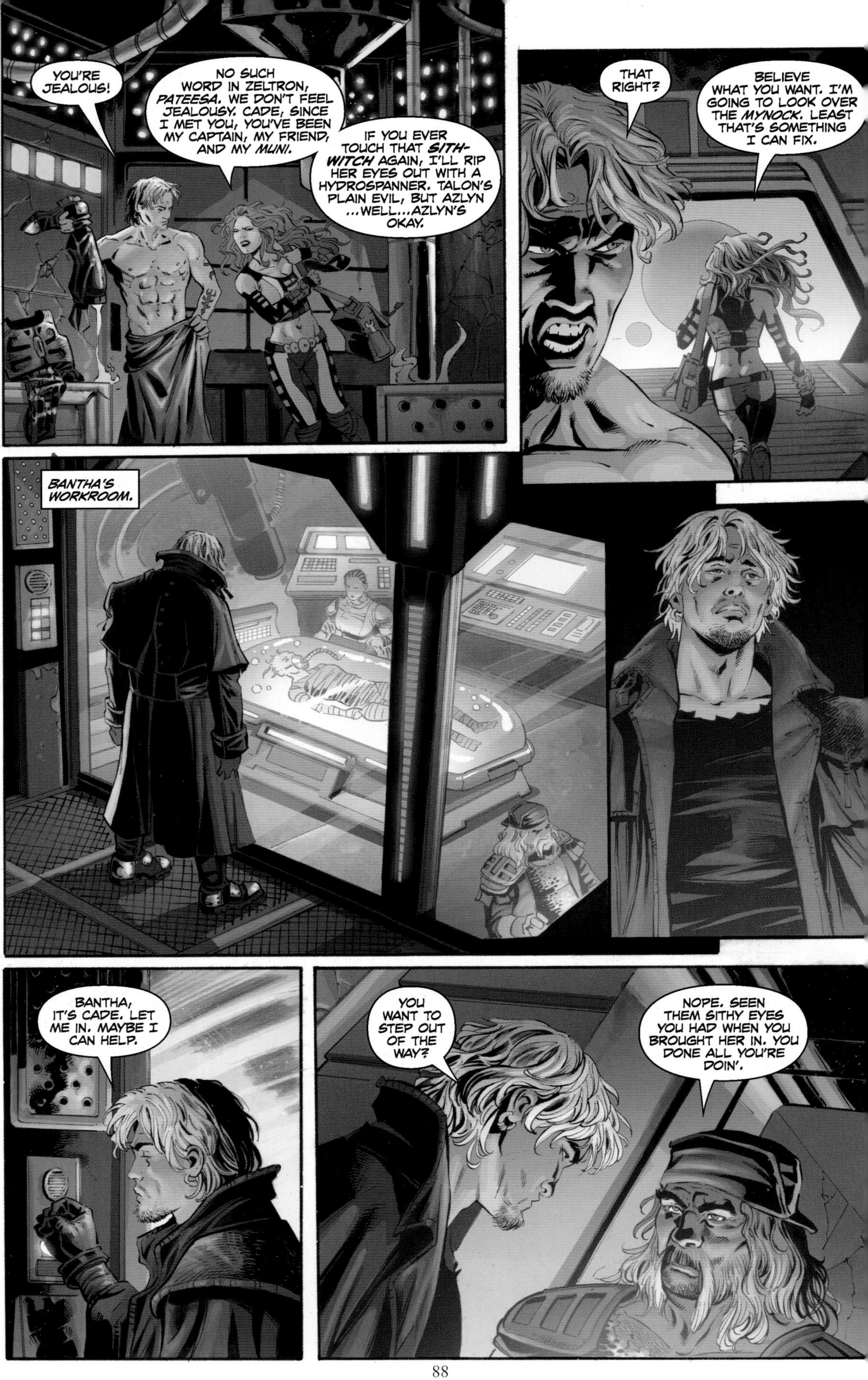
YOU'RE JEALOUS!
NO SUCH WORD IN ZELTRON, *PATEESA*. WE DON'T FEEL JEALOUSY. CADE, SINCE I MET YOU, YOU'VE BEEN MY CAPTAIN, MY FRIEND, AND MY *MUNI*.
IF YOU EVER TOUCH THAT *SITH-WITCH* AGAIN, I'LL RIP HER EYES OUT WITH A HYDROSPANNER. TALON'S PLAIN EVIL, BUT AZLYN ...WELL...AZLYN'S OKAY.
THAT RIGHT?
BELIEVE WHAT YOU WANT. I'M GOING TO LOOK OVER THE *MYNOCK*. LEAST THAT'S SOMETHING I CAN FIX.
BANTHA'S WORKROOM.
BANTHA, IT'S CADE. LET ME IN. MAYBE I CAN HELP.
YOU WANT TO STEP OUT OF THE WAY?
NOPE. SEEN THEM SITHY EYES YOU HAD WHEN YOU BROUGHT HER IN. YOU DONE ALL YOU'RE DOIN'.

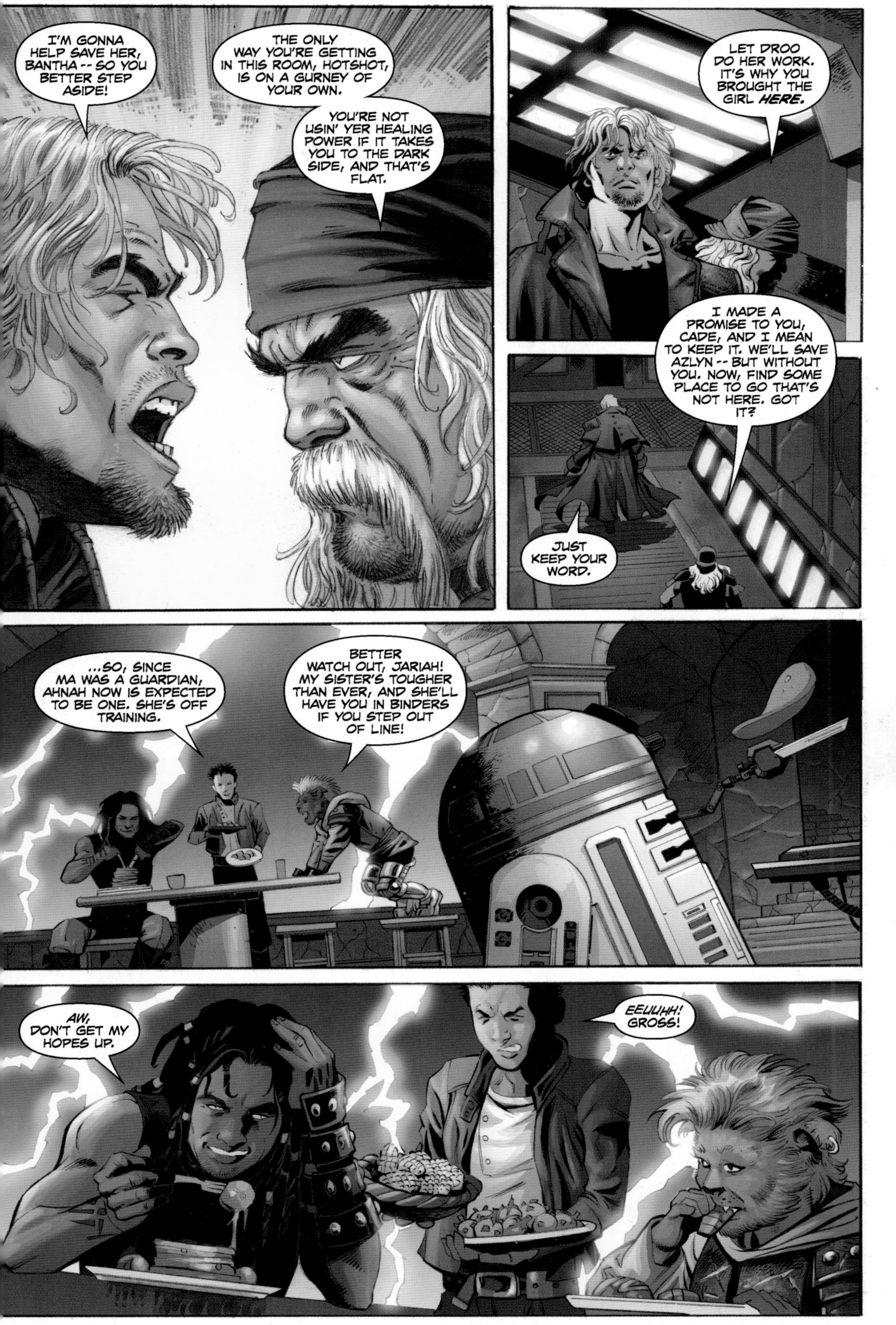

I'M GONNA HELP SAVE HER, BANTHA -- SO YOU BETTER STEP ASIDE!
THE ONLY WAY YOU'RE GETTING IN THIS ROOM, HOTSHOT, IS ON A GURNEY OF YOUR OWN.
YOU'RE NOT USIN' YER HEALING POWER IF IT TAKES YOU TO THE DARK SIDE, AND THAT'S FLAT.
LET DROO DO HER WORK. IT'S WHY YOU BROUGHT THE GIRL *HERE.*
I MADE A PROMISE TO YOU, CADE, AND I MEAN TO KEEP IT. WE'LL SAVE AZLYN -- BUT WITHOUT YOU. NOW, FIND SOME PLACE TO GO THAT'S NOT HERE. GOT IT?
JUST KEEP YOUR WORD.
...SO, SINCE MA WAS A GUARDIAN, AHNAH NOW IS EXPECTED TO BE ONE. SHE'S OFF TRAINING.
BETTER WATCH OUT, JARIAH! MY SISTER'S TOUGHER THAN EVER, AND SHE'LL HAVE YOU IN BINDERS IF YOU STEP OUT OF LINE!
AW, DON'T GET MY HOPES UP.
EEUUHH! GROSS!

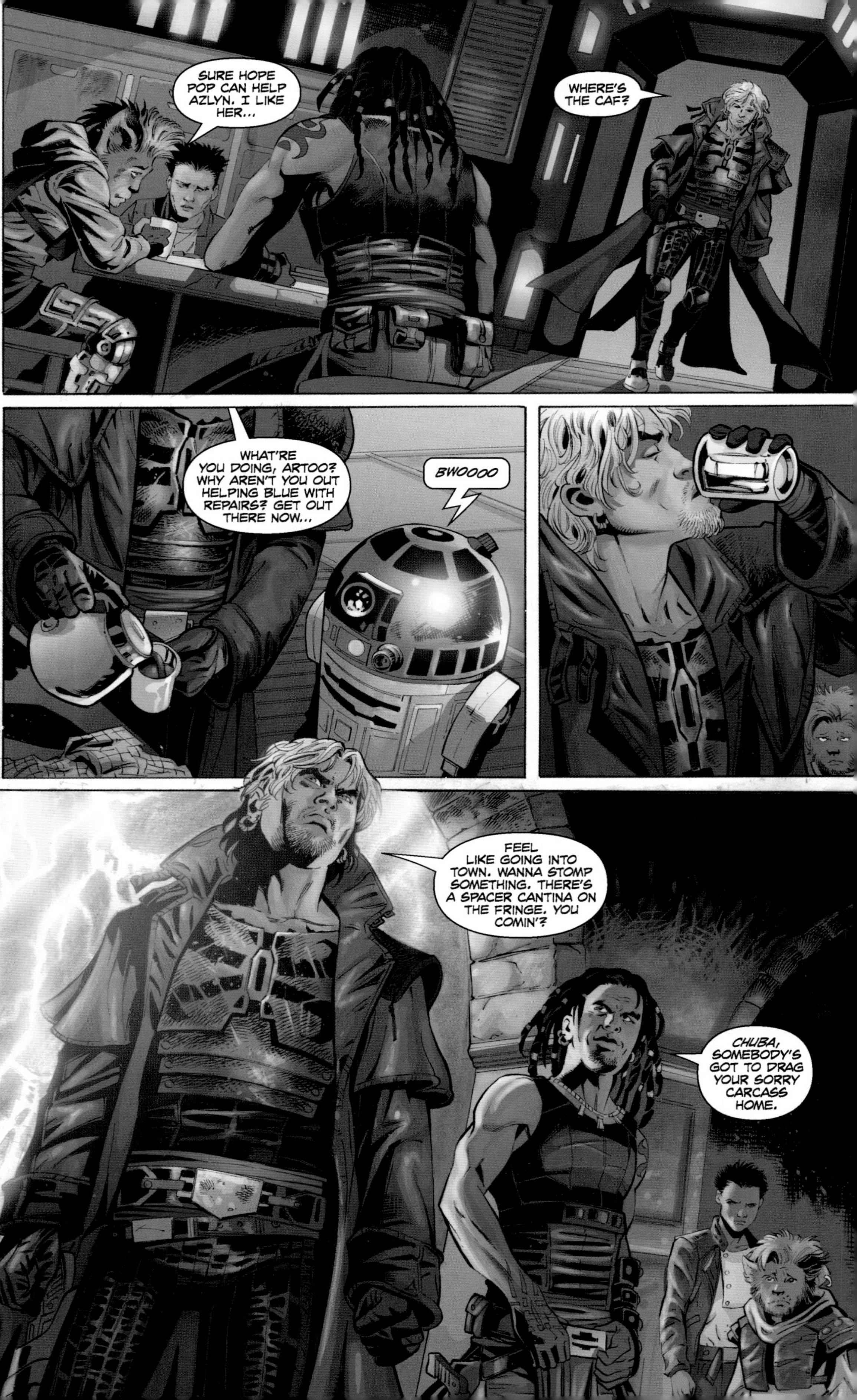
SURE HOPE POP CAN HELP AZLYN. I LIKE HER...
WHERE'S THE CAF?
WHAT'RE YOU DOING, ARTOO? WHY AREN'T YOU OUT HELPING BLUE WITH REPAIRS? GET OUT THERE NOW...
BWOOOO
FEEL LIKE GOING INTO TOWN. WANNA STOMP SOMETHING. THERE'S A SPACER CANTINA ON THE FRINGE. YOU COMIN'?
CHUBA, SOMEBODY'S GOT TO DRAG YOUR SORRY CARCASS HOME.

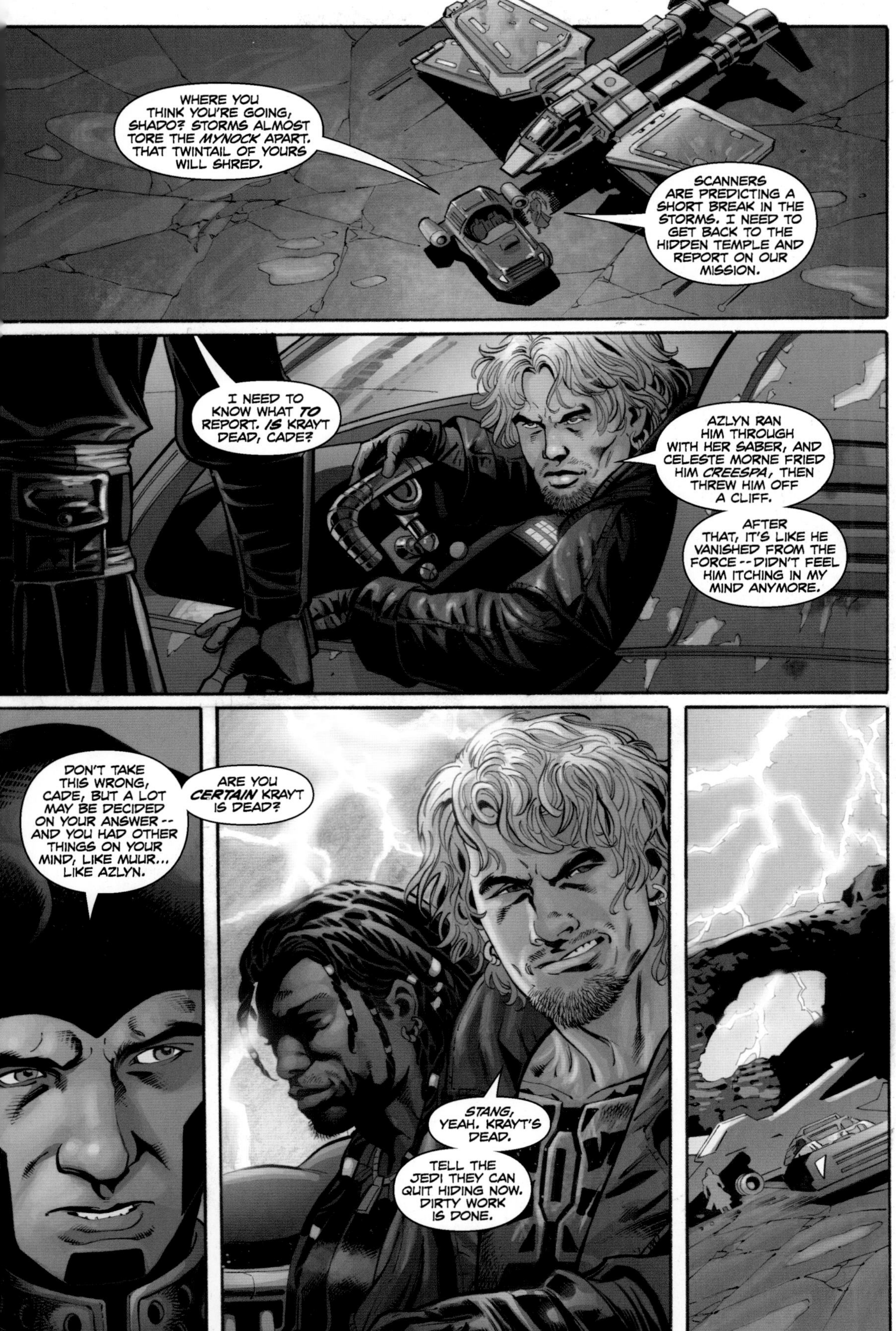
WHERE YOU THINK YOU'RE GOING, SHADO? STORMS ALMOST TORE THE *MYNOCK* APART. THAT TWINTAIL OF YOURS WILL SHRED.
SCANNERS ARE PREDICTING A SHORT BREAK IN THE STORMS. I NEED TO GET BACK TO THE HIDDEN TEMPLE AND REPORT ON OUR MISSION.
I NEED TO KNOW WHAT *TO* REPORT. *IS* KRAYT DEAD, CADE?
AZLYN RAN HIM THROUGH WITH HER SABER, AND CELESTE MORNE FRIED HIM *CREESPA*, THEN THREW HIM OFF A CLIFF.
AFTER THAT, IT'S LIKE HE VANISHED FROM THE FORCE--DIDN'T FEEL HIM ITCHING IN MY MIND ANYMORE.
DON'T TAKE THIS WRONG, CADE, BUT A LOT MAY BE DECIDED ON YOUR ANSWER-- AND YOU HAD OTHER THINGS ON YOUR MIND, LIKE MUUR... LIKE AZLYN.
ARE YOU *CERTAIN* KRAYT IS DEAD?
STANG, YEAH. KRAYT'S DEAD.
TELL THE JEDI THEY CAN QUIT HIDING NOW. DIRTY WORK IS DONE.

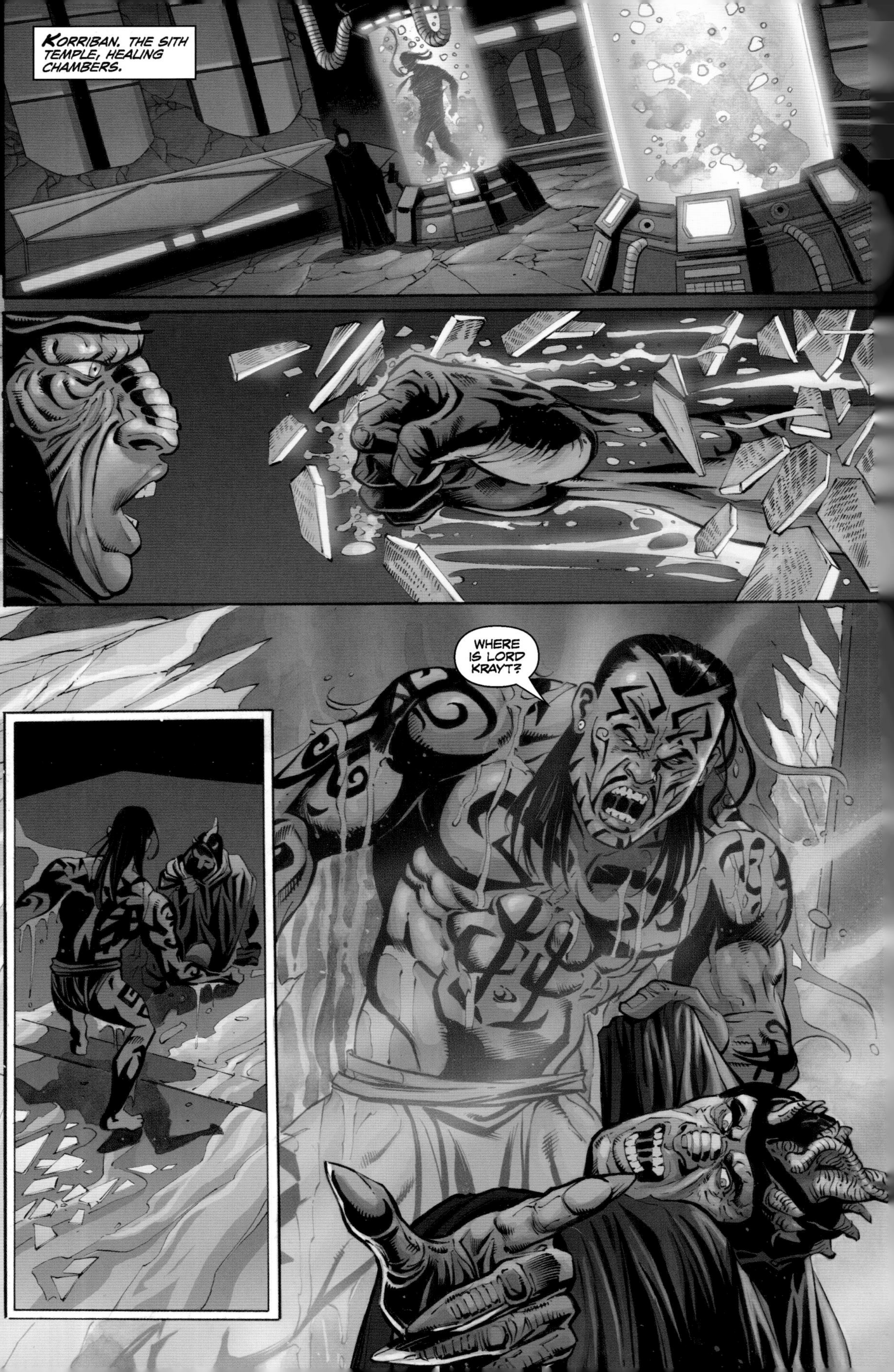
KORRIBAN. THE SITH TEMPLE, HEALING CHAMBERS.
WHERE IS LORD KRAYT?

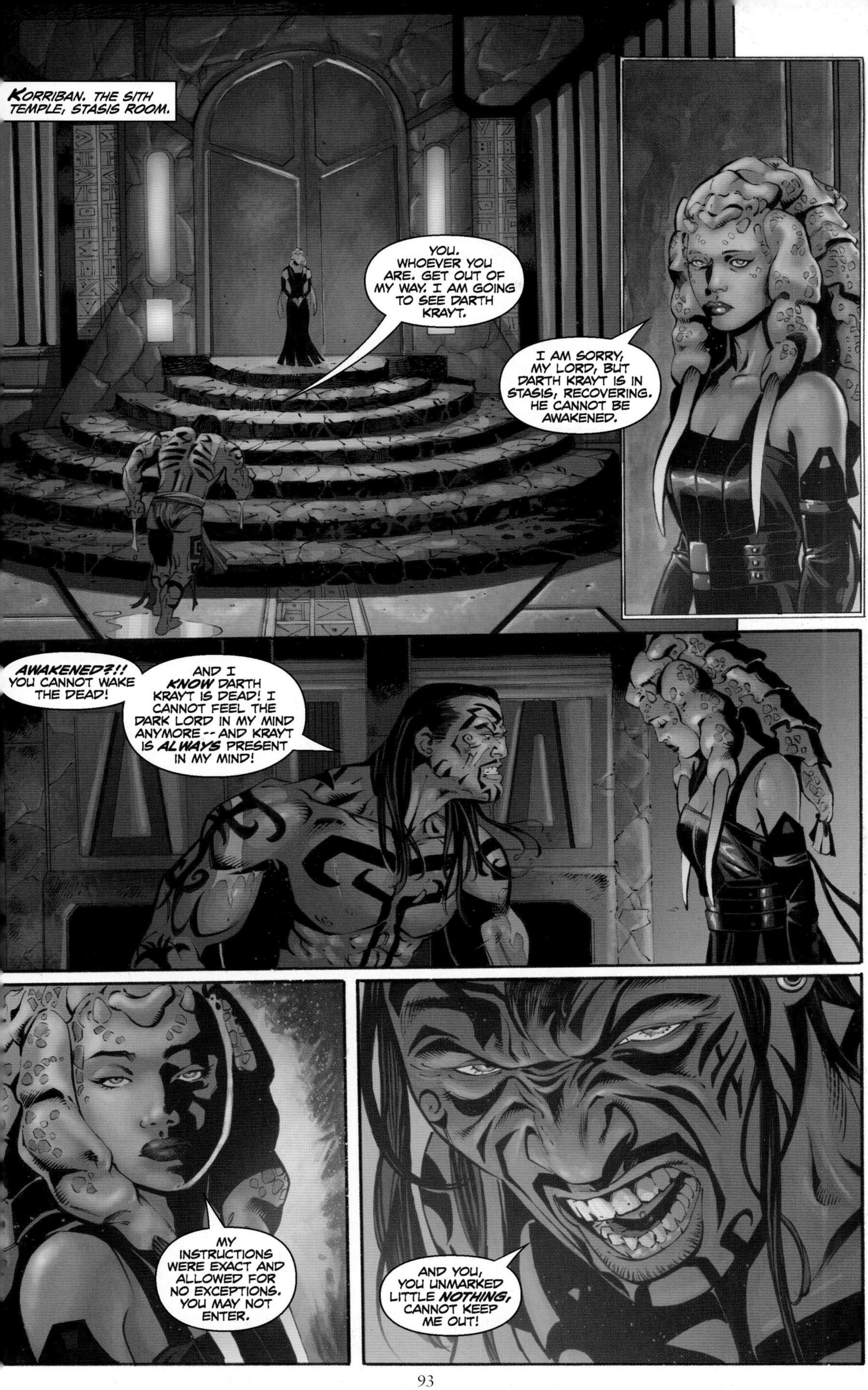
KORRIBAN. THE SITH TEMPLE; STASIS ROOM.
YOU. WHOEVER YOU ARE. GET OUT OF MY WAY. I AM GOING TO SEE DARTH KRAYT.
I AM SORRY, MY LORD, BUT DARTH KRAYT IS IN STASIS, RECOVERING. HE CANNOT BE AWAKENED.
AWAKENED?!! YOU CANNOT WAKE THE DEAD!
AND I KNOW DARTH KRAYT IS DEAD! I CANNOT FEEL THE DARK LORD IN MY MIND ANYMORE -- AND KRAYT IS ALWAYS PRESENT IN MY MIND!
MY INSTRUCTIONS WERE EXACT AND ALLOWED FOR NO EXCEPTIONS. YOU MAY NOT ENTER.
AND YOU, YOU UNMARKED LITTLE NOTHING, CANNOT KEEP ME OUT!

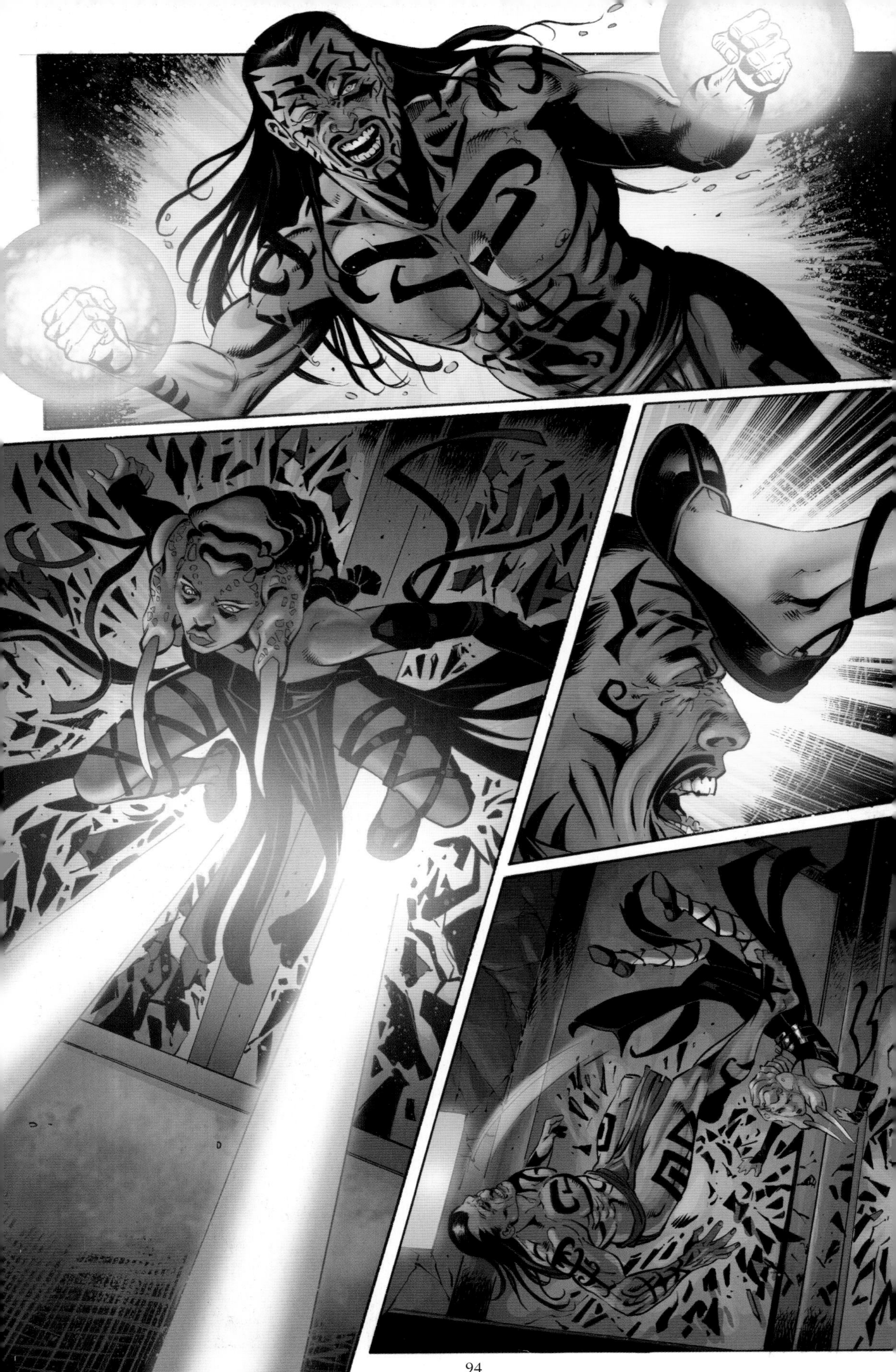

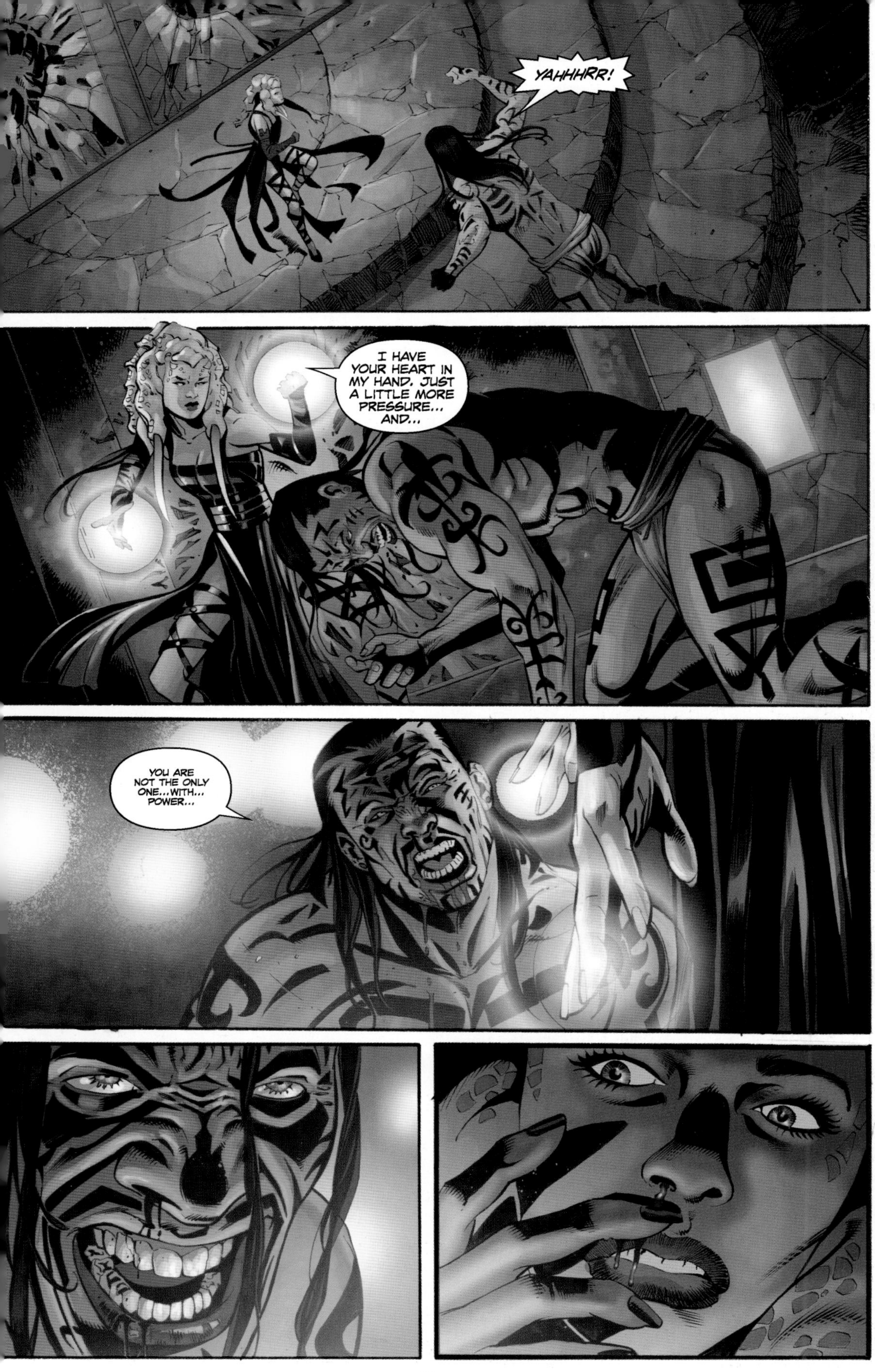
YAHHHRR!
I HAVE YOUR HEART IN MY HAND. JUST A LITTLE MORE PRESSURE... AND...
YOU ARE NOT THE ONLY ONE...WITH... POWER...

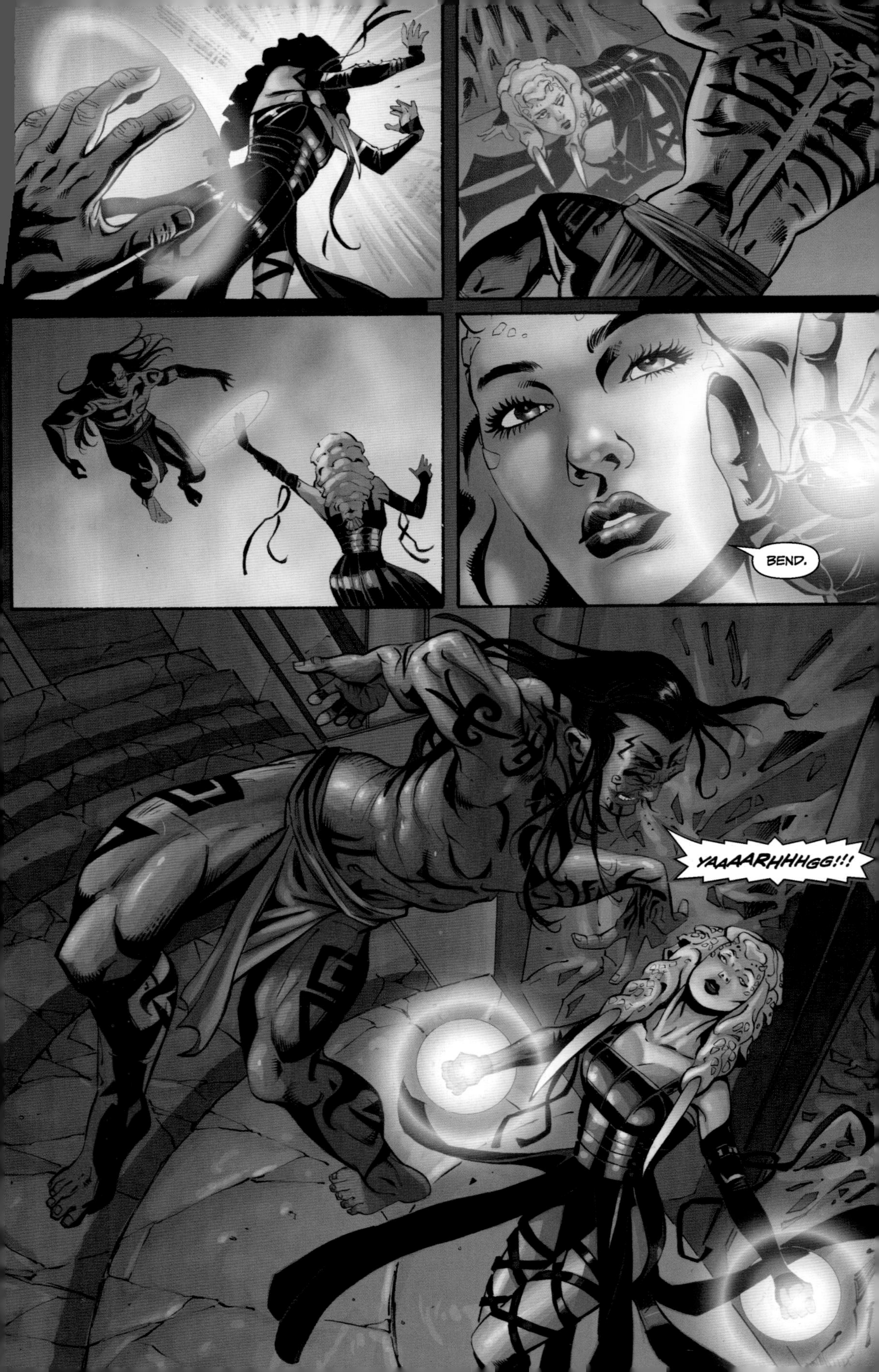
BEND.
YAAAARHHHGG!!!

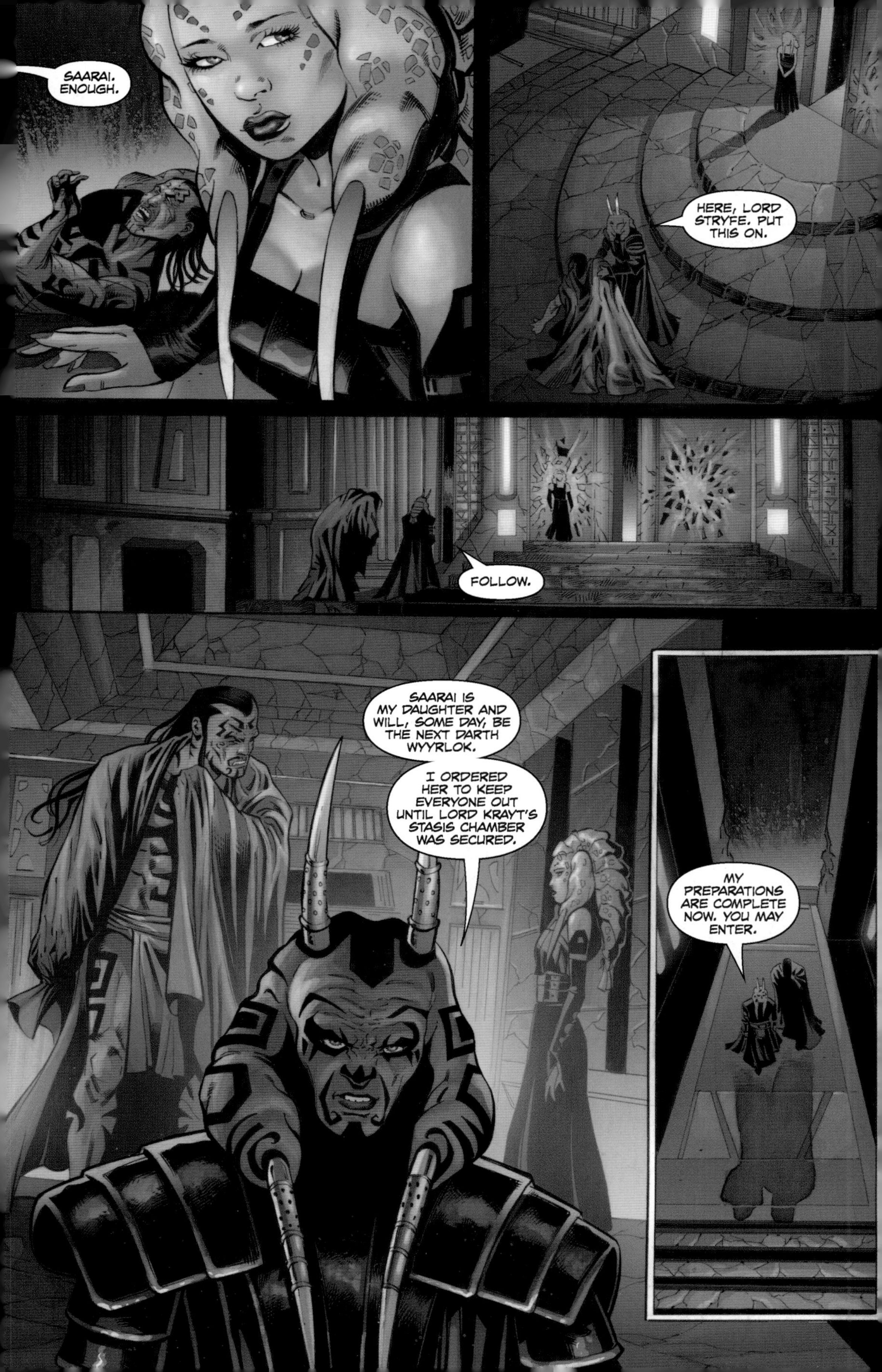
SAARAI. ENOUGH.
HERE, LORD STRYFE. PUT THIS ON.
FOLLOW.
SAARAI IS MY DAUGHTER AND WILL, SOME DAY, BE THE NEXT DARTH WYYRLOK.
I ORDERED HER TO KEEP EVERYONE OUT UNTIL LORD KRAYT'S STASIS CHAMBER WAS SECURED.
MY PREPARATIONS ARE COMPLETE NOW. YOU MAY ENTER.

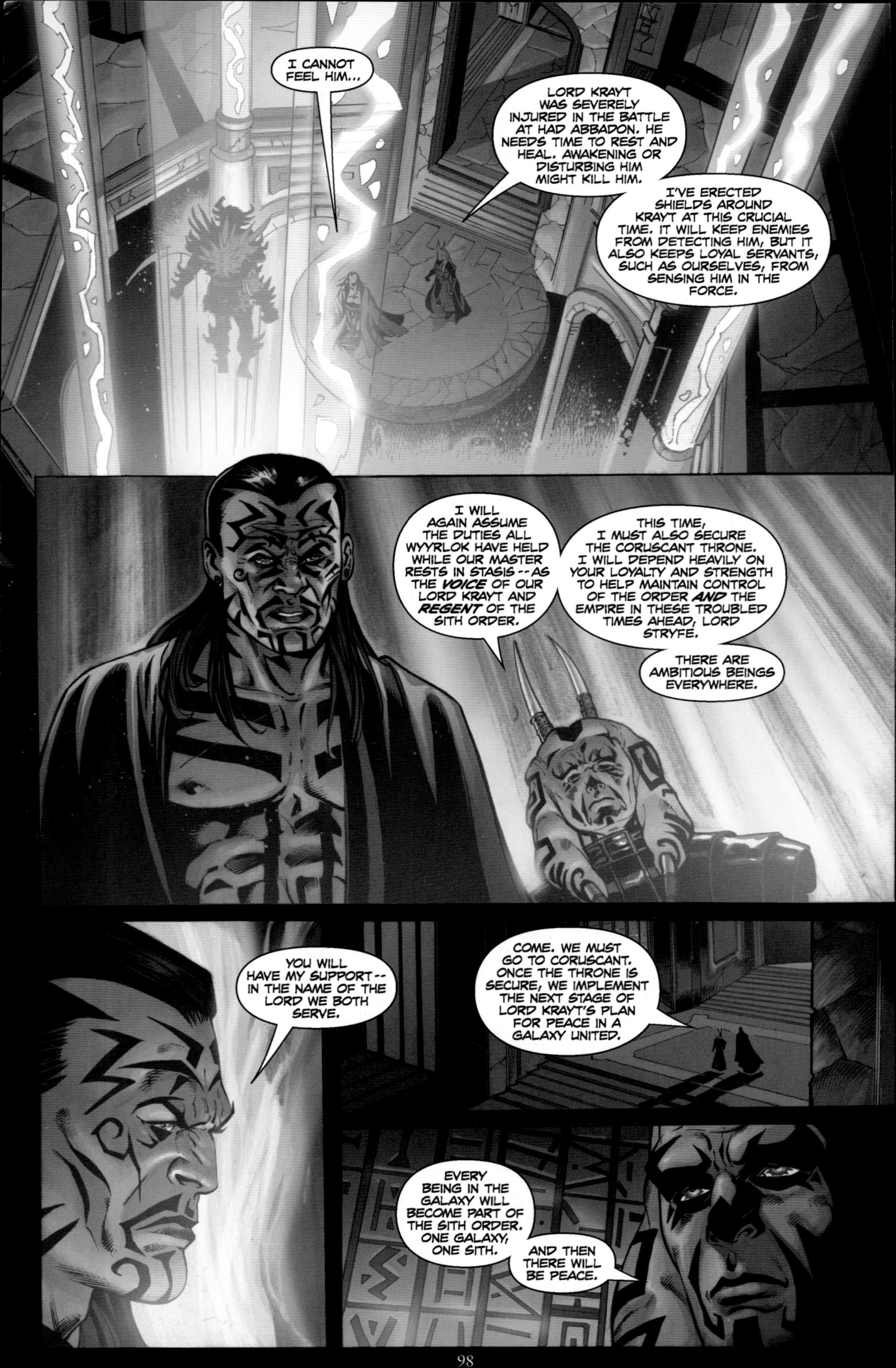
I CANNOT FEEL HIM...
LORD KRAYT WAS SEVERELY INJURED IN THE BATTLE AT HAD ABBADON. HE NEEDS TIME TO REST AND HEAL. AWAKENING OR DISTURBING HIM MIGHT KILL HIM.
I'VE ERECTED SHIELDS AROUND KRAYT AT THIS CRUCIAL TIME. IT WILL KEEP ENEMIES FROM DETECTING HIM, BUT IT ALSO KEEPS LOYAL SERVANTS, SUCH AS OURSELVES, FROM SENSING HIM IN THE FORCE.
I WILL AGAIN ASSUME THE DUTIES ALL WYYRLOK HAVE HELD WHILE OUR MASTER RESTS IN STASIS--AS THE *VOICE* OF OUR LORD KRAYT AND *REGENT* OF THE SITH ORDER.
THIS TIME, I MUST ALSO SECURE THE CORUSCANT THRONE. I WILL DEPEND HEAVILY ON YOUR LOYALTY AND STRENGTH TO HELP MAINTAIN CONTROL OF THE ORDER *AND* THE EMPIRE IN THESE TROUBLED TIMES AHEAD, LORD STRYFE.
THERE ARE AMBITIOUS BEINGS EVERYWHERE.
YOU WILL HAVE MY SUPPORT--IN THE NAME OF THE LORD WE BOTH SERVE.
COME. WE MUST GO TO CORUSCANT. ONCE THE THRONE IS SECURE, WE IMPLEMENT THE NEXT STAGE OF LORD KRAYT'S PLAN FOR PEACE IN A GALAXY UNITED.
EVERY BEING IN THE GALAXY WILL BECOME PART OF THE SITH ORDER. ONE GALAXY, ONE SITH.
AND THEN THERE WILL BE PEACE.

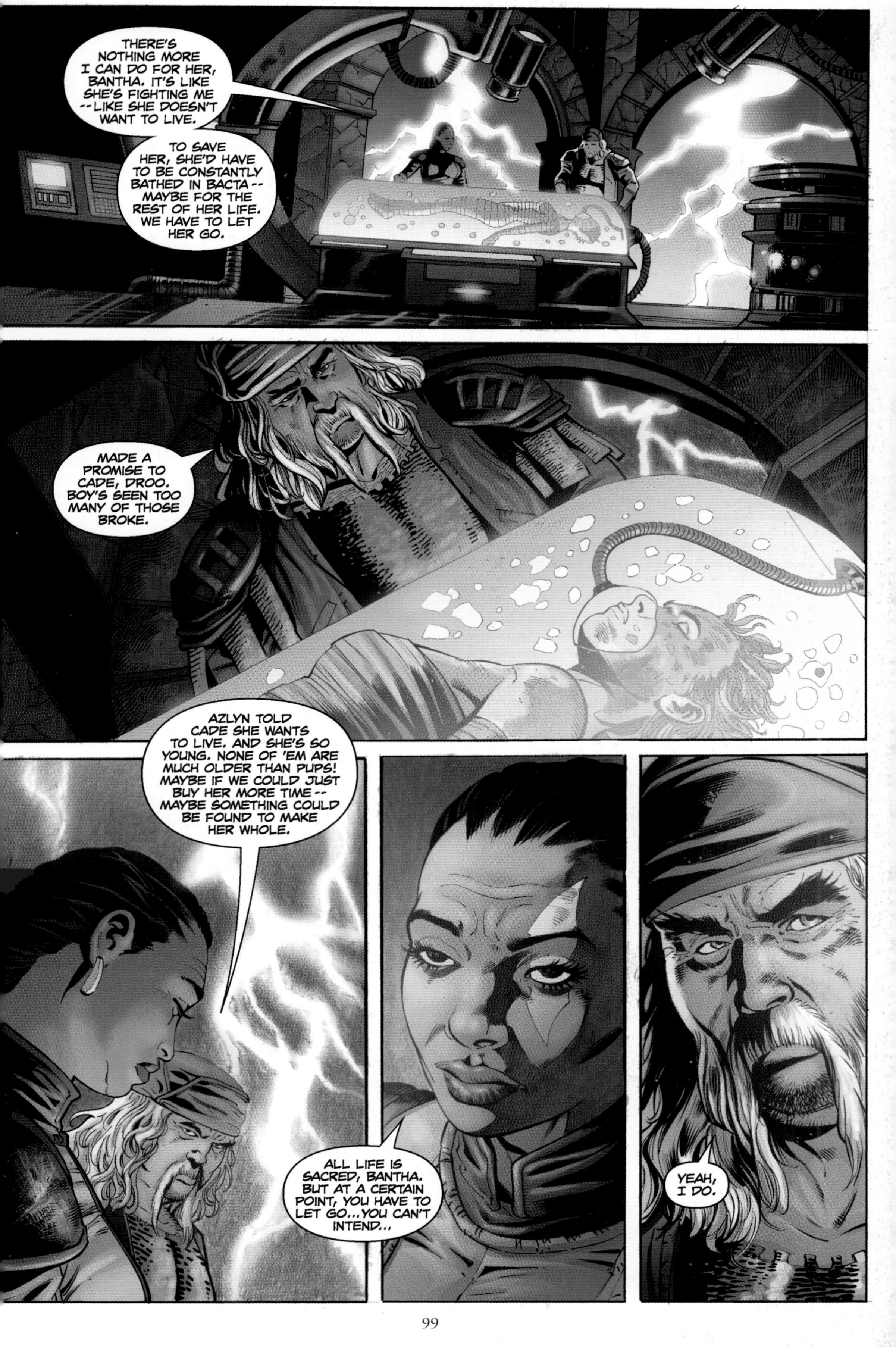
THERE'S NOTHING MORE I CAN DO FOR HER, BANTHA. IT'S LIKE SHE'S FIGHTING ME --LIKE SHE DOESN'T WANT TO LIVE.
TO SAVE HER, SHE'D HAVE TO BE CONSTANTLY BATHED IN BACTA-- MAYBE FOR THE REST OF HER LIFE. WE HAVE TO LET HER GO.
MADE A PROMISE TO CADE, DROO. BOY'S SEEN TOO MANY OF THOSE BROKE.
AZLYN TOLD CADE SHE WANTS TO LIVE. AND SHE'S SO YOUNG. NONE OF 'EM ARE MUCH OLDER THAN PUPS! MAYBE IF WE COULD JUST BUY HER MORE TIME-- MAYBE SOMETHING COULD BE FOUND TO MAKE HER WHOLE.
ALL LIFE IS SACRED, BANTHA. BUT AT A CERTAIN POINT, YOU HAVE TO LET GO...YOU CAN'T INTEND...
YEAH, I DO.

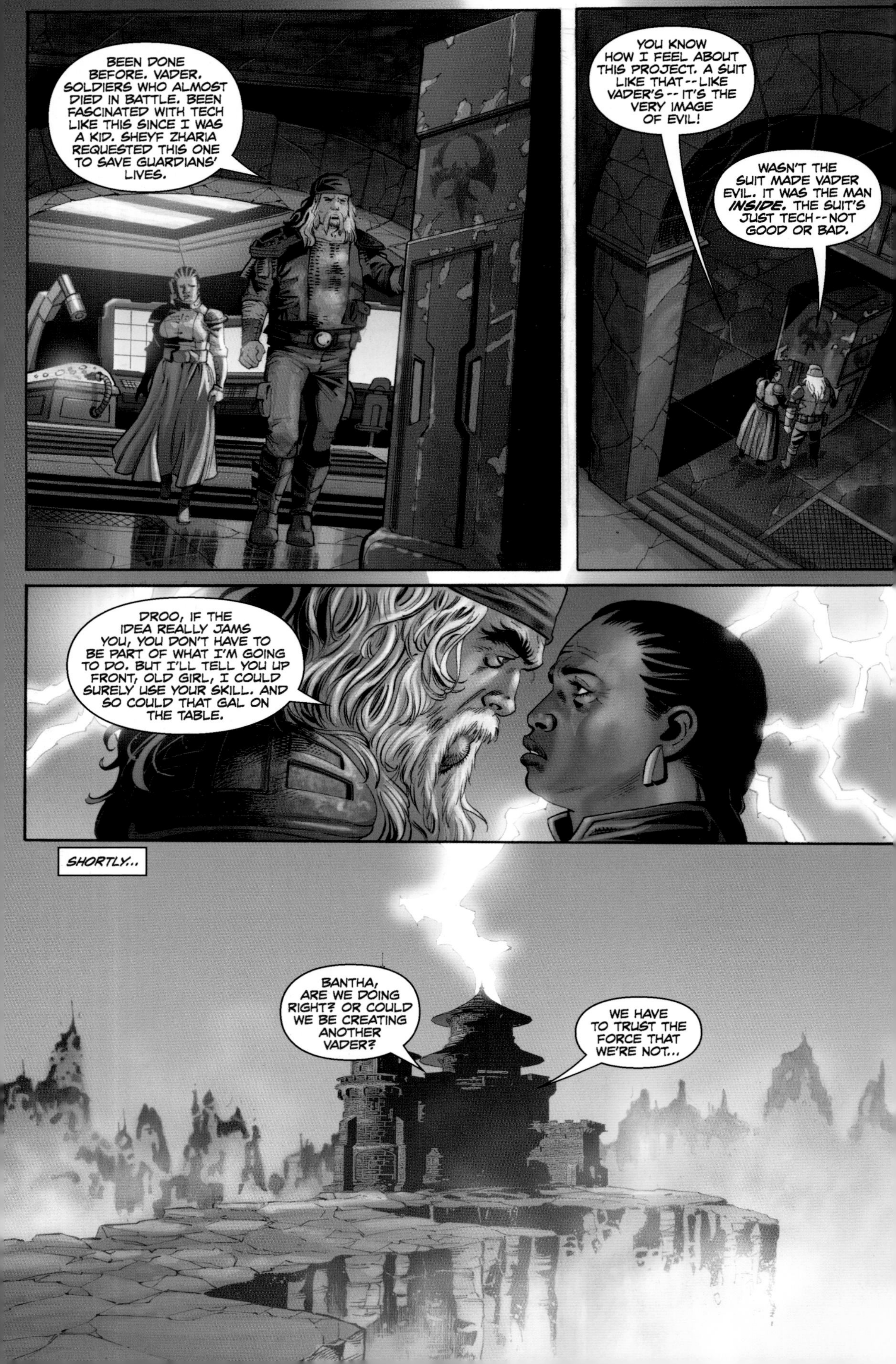
BEEN DONE BEFORE. VADER. SOLDIERS WHO ALMOST DIED IN BATTLE. BEEN FASCINATED WITH TECH LIKE THIS SINCE I WAS A KID. SHEYF ZHARIA REQUESTED THIS ONE TO SAVE GUARDIANS' LIVES.
YOU KNOW HOW I FEEL ABOUT THIS PROJECT. A SUIT LIKE THAT--LIKE VADER'S--IT'S THE VERY IMAGE OF EVIL!
WASN'T THE SUIT MADE VADER EVIL. IT WAS THE MAN INSIDE. THE SUIT'S JUST TECH--NOT GOOD OR BAD.
DROO, IF THE IDEA REALLY JAMS YOU, YOU DON'T HAVE TO BE PART OF WHAT I'M GOING TO DO. BUT I'LL TELL YOU UP FRONT, OLD GIRL, I COULD SURELY USE YOUR SKILL. AND SO COULD THAT GAL ON THE TABLE.
SHORTLY...
BANTHA, ARE WE DOING RIGHT? OR COULD WE BE CREATING ANOTHER VADER?
WE HAVE TO TRUST THE FORCE THAT WE'RE NOT...

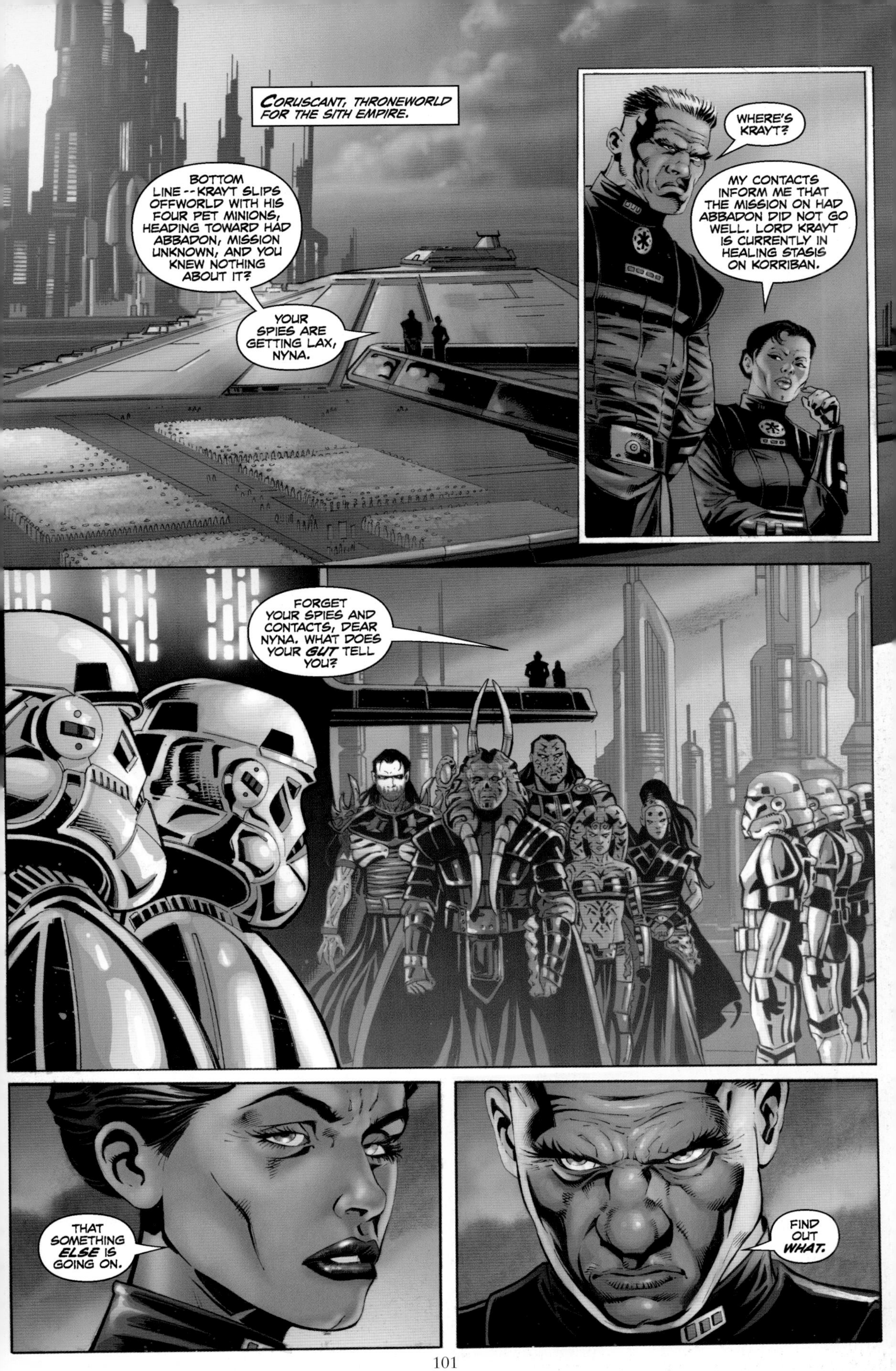
CORUSCANT, THRONEWORLD FOR THE SITH EMPIRE.
BOTTOM LINE--KRAYT SLIPS OFFWORLD WITH HIS FOUR PET MINIONS, HEADING TOWARD HAD ABBADON, MISSION UNKNOWN, AND YOU KNEW NOTHING ABOUT IT?
YOUR SPIES ARE GETTING LAX, NYNA.
WHERE'S KRAYT?
MY CONTACTS INFORM ME THAT THE MISSION ON HAD ABBADON DID NOT GO WELL. LORD KRAYT IS CURRENTLY IN HEALING STASIS ON KORRIBAN.
FORGET YOUR SPIES AND CONTACTS, DEAR NYNA. WHAT DOES YOUR *GUT* TELL YOU?
THAT SOMETHING *ELSE* IS GOING ON.
FIND OUT *WHAT.*

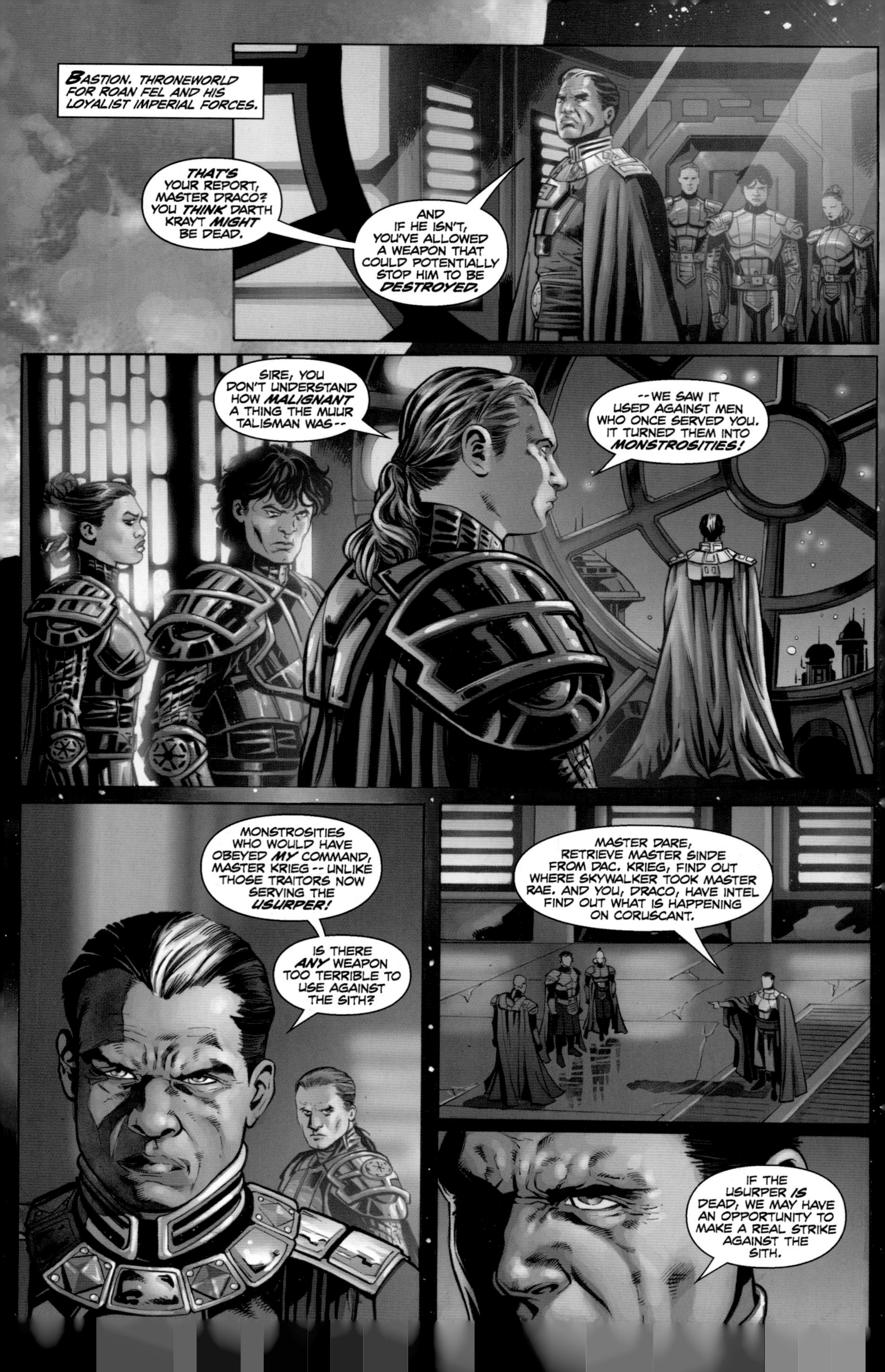
BASTION. THRONEWORLD FOR ROAN FEL AND HIS LOYALIST IMPERIAL FORCES.
THAT'S YOUR REPORT, MASTER DRACO? YOU THINK DARTH KRAY'T MIGHT BE DEAD.
AND IF HE ISN'T, YOU'VE ALLOWED A WEAPON THAT COULD POTENTIALLY STOP HIM TO BE DESTROYED.
SIRE, YOU DON'T UNDERSTAND HOW MALIGNANT A THING THE MUUR TALISMAN WAS--
--WE SAW IT USED AGAINST MEN WHO ONCE SERVED YOU. IT TURNED THEM INTO MONSTROSITIES!
MONSTROSITIES WHO WOULD HAVE OBEYED MY COMMAND, MASTER KRIEG--UNLIKE THOSE TRAITORS NOW SERVING THE USURPER!
IS THERE ANY WEAPON TOO TERRIBLE TO USE AGAINST THE SITH?
MASTER DARE, RETRIEVE MASTER SINDE FROM DAC. KRIEG, FIND OUT WHERE SKYWALKER TOOK MASTER RAE. AND YOU, DRACO, HAVE INTEL FIND OUT WHAT IS HAPPENING ON CORUSCANT.
IF THE USURPER IS DEAD, WE MAY HAVE AN OPPORTUNITY TO MAKE A REAL STRIKE AGAINST THE SITH.

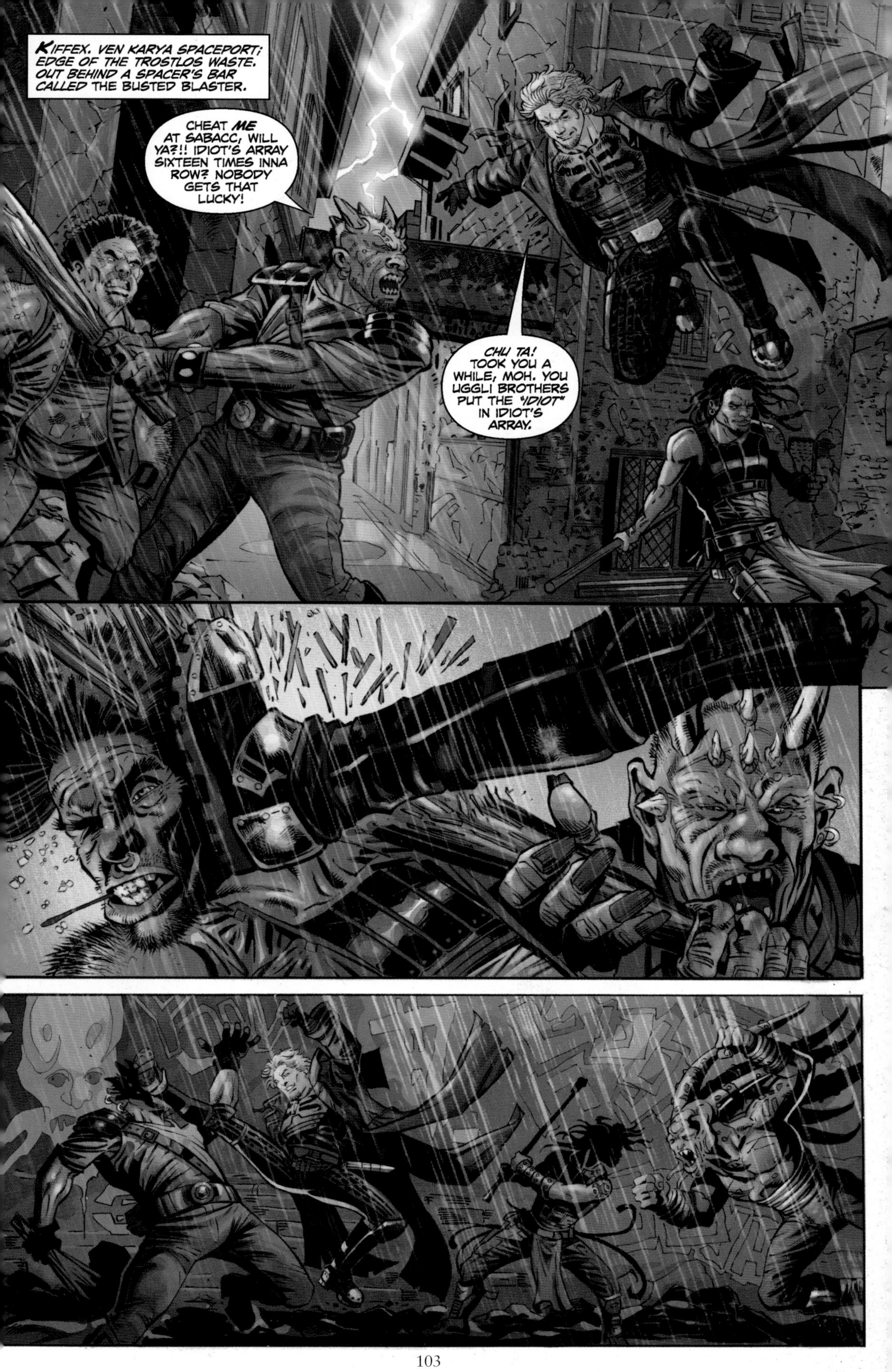
KIFFEX. VEN KARYA SPACEPORT; EDGE OF THE TROSTLOS WASTE. OUT BEHIND A SPACER'S BAR CALLED THE BUSTED BLASTER.
CHEAT ME AT SABACC, WILL YA?!! IDIOT'S ARRAY SIXTEEN TIMES INNA ROW? NOBODY GETS THAT LUCKY!
CHU TA! TOOK YOU A WHILE, MOH. YOU UGGLI BROTHERS PUT THE "IDIOT" IN IDIOT'S ARRAY.

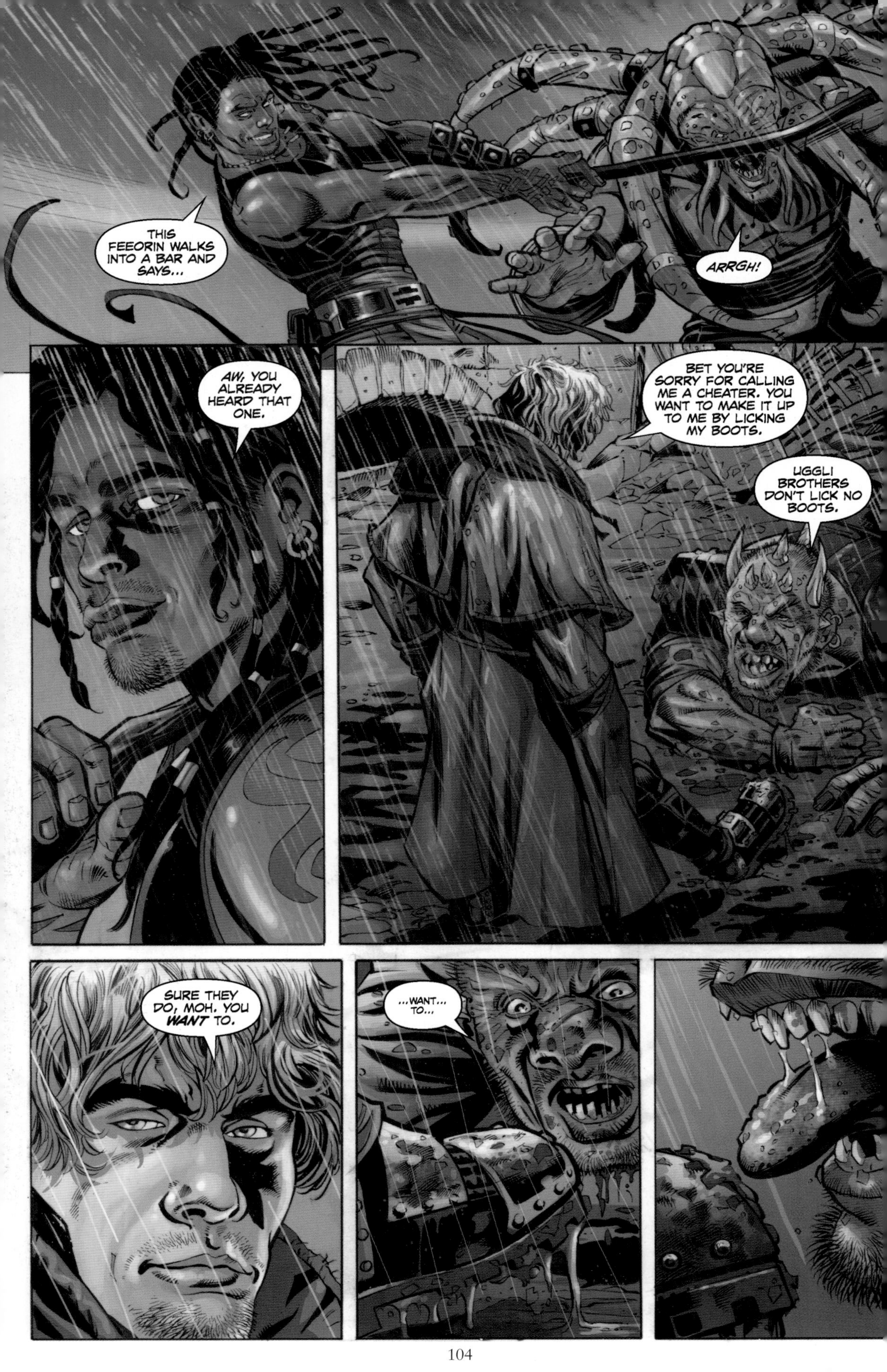

THIS FEEORIN WALKS INTO A BAR AND SAYS...
ARRGH!
AW, YOU ALREADY HEARD THAT ONE.
BET YOU'RE SORRY FOR CALLING ME A CHEATER. YOU WANT TO MAKE IT UP TO ME BY LICKING MY BOOTS.
UGGLI BROTHERS DON'T LICK NO BOOTS.
SURE THEY DO, MOH. YOU *WANT* TO.
...WANT... TO...

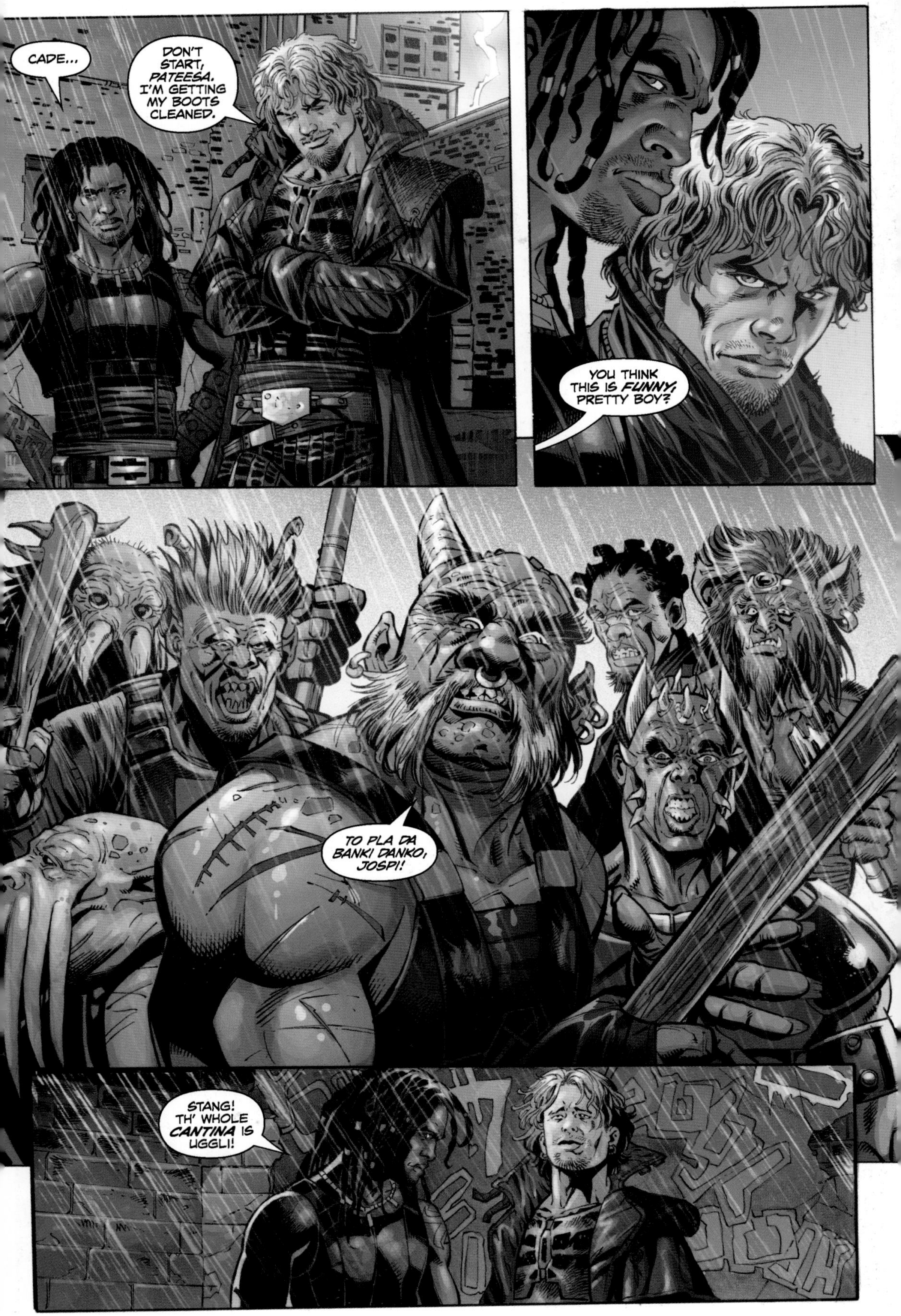
CADE...
DON'T START, *PATEESA.* I'M GETTING MY BOOTS CLEANED.
YOU THINK THIS IS *FUNNY,* PRETTY BOY?
TO PLA DA BANKI DANKO, JOSPI!
STANG! TH' WHOLE *CANTINA* IS UGGLI!

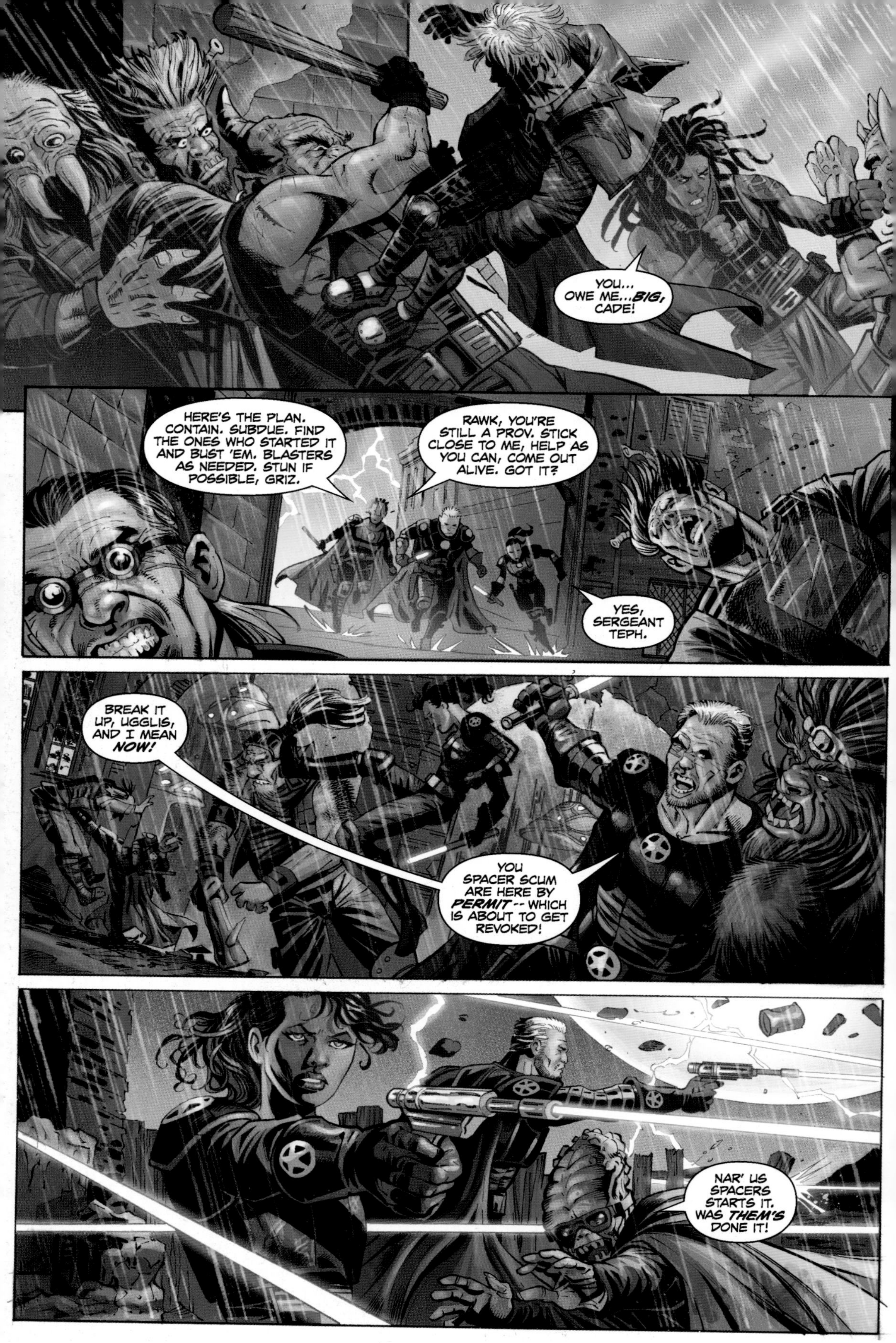
YOU... OWE ME... BIG, CADE!
HERE'S THE PLAN. CONTAIN. SUBDUE. FIND THE ONES WHO STARTED IT AND BUST 'EM. BLASTERS AS NEEDED. STUN IF POSSIBLE, GRIZ.
RAWK, YOU'RE STILL A PROV. STICK CLOSE TO ME, HELP AS YOU CAN, COME OUT ALIVE. GOT IT?
YES, SERGEANT TEPH.
BREAK IT UP, UGGLIS, AND I MEAN NOW!
YOU SPACER SCUM ARE HERE BY PERMIT -- WHICH IS ABOUT TO GET REVOKED!
NAR' US SPACERS STARTS IT. WAS THEM'S DONE IT!

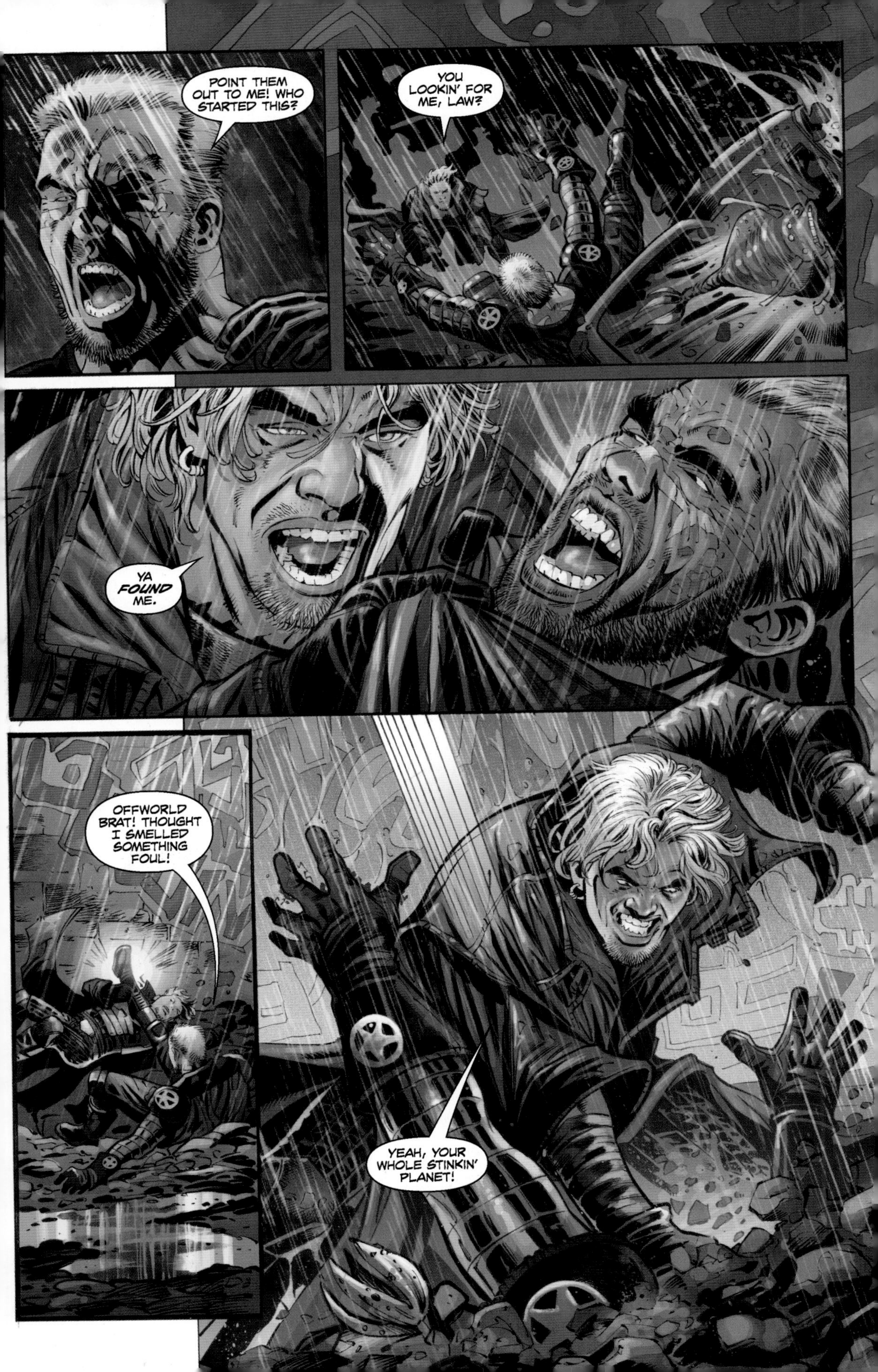
POINT THEM OUT TO ME! WHO STARTED THIS?
YOU LOOKIN' FOR ME, LAW?
YA *FOUND* ME.
OFFWORLD BRAT! THOUGHT I SMELLED SOMETHING FOUL!
YEAH, YOUR WHOLE STINKIN' PLANET!

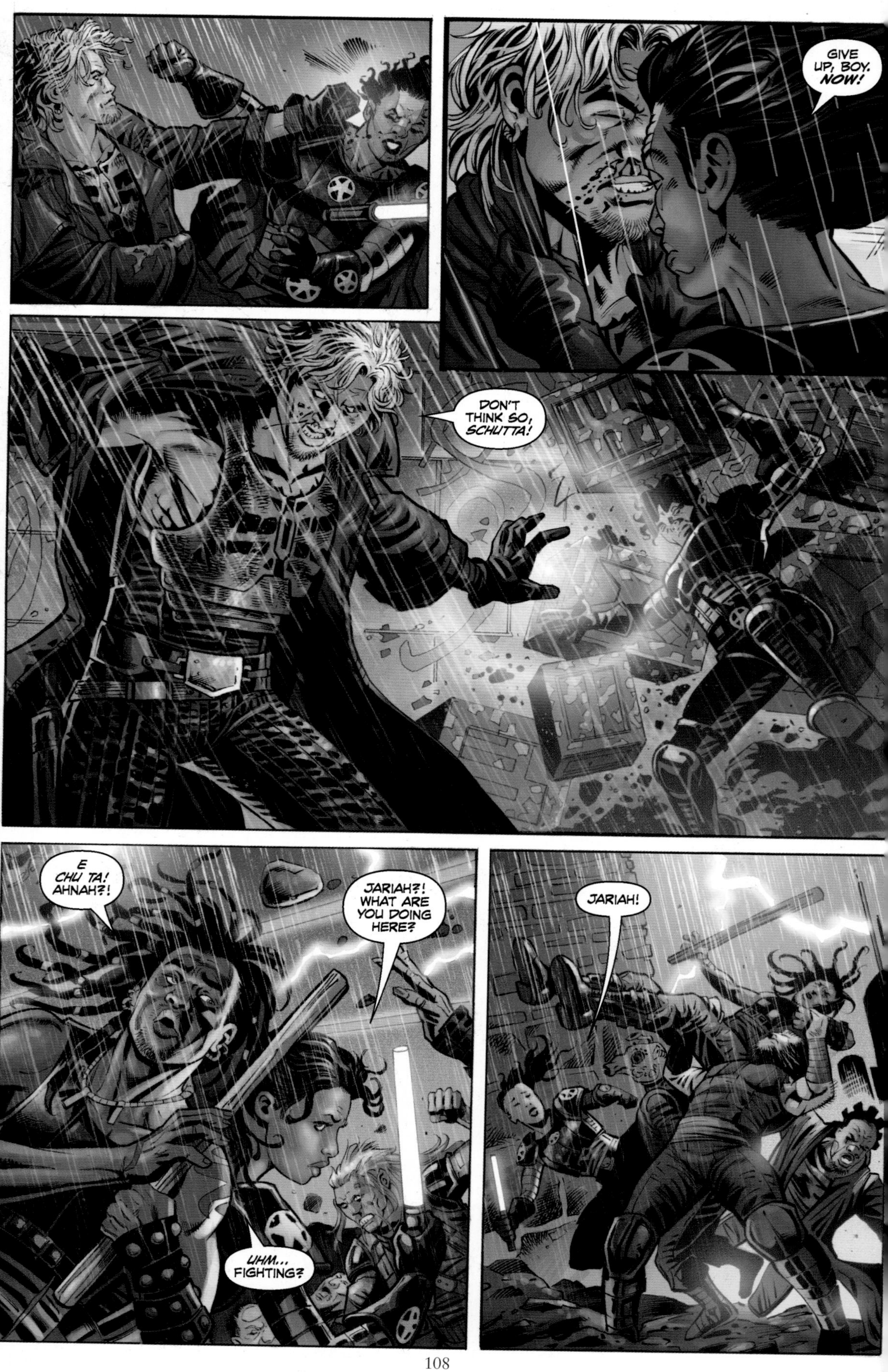
GIVE UP, BOY. NOW!
DON'T THINK SO, SCHUTTA!
E CHU TA! AHNAH?!
JARIAH?! WHAT ARE YOU DOING HERE?
UHM... FIGHTING?
JARIAH!

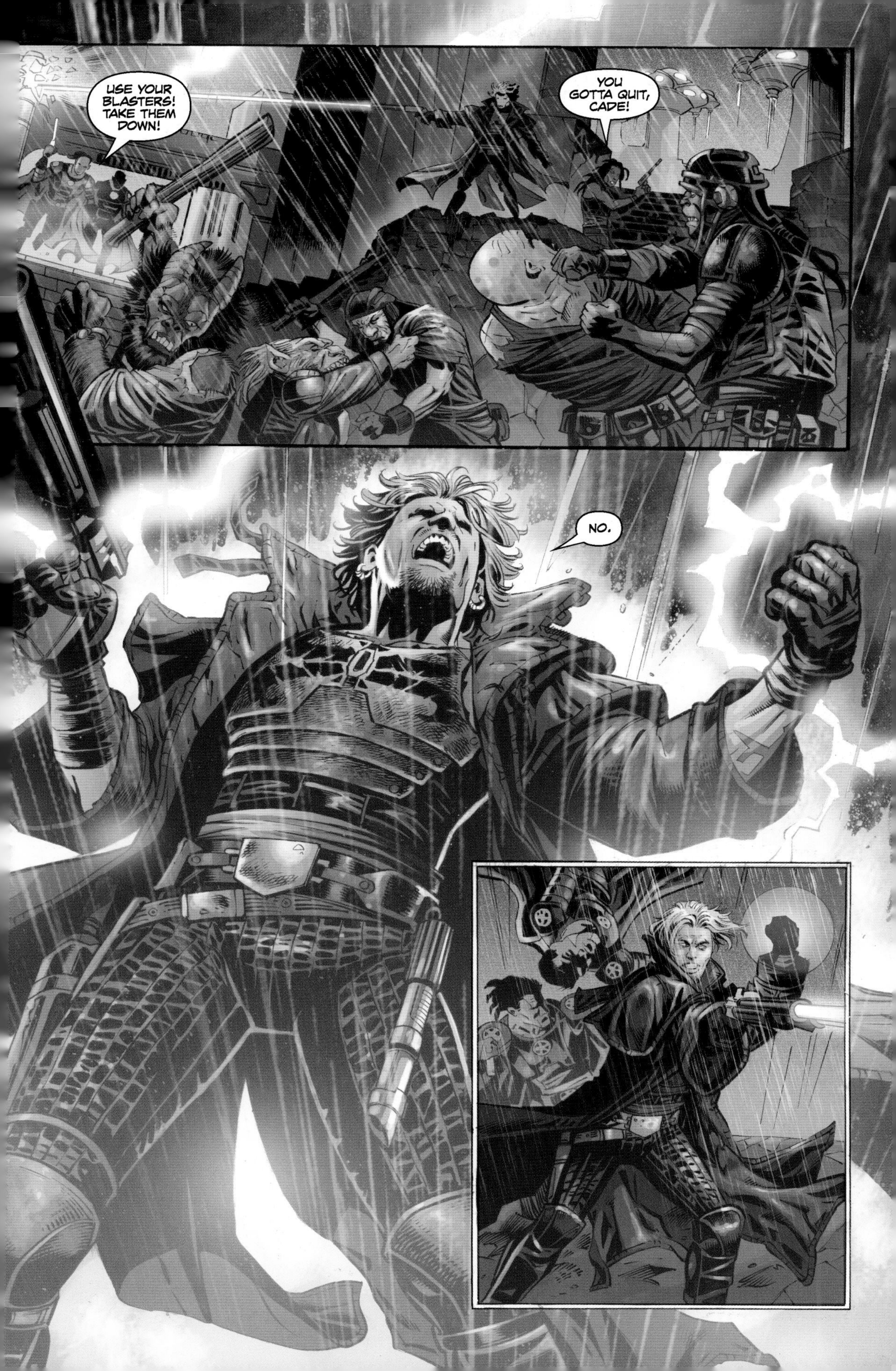
USE YOUR BLASTERS! TAKE THEM DOWN!
YOU GOTTA QUIT, CADE!
NO.

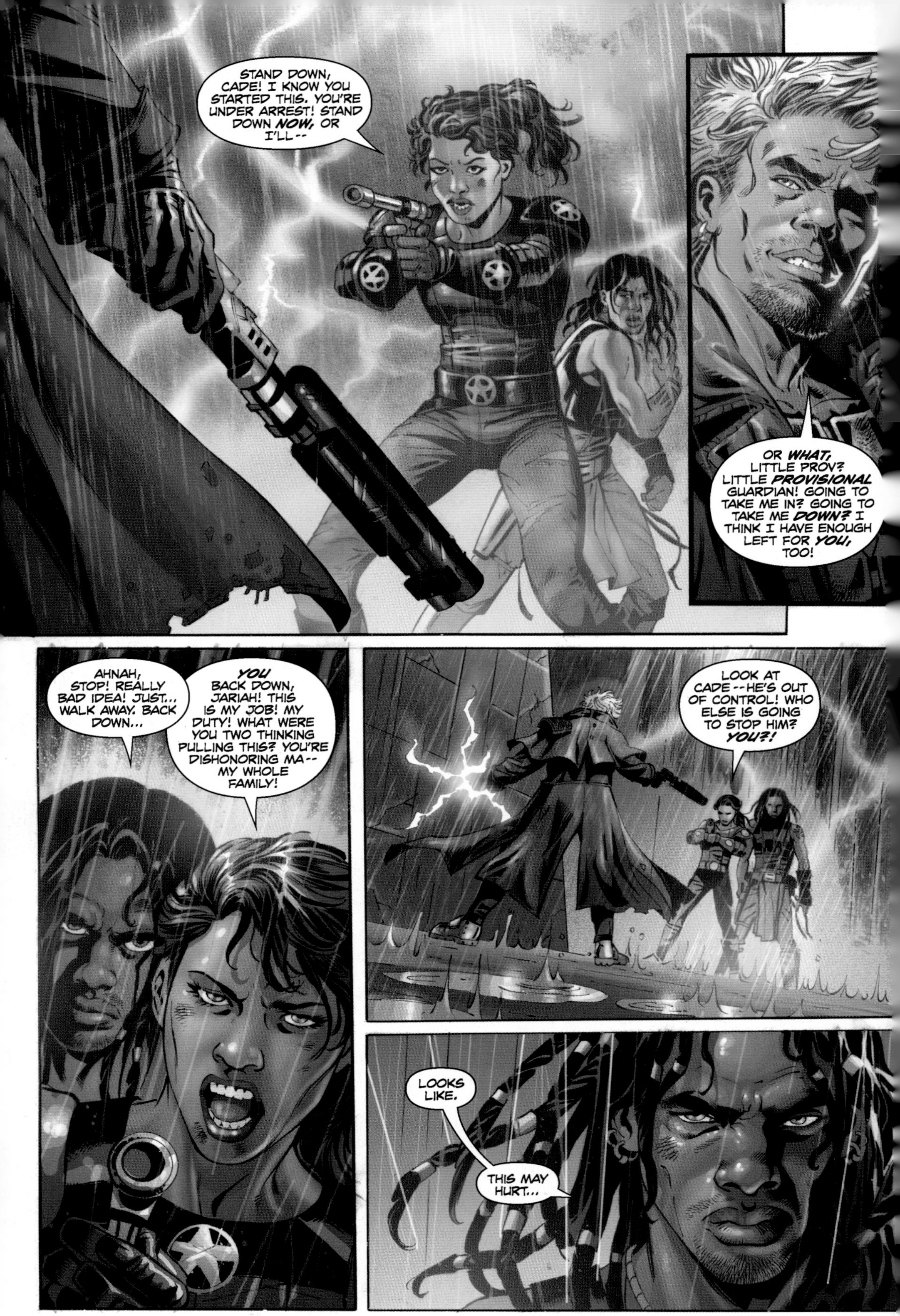
STAND DOWN, CADE! I KNOW YOU STARTED THIS. YOU'RE UNDER ARREST! STAND DOWN NOW, OR I'LL--
OR WHAT, LITTLE PROV? LITTLE PROVISIONAL GUARDIAN! GOING TO TAKE ME IN? GOING TO TAKE ME DOWN? I THINK I HAVE ENOUGH LEFT FOR YOU, TOO!
AHNAH, STOP! REALLY BAD IDEA! JUST... WALK AWAY. BACK DOWN...
YOU BACK DOWN, JARIAH! THIS IS MY JOB! MY DUTY! WHAT WERE YOU TWO THINKING PULLING THIS? YOU'RE DISHONORING MA-- MY WHOLE FAMILY!
LOOK AT CADE--HE'S OUT OF CONTROL! WHO ELSE IS GOING TO STOP HIM? YOU?!
LOOKS LIKE.
THIS MAY HURT...

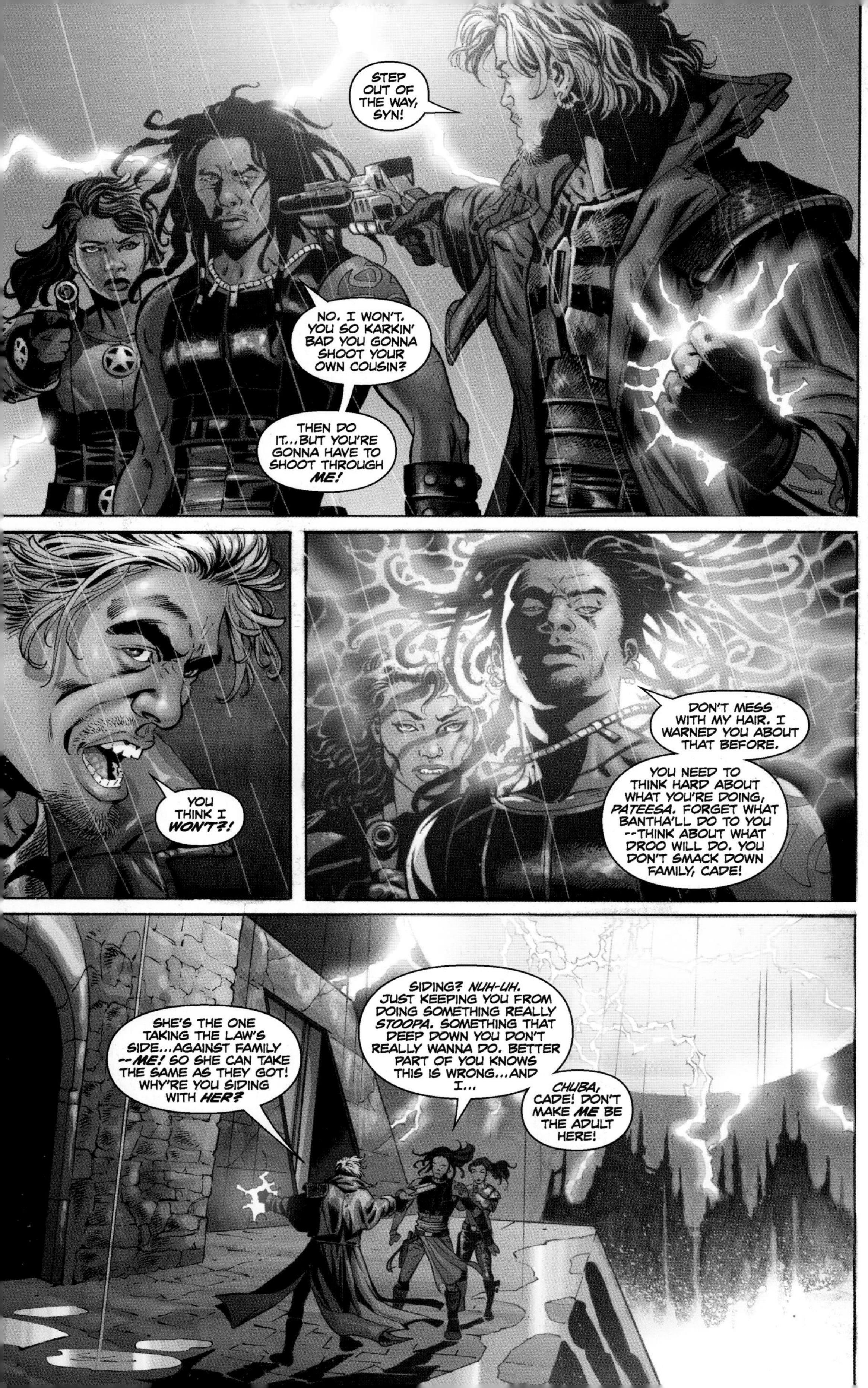
STEP OUT OF THE WAY, SYN!
NO. I WON'T. YOU SO KARKIN' BAD YOU GONNA SHOOT YOUR OWN COUSIN?
THEN DO IT...BUT YOU'RE GONNA HAVE TO SHOOT THROUGH *ME!*
YOU THINK I *WON'T?!*
DON'T MESS WITH MY HAIR. I WARNED YOU ABOUT THAT BEFORE.
YOU NEED TO THINK HARD ABOUT WHAT YOU'RE DOING, *PATEESA*. FORGET WHAT BANTHA'LL DO TO YOU --THINK ABOUT WHAT DROO WILL DO. YOU DON'T SMACK DOWN FAMILY, CADE!
SHE'S THE ONE TAKING THE LAW'S SIDE...AGAINST FAMILY *--ME!* SO SHE CAN TAKE THE SAME AS THEY GOT! WHY'RE YOU SIDING WITH *HER?*
SIDING? *NUH-UH.* JUST KEEPING YOU FROM DOING SOMETHING REALLY *STOOPA*. SOMETHING THAT DEEP DOWN YOU DON'T REALLY WANNA DO. BETTER PART OF YOU KNOWS THIS IS WRONG...AND I...
CHUBA, CADE! DON'T MAKE *ME* BE THE ADULT HERE!

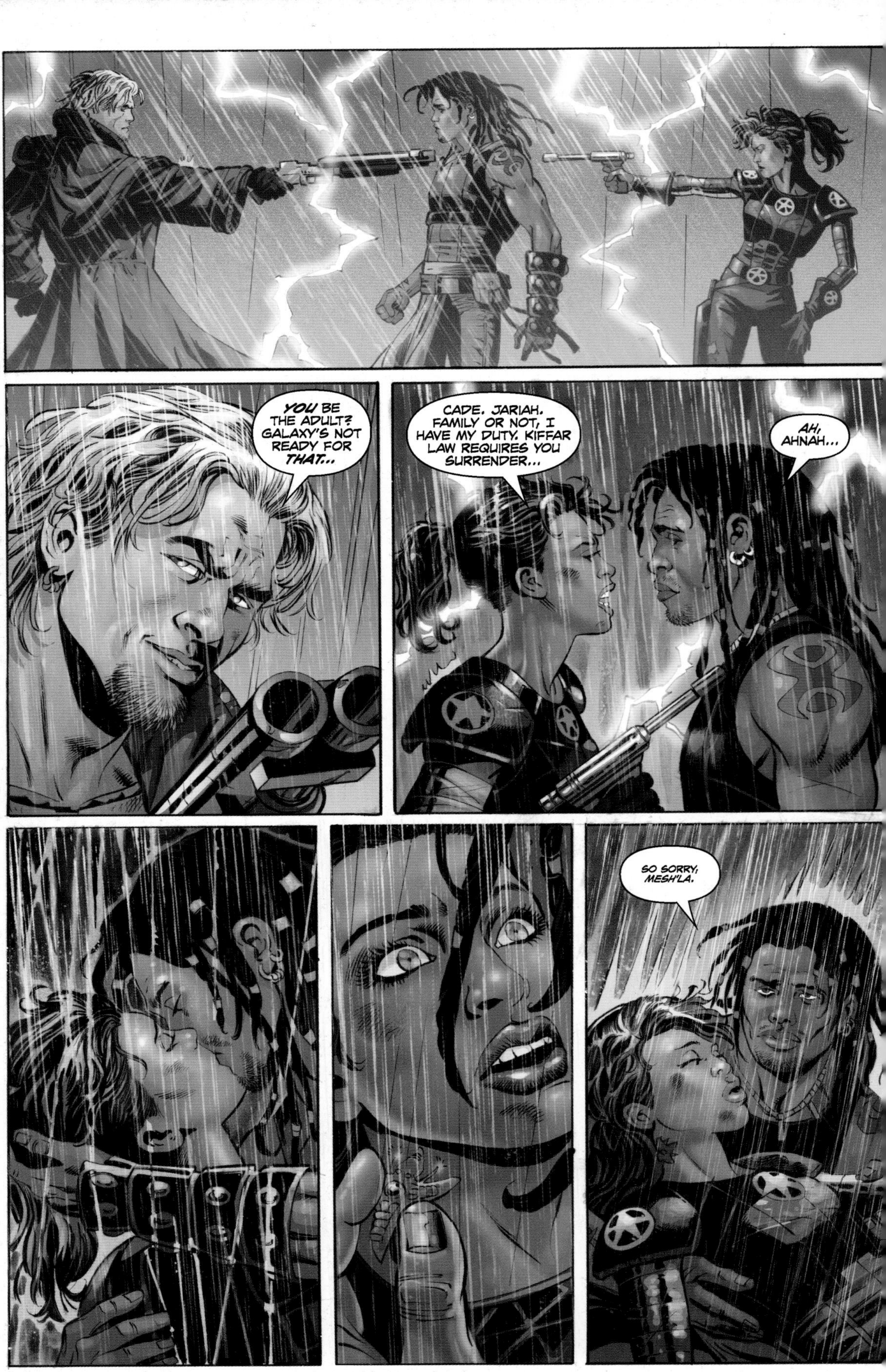
YOU BE THE ADULT? GALAXY'S NOT READY FOR THAT...
CADE. JARIAH. FAMILY OR NOT, I HAVE MY DUTY. KIFFAR LAW REQUIRES YOU SURRENDER...
AH, AHNAH...
SO SORRY, MESH'LA.

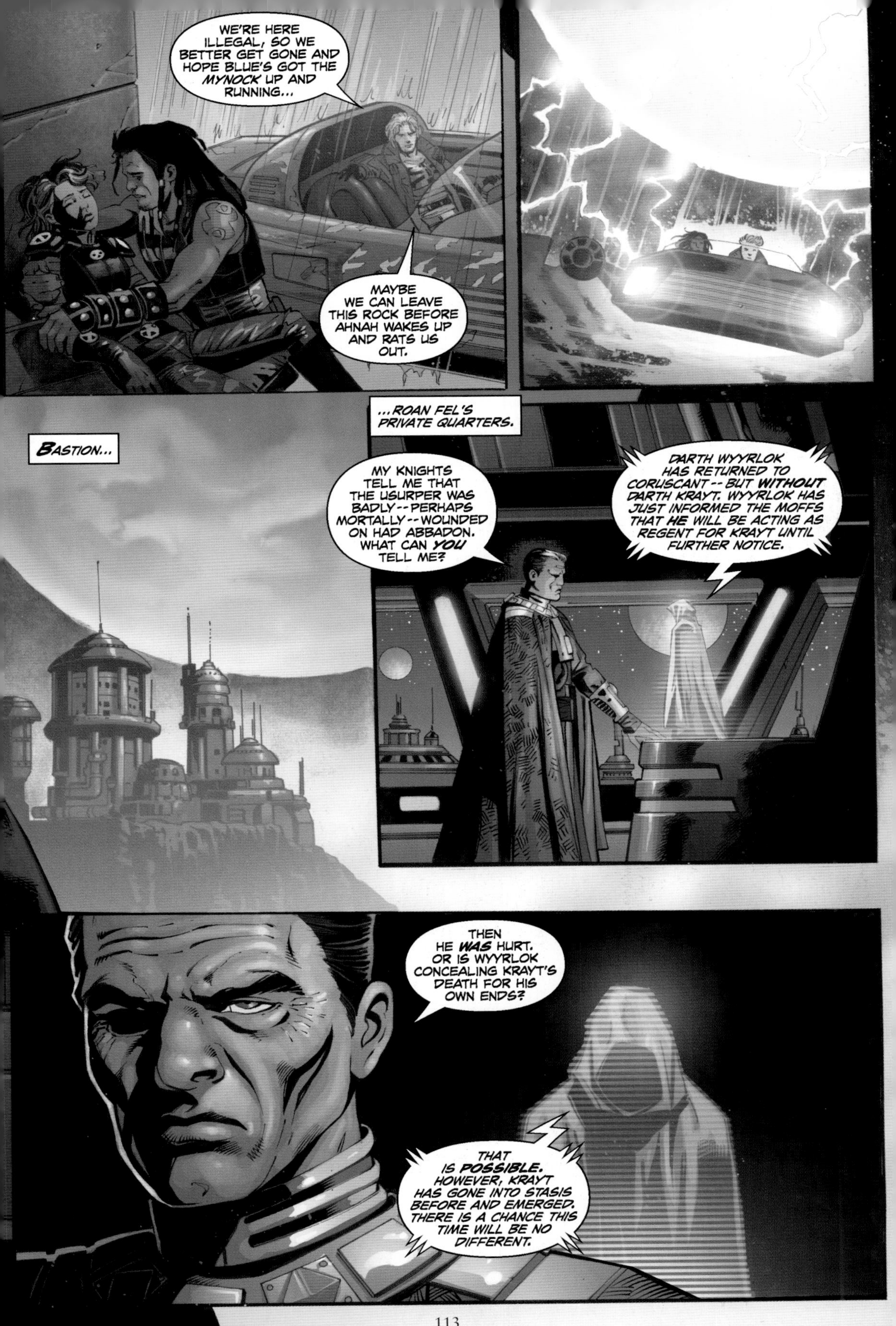
WE'RE HERE ILLEGAL, SO WE BETTER GET GONE AND HOPE BLUE'S GOT THE *MYNOCK* UP AND RUNNING...
MAYBE WE CAN LEAVE THIS ROCK BEFORE AHNAH WAKES UP AND RATS US OUT.
BASTION...
...ROAN FEL'S PRIVATE QUARTERS.
MY KNIGHTS TELL ME THAT THE USURPER WAS BADLY--PERHAPS MORTALLY--WOUNDED ON HAD ABBADON. WHAT CAN *YOU* TELL ME?
DARTH WYYRLOK HAS RETURNED TO CORUSCANT--BUT **WITHOUT** DARTH KRAYT. WYYRLOK HAS JUST INFORMED THE MOFFS THAT **HE** WILL BE ACTING AS REGENT FOR KRAYT UNTIL FURTHER NOTICE.
THEN HE ***WAS*** HURT. OR IS WYYRLOK CONCEALING KRAYT'S DEATH FOR HIS OWN ENDS?
THAT IS **POSSIBLE.** HOWEVER, KRAYT HAS GONE INTO STASIS BEFORE AND EMERGED. THERE IS A CHANCE THIS TIME WILL BE NO DIFFERENT.

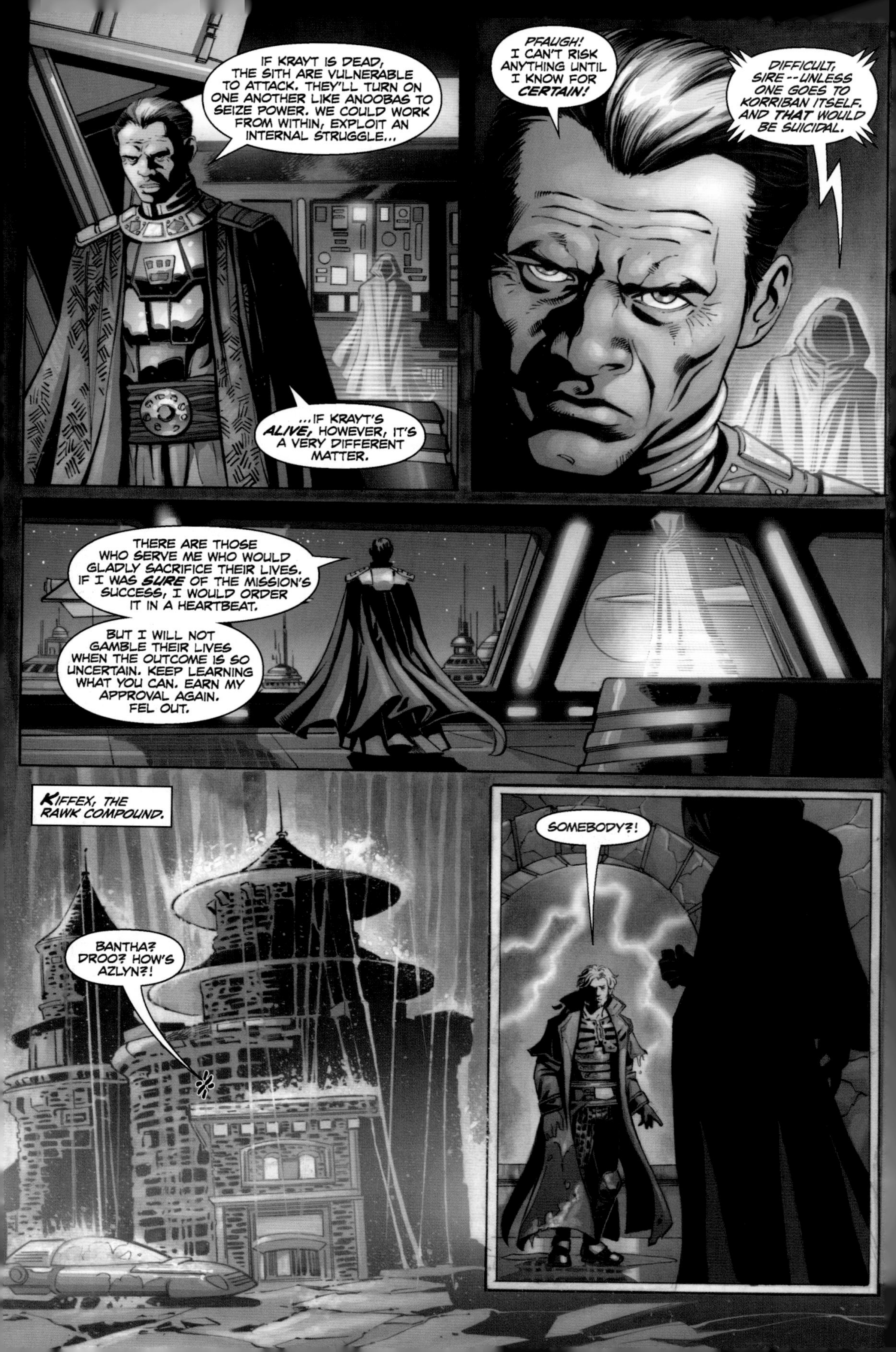
IF KRAYT IS DEAD, THE SITH ARE VULNERABLE TO ATTACK. THEY'LL TURN ON ONE ANOTHER LIKE ANOOBAS TO SEIZE POWER. WE COULD WORK FROM WITHIN, EXPLOIT AN INTERNAL STRUGGLE...
...IF KRAYT'S ALIVE, HOWEVER, IT'S A VERY DIFFERENT MATTER.
PFAUGH! I CAN'T RISK ANYTHING UNTIL I KNOW FOR CERTAIN!
DIFFICULT, SIRE--UNLESS ONE GOES TO KORRIBAN ITSELF. AND THAT WOULD BE SUICIDAL.
THERE ARE THOSE WHO SERVE ME WHO WOULD GLADLY SACRIFICE THEIR LIVES. IF I WAS SURE OF THE MISSION'S SUCCESS, I WOULD ORDER IT IN A HEARTBEAT.
BUT I WILL NOT GAMBLE THEIR LIVES WHEN THE OUTCOME IS SO UNCERTAIN. KEEP LEARNING WHAT YOU CAN. EARN MY APPROVAL AGAIN. FEL OUT.
KIFFEX, THE RAWK COMPOUND.
BANTHA? DROO? HOW'S AZLYN?!
SOMEBODY?!

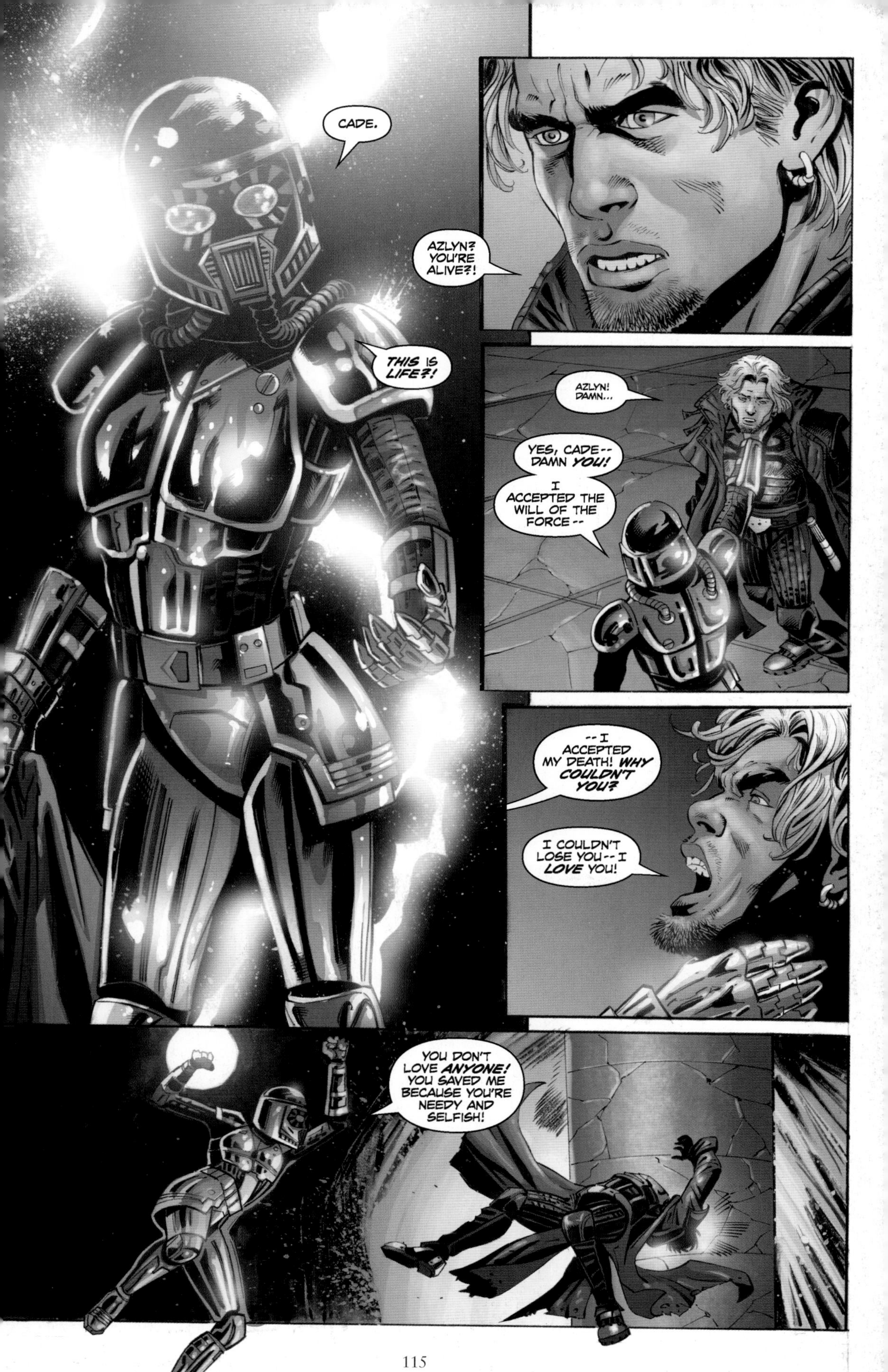
CADE.
AZLYN? YOU'RE ALIVE?!
THIS IS LIFE?!
AZLYN! DAMN...
YES, CADE-- DAMN YOU!
I ACCEPTED THE WILL OF THE FORCE --
--I ACCEPTED MY DEATH! WHY COULDN'T YOU?
I COULDN'T LOSE YOU--I LOVE YOU!
YOU DON'T LOVE ANYONE! YOU SAVED ME BECAUSE YOU'RE NEEDY AND SELFISH!

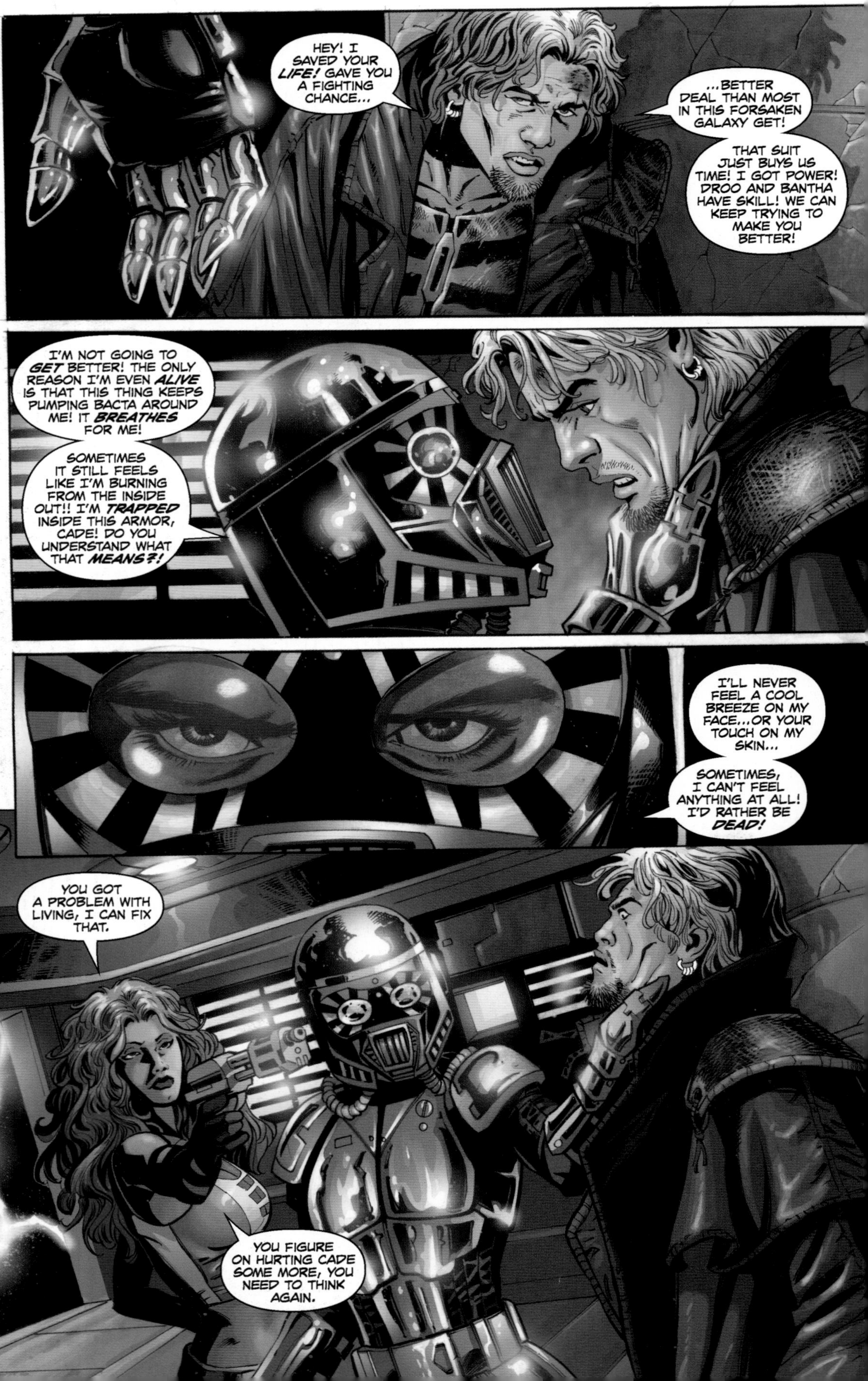
HEY! I SAVED YOUR *LIFE!* GAVE YOU A FIGHTING CHANCE...
...BETTER DEAL THAN MOST IN THIS FORSAKEN GALAXY GET!
THAT SUIT JUST BUYS US TIME! I GOT POWER! DROO AND BANTHA HAVE SKILL! WE CAN KEEP TRYING TO MAKE YOU BETTER!
I'M NOT GOING TO *GET* BETTER! THE ONLY REASON I'M EVEN *ALIVE* IS THAT THIS THING KEEPS PUMPING BACTA AROUND ME! IT *BREATHES* FOR ME!
SOMETIMES IT STILL FEELS LIKE I'M BURNING FROM THE INSIDE OUT!! I'M *TRAPPED* INSIDE THIS ARMOR, CADE! DO YOU UNDERSTAND WHAT THAT *MEANS?!*
I'LL NEVER FEEL A COOL BREEZE ON MY FACE...OR YOUR TOUCH ON MY SKIN...
SOMETIMES, I CAN'T FEEL ANYTHING AT ALL! I'D RATHER BE *DEAD!*
YOU GOT A PROBLEM WITH LIVING, I CAN FIX THAT.
YOU FIGURE ON HURTING CADE SOME MORE, YOU NEED TO THINK AGAIN.

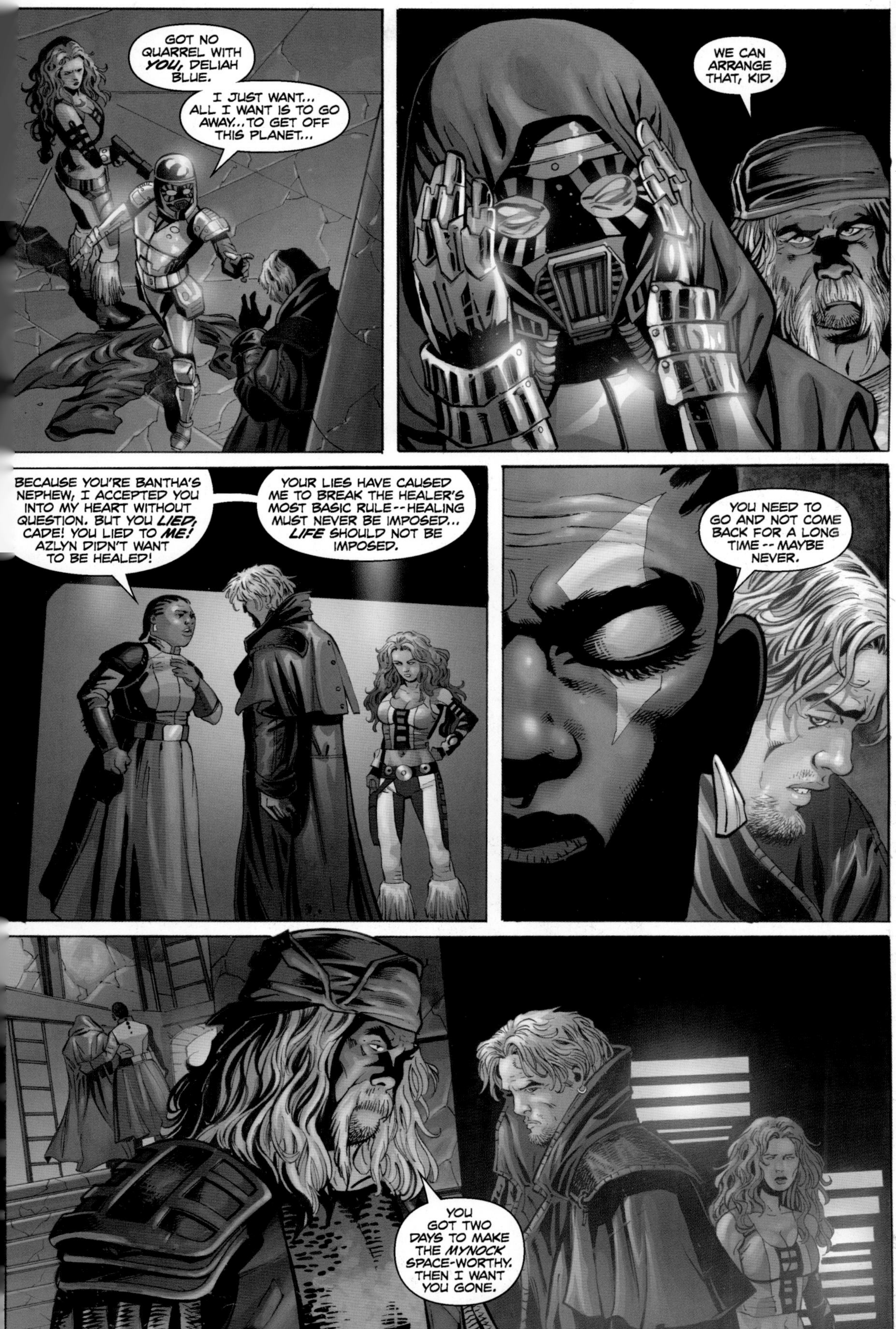
GOT NO QUARREL WITH *YOU,* DELIAH BLUE.
I JUST WANT... ALL I WANT IS TO GO AWAY...TO GET OFF THIS PLANET...
WE CAN ARRANGE THAT, KID.
BECAUSE YOU'RE BANTHA'S NEPHEW, I ACCEPTED YOU INTO MY HEART WITHOUT QUESTION. BUT YOU *LIED,* CADE! YOU LIED TO *ME!* AZLYN DIDN'T WANT TO BE HEALED!
YOUR LIES HAVE CAUSED ME TO BREAK THE HEALER'S MOST BASIC RULE--HEALING MUST NEVER BE IMPOSED... *LIFE* SHOULD NOT BE IMPOSED.
YOU NEED TO GO AND NOT COME BACK FOR A LONG TIME--MAYBE NEVER.
YOU GOT TWO DAYS TO MAKE THE *MYNOCK* SPACE-WORTHY. THEN I WANT YOU GONE.

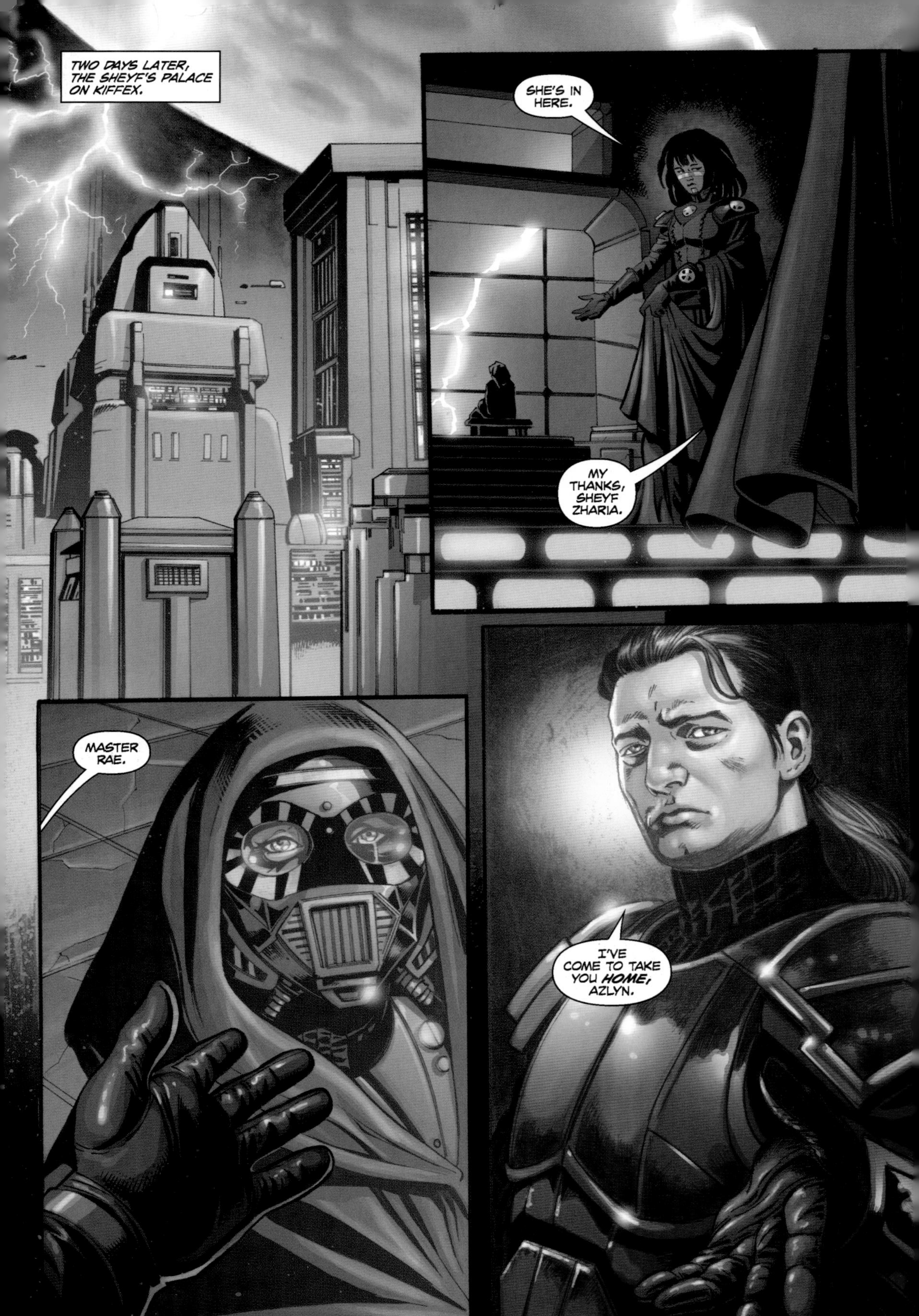
TWO DAYS LATER, THE SHEYF'S PALACE ON KIFFEX.
SHE'S IN HERE.
MY THANKS, SHEYF ZHARIA.
MASTER RAE.
I'VE COME TO TAKE YOU HOME, AZLYN.

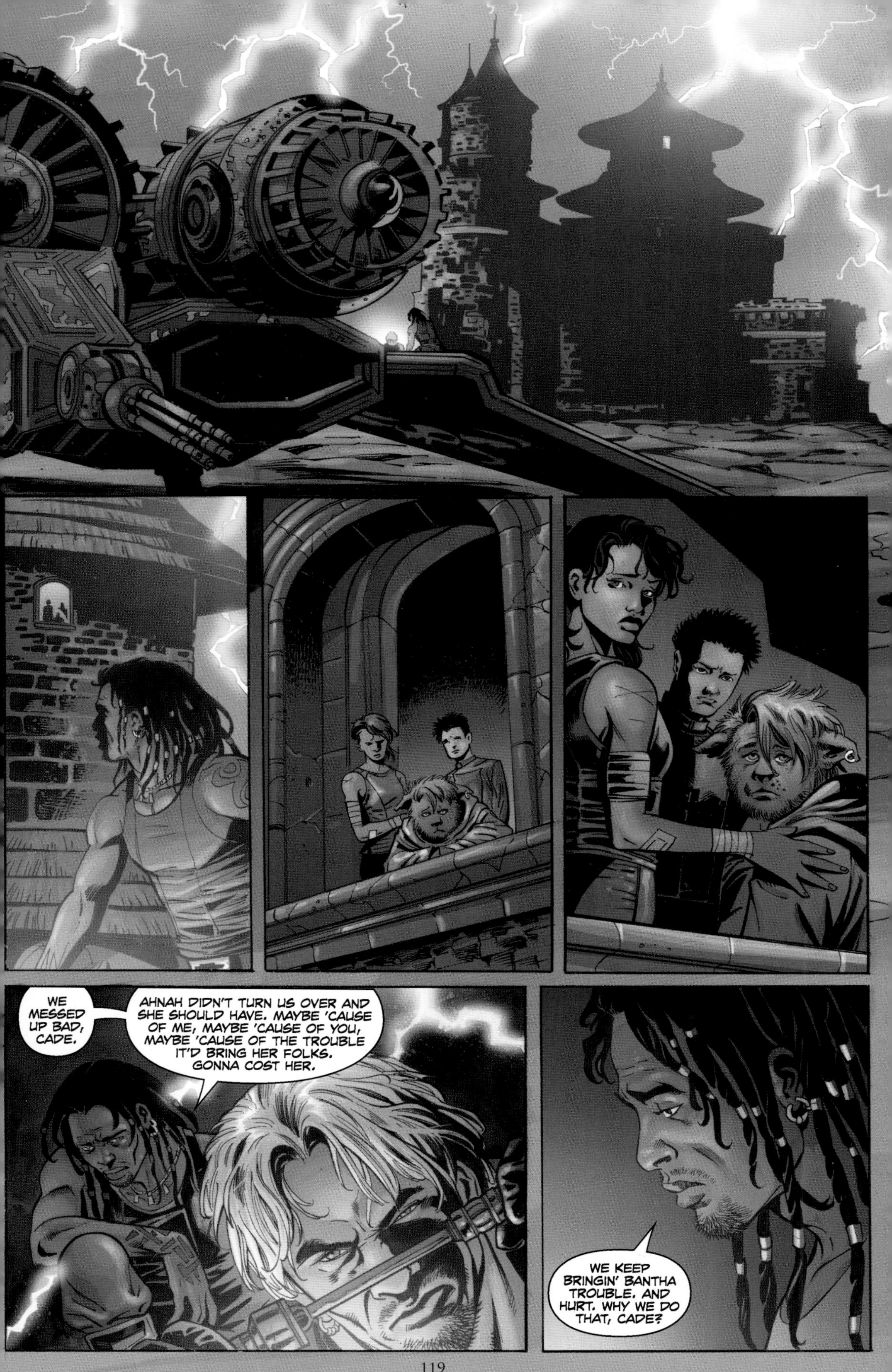
WE MESSED UP BAD, CADE.
AHNAH DIDN'T TURN US OVER AND SHE SHOULD HAVE. MAYBE 'CAUSE OF ME, MAYBE 'CAUSE OF YOU, MAYBE 'CAUSE OF THE TROUBLE IT'D BRING HER FOLKS. GONNA COST HER.
WE KEEP BRINGIN' BANTHA TROUBLE. AND HURT. WHY WE DO THAT, CADE?

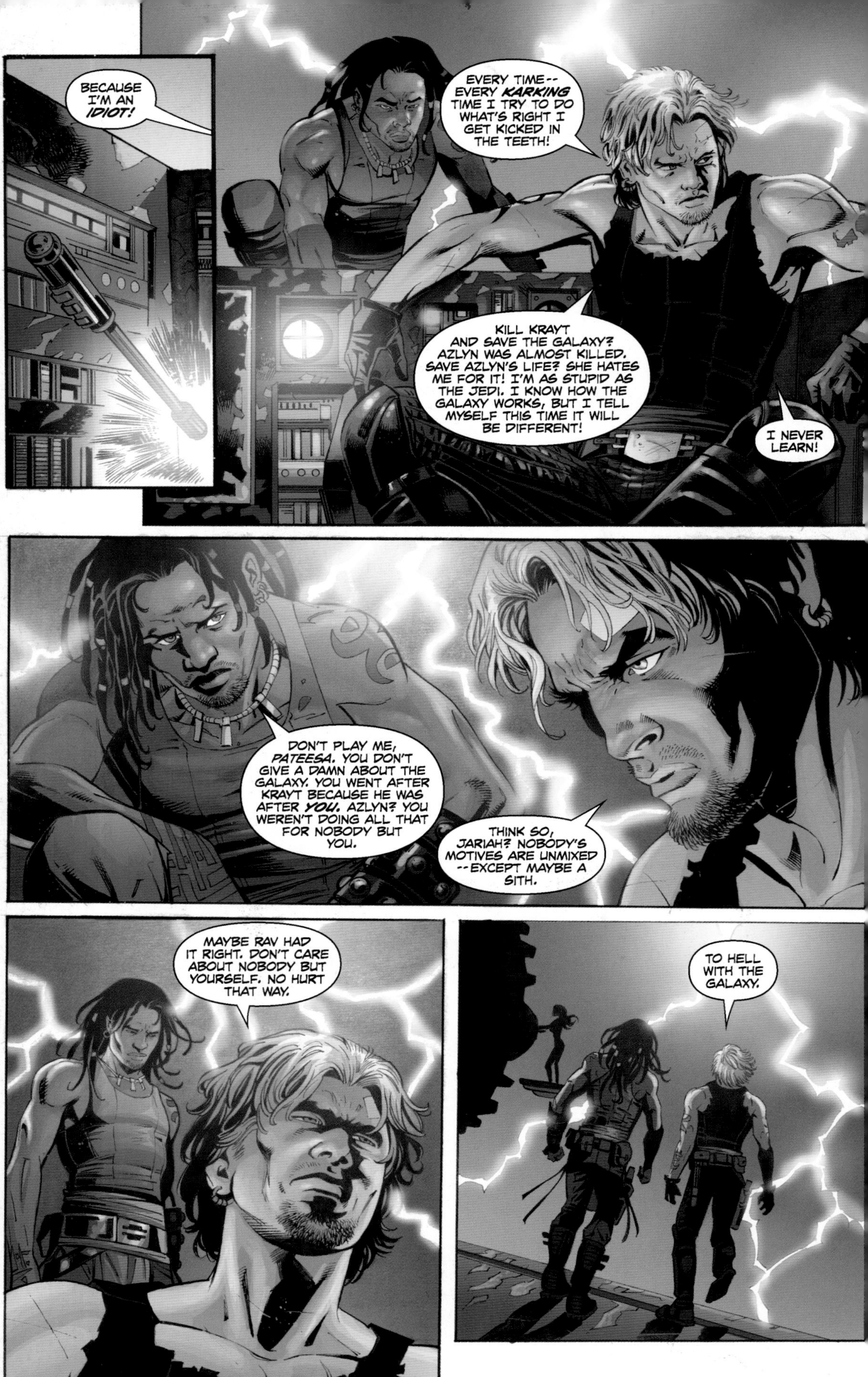
BECAUSE I'M AN *IDIOT!*
EVERY TIME-- EVERY ***KARKING*** TIME I TRY TO DO WHAT'S RIGHT I GET KICKED IN THE TEETH!
KILL KRAYT AND SAVE THE GALAXY? AZLYN WAS ALMOST KILLED. SAVE AZLYN'S LIFE? SHE HATES ME FOR IT! I'M AS STUPID AS THE JEDI. I KNOW HOW THE GALAXY WORKS, BUT I TELL MYSELF THIS TIME IT WILL BE DIFFERENT!
I NEVER LEARN!
DON'T PLAY ME, *PATEESA*. YOU DON'T GIVE A DAMN ABOUT THE GALAXY. YOU WENT AFTER KRAYT BECAUSE HE WAS AFTER ***YOU.*** AZLYN? YOU WEREN'T DOING ALL THAT FOR NOBODY BUT YOU.
THINK SO, JARIAH? NOBODY'S MOTIVES ARE UNMIXED --EXCEPT MAYBE A SITH.
MAYBE RAV HAD IT RIGHT. DON'T CARE ABOUT NOBODY BUT YOURSELF. NO HURT THAT WAY.
TO HELL WITH THE GALAXY.

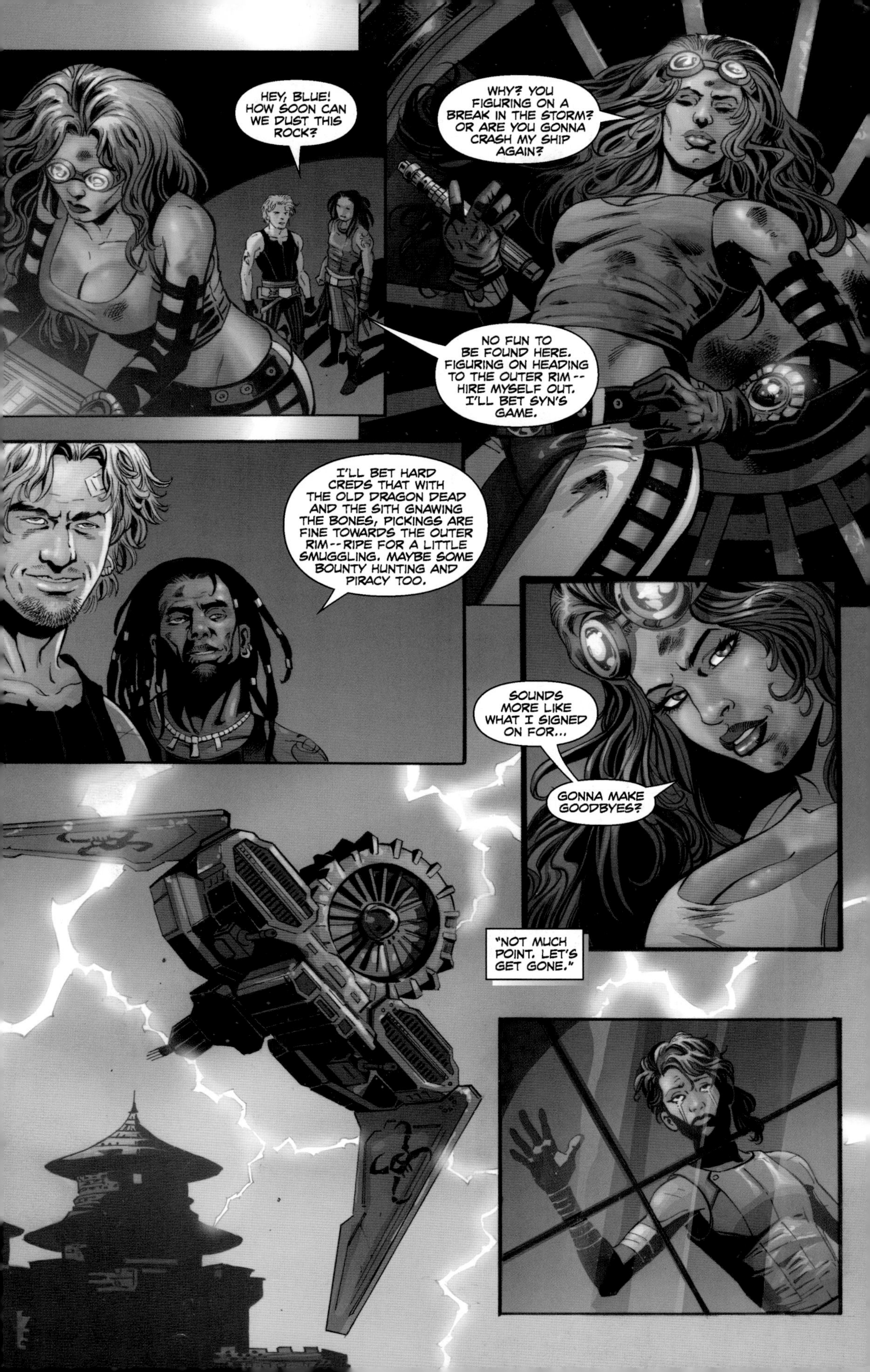
HEY, BLUE! HOW SOON CAN WE DUST THIS ROCK?
WHY? YOU FIGURING ON A BREAK IN THE STORM? OR ARE YOU GONNA CRASH MY SHIP AGAIN?
NO FUN TO BE FOUND HERE. FIGURING ON HEADING TO THE OUTER RIM-- HIRE MYSELF OUT. I'LL BET SYN'S GAME.
I'LL BET HARD CREDS THAT WITH THE OLD DRAGON DEAD AND THE SITH GNAWING THE BONES, PICKINGS ARE FINE TOWARDS THE OUTER RIM--RIPE FOR A LITTLE SMUGGLING. MAYBE SOME BOUNTY HUNTING AND PIRACY TOO.
SOUNDS MORE LIKE WHAT I SIGNED ON FOR...
GONNA MAKE GOODBYES?
"NOT MUCH POINT. LET'S GET GONE."

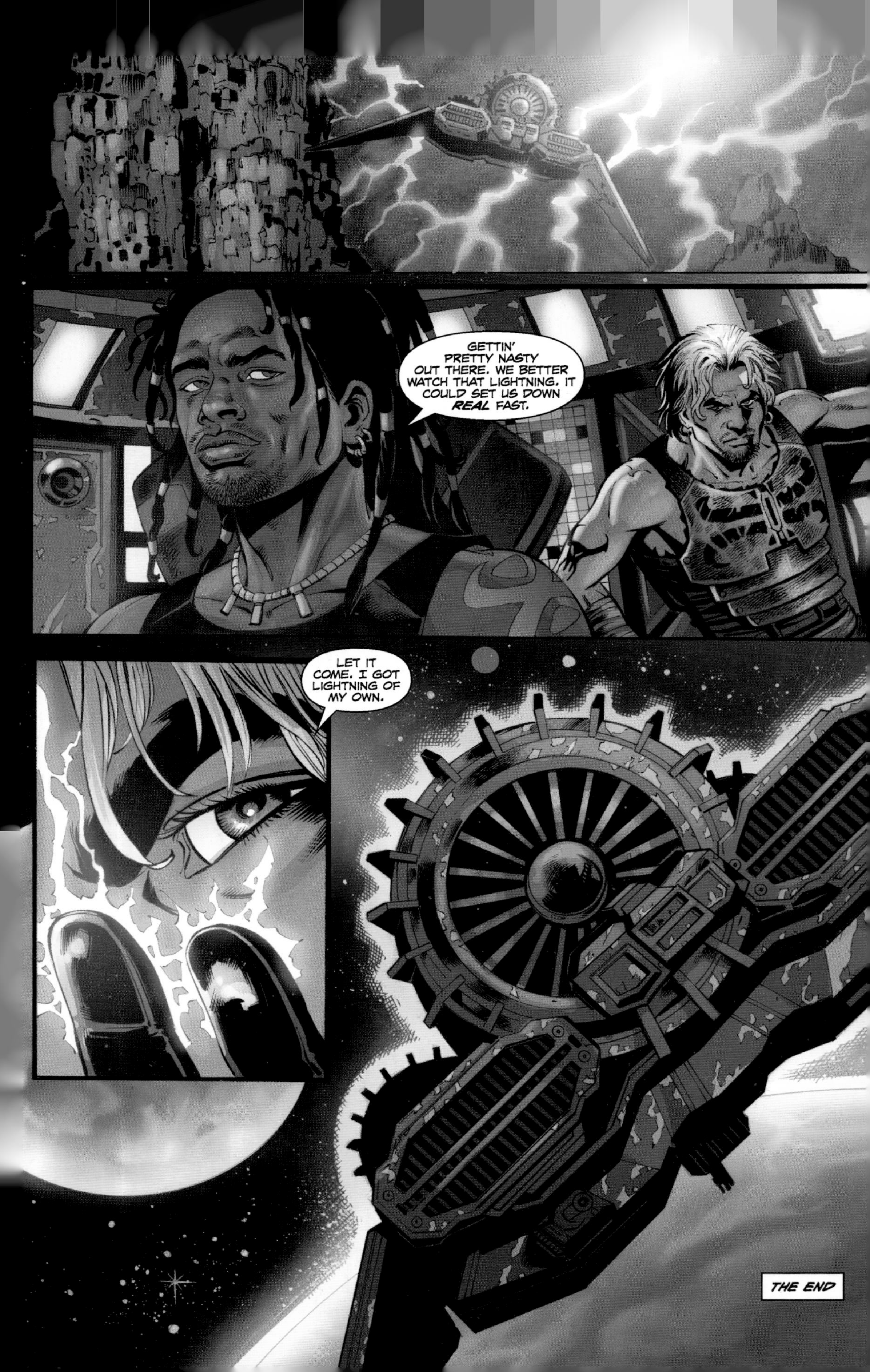
GETTIN' PRETTY NASTY OUT THERE. WE BETTER WATCH THAT LIGHTNING. IT COULD SET US DOWN REAL FAST.
LET IT COME. I GOT LIGHTNING OF MY OWN.
THE END

GLOSSARY

creespa: crispy

kark: derogatory expletive

karkin': derogatory modifier

mesh'la: beautiful

muni: lover

nagoola: not bad

pateesa: friend; sweetie; darling

schutta: insult specific to Twi'lek females

stoopa: stupid

E chu ta!: exclamation

"**To pla da banki danko, jospi!**": You better go home, fly zool!

STAR WARS®

❯ S K E T C H B O O K ❮
DESIGNS BY OMAR FRANCIA

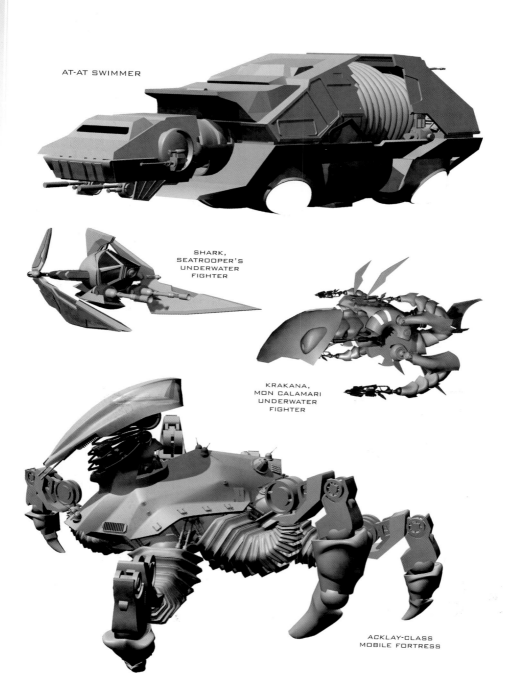

AT-AT SWIMMER

SHARK,
SEATROOPER'S
UNDERWATER
FIGHTER

KRAKANA,
MON CALAMARI
UNDERWATER
FIGHTER

ACKLAY-CLASS
MOBILE FORTRESS

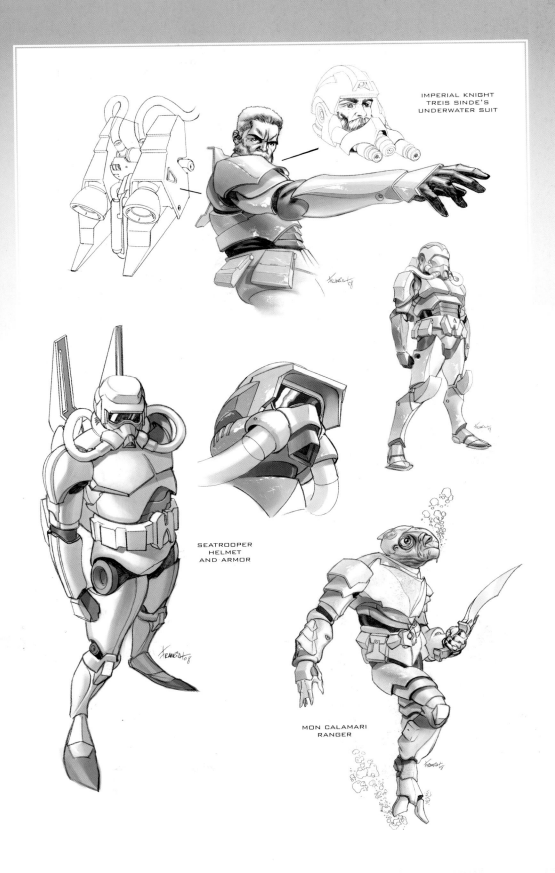

IMPERIAL KNIGHT
TREIS SINDE'S
UNDERWATER SUIT

SEATROOPER
HELMET
AND ARMOR

MON CALAMARI
RANGER

STAR WARS GRAPHIC NOVEL TIMELINE (IN YEARS)

Omnibus: Tales of the Jedi—5,000–3,986 BSW4
Knights of the Old Republic—3,964–3,963 BSW4
Jedi vs. Sith—1,000 BSW4
Omnibus: Rise of the Sith—33 BSW4
Episode I: The Phantom Menace—32 BSW4
Omnibus: Emissaries and Assassins—32 BSW4
Twilight—31 BSW4
Bounty Hunters—31 BSW4
The Hunt for Aurra Sing—30 BSW4
Darkness—30 BSW4
The Stark Hyperspace War—30 BSW4
Rite of Passage—28 BSW4
Jango Fett—27 BSW4
Zam Wesell—27 BSW4
Honor and Duty—24 BSW4
Episode II: Attack of the Clones—22 BSW4
Clone Wars—22–19 BSW4
Clone Wars Adventures—22–19 BSW4
General Grievous—22–19 BSW4
Episode III: Revenge of the Sith—19 BSW4
Dark Times—19 BSW4
Omnibus: Droids—5.5 BSW4
Boba Fett: Enemy of the Empire—3 BSW4
Underworld—1 BSW4
Episode IV: A New Hope—SW4
Classic Star Wars—0–3 ASW4
A Long Time Ago . . . —0–4 ASW4
Empire—0 ASW4
Rebellion—0 ASW4
Boba Fett: Man with a Mission—0 ASW4
Omnibus: Early Victories—0–3 ASW4
Jabba the Hutt: The Art of the Deal—1 ASW4
Episode V: The Empire Strikes Back—3 ASW4
Shadows of the Empire—3.5 ASW4
Episode VI: Return of the Jedi—4 ASW4
Mara Jade: By the Emperor's Hand—4 ASW4
Omnibus: X-Wing Rogue Squadron—4–5 ASW4
Heir to the Empire—9 ASW4
Dark Force Rising—9 ASW4
The Last Command—9 ASW4
Dark Empire—10 ASW4
Boba Fett: Death, Lies, and Treachery—10 ASW4
Crimson Empire—11 ASW4
Jedi Academy: Leviathan—12 ASW4
Union—19 ASW4
Chewbacca—25 ASW4
Legacy—130–137 ASW4

Old Republic Era
25,000 – 1000 years before
Star Wars: A New Hope

Rise of the Empire Era
1000 – 0 years before
Star Wars: A New Hope

Rebellion Era
0 – 5 years after
Star Wars: A New Hope

New Republic Era
5 – 25 years after
Star Wars: A New Hope

New Jedi Order Era
25+ years after
Star Wars: A New Hope

Legacy Era
130+ years after
Star Wars: A New Hope

Infinities
Does not apply to timeline

Sergio Aragonés Stomps Star Wars
Star Wars Tales
Star Wars Infinities
Tag and Bink
Star Wars Visionaries

BSW4 = before *Episode IV: A New Hope*. ASW4 = after *Episode IV: A New Hope*.

STAR WARS®

VECTOR

An event with repercussions for every era and every hero in the *Star Wars* galaxy begins here! For anyone who never knew where to start with *Star Wars* comics, *Vector* is the perfect introduction to the entire *Star Wars* line! For any serious *Star Wars* fan, *Vector* is a must-see event with major happenings throughout the most important moments of the galaxy's history!

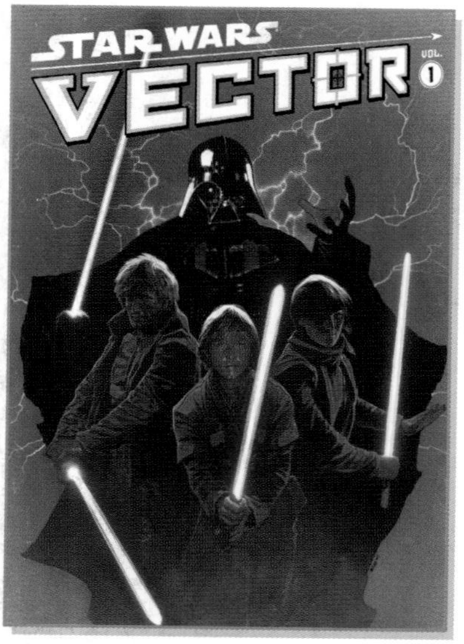
STAR WARS
VECTOR
VOL. 1

VOLUME ONE
(*Knights of the Old Republic* Vol. 5; *Dark Times* Vol. 3)
ISBN 978-1-59582-226-0 | $17.95

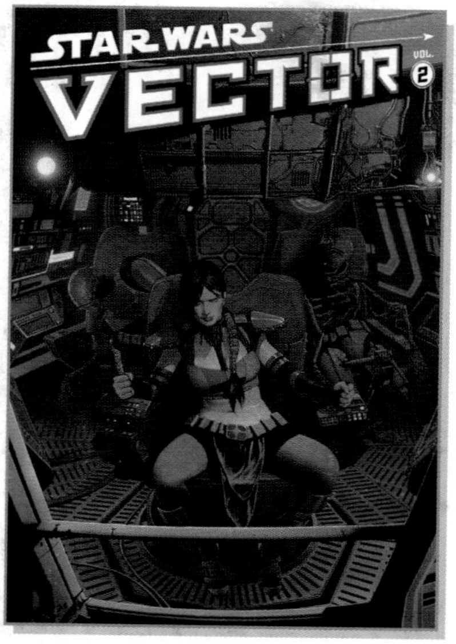
STAR WARS
VECTOR
VOL. 2

VOLUME TWO
(*Rebellion* Vol. 4; *Legacy* Vol. 6)
ISBN 978-1-59582-227-7 | $17.95

KNIGHTS OF THE OLD REPUBLIC

Volume One: Commencement
ISBN 978-1-59307-640-5 | $18.95

Volume Two: Flashpoint
ISBN 978-1-59307-761-7 | $18.95

Volume Three: Days of Fear, Nights of Anger
ISBN 978-1-59307-867-6 | $18.95

Volume Four: Daze of Hate, Knights of Suffering
ISBN 978-1-59582-208-6 | $18.95

Volume Six: Vindication
ISBN 978-1-59582-274-1 | $19.95

Volume Seven: Dueling Ambitions
ISBN 978-1-59582-348-9 | $18.95

REBELLION

Volume One: My Brother, My Enemy
ISBN 978-1-59307-711-2 | $14.95

Volume Two: The Ahakista Gambit
ISBN 978-1-59307-890-4 | $17.95

Volume Three: Small Victories
ISBN 978-1-59582-166-9 | $12.95

LEGACY

Volume One: Broken
ISBN 978-1-59307-716-7 | $17.95

Volume Two: Shards
ISBN 978-1-59307-879-9 | $19.95

Volume Three: Claws of the Dragon
ISBN 978-1-59307-946-8 | $17.95

Volume Four: Alliance
ISBN 978-1-59582-223-9 | $15.95

Volume Five: The Hidden Temple
ISBN 978-1-59582-224-6 | $15.95

DARK TIMES

Volume One: The Path to Nowhere
ISBN 978-1-59307-792-1 | $17.95

Volume Two: Parallels
ISBN 978-1-59307-945-1 | $17.95

darkhorse.com

AVAILABLE AT YOUR LOCAL COMICS SHOP OR BOOKSTORE.
TO FIND A COMICS SHOP IN YOUR AREA, CALL 1-888-266-4226
For more information or to order direct: On the web: darkhorse.com
E-mail: mailorder@darkhorse.com • Phone: 1-800-862-0052 Mon.–Fri.
9 AM to 5 PM Pacific Time.

DARK HORSE BOOKS